T0064748

THE
Remarkable
Millard Fillmore

THE
Remarkable
Millard Fillmore

*The Unbelievable Life
of a Forgotten President*

George Pendle

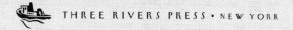

THREE RIVERS PRESS • NEW YORK

Copyright © 2007 by George Pendle

Published in the United States by Three Rivers Press, an imprint of the
Crown Publishing Group, a division of Random House, Inc., New York.
www.crownpublishing.com

Three Rivers Press and the Tugboat design are registered trademarks of
Random House, Inc.

Library of Congress Cataloging-in-Publication Data

Pendle, George, 1976–.
The remarkable Millard Fillmore : the unbelievable life of a forgotten
president / George Pendle.—1st ed.
    p. cm.
Includes bibliographical references.
1. Fillmore, Millard, 1800–1874.   2. Presidents—United States—
Biography.   I. Title.
E427.P465 2007
973.6'4092—dc22
    [B]   2006029390

ISBN 978-0-307-33962-1

Design by Maria Elias

First Edition

TO CHARLOTTE—
First Lady

Contents

Author's Note

The Remarkable Millard Fillmore is the first comprehensive biography ever to be written of the thirteenth president of the United States of America. Through a thorough reevaluation of the recognized facts, as well as the unearthing of previously unknown sources, it is my hope to redeem the reputation of a forgotten giant.

It cannot be denied that the official record of Millard Fillmore's life seems to leave little to contemplate. The history books state that during his presidency he held to an unwavering course of inaction, straying from it only to demonstrate an astounding ability to compromise his principles. Compared to recent depictions of the Founding Fathers, the Fillmore that has been passed down to us seems to lack the vigor and depth we tend to associate with great Americans. Unlike Alexander Hamilton or Benjamin Franklin, it is said that Fillmore failed to imprint his personality upon the country's institutions, preferring instead to be carried along like flotsam by the inertial force of politics. And while recent portraits of George Washington and Abraham Lincoln have confirmed both presidents as deeply complex and emotional men, as well as figureheads to the nation, Millard Fillmore has been depicted as nothing other than a blundering, pompous, ultimately shallow failure.

This could not be more wrong.

As knowing the genesis of a book can often aid the reader in understanding its subject, it should be acknowledged that from conception to completion the writing of this biography has been an intensely personal experience. Three decades ago, when I first pushed open the imposing oak doors of the Biographers Club in Washington, D.C., I was overawed by the grandeur and eminence of that institution. What great minds worked here! What mighty tomes had their genesis in these majestic corridors! No sooner had I entered the club on that cold December day than Carl Sandburg, that stormy, husky, brawling old man of American letters (and Pulitzer Prize–winning biographer of Abraham Lincoln), called to me from across the imposing marble lobby. "Boy," he said—for I was barely out of my teens—"what's your subject?" His surrounding cohort of cronies tittered sycophantically. It had been during my college years that I first discovered the black hole in American history covering the years of the presidency from 1850 to 1853. A little delicate probing found that the figure at the center of this factual vacuum was none other than the subject of the biography you hold in front of you. In a stammering voice I replied, "Millard Fillmore, Mr. Sandburg, sir." He paused and looked at me with widening eyes as a hush fell on the other members. His shock of white hair surrounded his skull like an oddly menacing halo. And then, in a booming voice, he cruelly shouted, "Fillmore? You idiot! That pecker never did a damn thing in his life!" The color drained from my face as his minions guffawed obsequiously. I was about to retreat out of the door when Arthur Schlesinger Jr. crept up behind me and, grabbing the top of my underpants, hoisted them halfway up my back.

From that day on, anonymous notes began to appear in my club locker describing me as "a vain mediocrity," as the popular press had once labeled Fillmore. I was referred to as "His Accidency"—a nickname that had been given to Fillmore upon his succession to the presidency following the death of President Zachary Taylor—and my colleagues made sure that I constantly suffered "accidents" of my own on visits to the club. A bucket of ice water once fell on me from the gallery, causing me significant distress, and upon leaving my overcoat in the cloakroom I would often return to find that the sleeves had been sewn shut.

This sort of abuse would continue for thirty years. But I am of a stubborn disposition and not easily cowed by criticism. As my peers gained acclaim for their presidential biographies of Washington, Jefferson, and Lincoln, I kept to myself, and through the years of insult and injury, I drew strength from Millard Fillmore.

I often imagined myself walking next to his robust form, the light dappling his fine head of hair, as I vainly tried to keep up with his powerful, thrusting stride. During these reveries he might offer me some deep insight into human nature, help me climb a stile, or calm a wild bull into whose pasture we had wandered by accident. I pictured us lounging beneath a mighty oak, Fillmore's weighty words painting the night air in fantastical colors. Gazing upon him was like looking upon the embodiment of the United States itself: imperious, brave, beautiful.

In 2001, I received a phone call in the early hours of a spring morning. This was not an uncommon experience. When the older members of the Biographers Club convened after a long supper they would often telephone my house shouting out such childish jibes as "Three more years!" (a taunt at the length of Fillmore's presidency) before hanging up amidst much drunken snickering. Yet this phone call was different. A voice insisted that I take the next plane to Arua, a small village in northern Uganda. When I asked who my midnight interlocutor might be, he introduced himself as Dr. Pepe Rockefeller, professor of anthropology at New York University. Having heard of my three-decade-long quest to publish Fillmore's definitive biography, Dr. Rockefeller said he had uncovered something that might be of interest to me.

While studying the Aka pygmies in their tribal homelands within the rainforest, my contact had found an old portmanteau bearing the presidential seal. The case dated back to 1873—the year before Fillmore's death—and was filled, he said, with letters and journals signed "Millard Fillmore." My heart skipped a beat. As if in a dream, I was soon stepping down onto an earthen airstrip in the midst of the African jungle, my life savings in a briefcase handcuffed to my wrist. I was thrilled to find that the documents were in remarkably good condition considering the humidity, the rainfall, and the attentions of the Aka, who, said my contact, had been worshiping them as sacred objects for generations.

It must be acknowledged that some scholars of American history have claimed the handwriting in these documents does not match that found in official government papers. Some have even hypothesized that as the journal and letters appear to have been written in ballpoint pen (which was supposedly not invented until 1938), they are obviously counterfeit. To my eyes it is obvious that these alleged "inconsistencies" merely confirm the vast and unheralded accomplishments of Millard Fillmore's own life. Imagine! A president of the United States inventing the ballpoint pen some ninety years before László Biró fraudulently affixed his name to the invention. This fact alone would change the history books forever, and put to shame Lincoln's patent no. 6469 for a device to lift boats over shoals—an invention, I hasten to add, that was never even manufactured.

In addition to his other virtues, Fillmore was a world-class journal keeper, and the multiple volumes of his daily record provide a rich source for the re-creating of his life story. Within the soiled but readable pages there were intimations of personal intrigues, tales of passion and despair, and revelations of iniquity perpetrated at the highest levels of government. When the journals were appended to what we already know of Fillmore, the supposed colorlessness of Fillmore's life blossomed into audacious Technicolor.

Convinced of the papers' authenticity, and needing urgent medical attention for the malaria that was wracking my body, a deal was quickly struck with Dr. Rockefeller. As I lay in a dugout canoe, heading down the Nile back toward civilization, I began piecing together a true history of the upheavals and betrayals that convulsed the United States more than 150 years ago.

It is an incontrovertible fact that the American people have long looked toward the office of the president to guide them. The most recent presidential election, in which a president's "moral values" were seen as being of the utmost importance, only clarified the fact that it is a president's immaculate character that allows him to hold our country's most revered post. Yet while we constantly search for heroism and nobility in our chief executive's character, perhaps no one has been able to satisfy our yearning desires as much as Millard Fillmore. In this book I will assert that there has been no American, not Washington, not Jefferson, not even Lincoln, who stood as firm nor who succeeded in his duties to his country as successfully as Fillmore. It is my most devout wish that by the end of this book Millard Fillmore will be shown in his true glory, his bright achievements removed from under the bushel of history.

It is an auspicious time to reexamine the life of Millard Fillmore, for today we are indisputably the heirs to his America—an America of unassuming heroism and undeniable moral superiority, which feels deeply its responsibility to the world at large and never rests until a job is done. To repudiate Fillmore's legacy, as historians and critics have done for so long, is to repudiate the modern world. The resulting portrait, I hope, will seem fresh and surprising even to those best versed in the literature of the period—even those, I must point out, who frequent the reading rooms of Washington, D.C.'s wretched Biographers Club.

Millard Fillmore demonstrated that through methodical industry and some competence an uninspiring man could make the American dream come true.
—The White House (official Web site)

Fillmore was a pompous, colorless individual who rose far beyond his ability.
—*The Reader's Companion to American History*

To discuss Millard Fillmore is to overrate him.
—*American Heritage* magazine

Mr. Fillmore is a remarkable man.

—*Woodworth's Youth's Cabinet*, September 1850

THE
Remarkable
Millard Fillmore

1.

I, Fillmore

(1800–1819)

A Noble Birth—The Family Tree—Piratical Melancholia—Edible

Pants—The Forbidden Excitements of the Frontier—The Disease of

Education—Signs of Presidential Fortitude

"*I* was born," the first page of Fillmore's first journal reads, "on the snowy night of the seventh day of January, 1800."[1] The second child and eldest son in a family of nine, Fillmore would later recount that his birth was not "marked by any striking signs in the heavens above or the earth beneath calculated to alarm the superstitious fears of the scattered inhabitants of that howling wilderness." Nevertheless, Johann Wilson, a neighbor of the family, chose the night of Fillmore's birth to be convinced that men from the "outer depths of the sky" had come to "vanish me away," and threw himself under his own plow.

Fillmore's mother and father were simple dirt farmers, poor beyond their wildest dreams, and it showed in the naming of their son.[2] *Millard* was his mother's unused maiden name, and such was their poverty that they could not afford to bestow upon their eldest son a middle name (unlike the wealthy family of Thomas Jebediah Birchard Gamaliel Redondo Jefferson). Too honest to steal even a letter, as future president Harry S. Truman would do years later, their son would become known to the world simply as Millard Fillmore.[3]

Fillmore would fondly remember his birthplace as being "completely

1. Throughout this biography, the majority of Millard Fillmore's quotations are taken from the recently discovered and unpublished *Journals of Millard Fillmore, Vols. 1–53.* Other quotes are taken from his unpublished letters, his unpublished notebooks, and his soon-to-be published napkin doodles.

2. Dirt farming was common in North America ever since colonial times, with the four categories of dirt—slime, dreck, grime, and crud—all in abundance. (Though sometimes wrongly classified as dirt, dust is in fact a totally different species.) Dirt farming reached its zenith by the middle of the nineteenth century, yet despite the discovery of guck in 1873 and scuzz in 1889, the increasing popularity of mirrors caused the dirt industry to all but vanish by the turn of the century.

3. There has been some conjecture, postulated by A. Davidson, Ph.D. (Phys. Ed.), in her book *Lincoln's Diphthong,* that the correct pronunciation of *Millard* is with an open front unrounded vowel sound, in order that it rhymes with *retard.* This author maintains that *Millard* should be pronounced with a mid-central unstressed and neutral resonance, so that it can be rhymed with *dullard.*

shut out from all the enterprises of civilization and advancement." The typical pioneer could often be seen clad in simple bearskin and deerhide, with leather jerkin, cowhide boots, britches made of guts, ties woven of pig hair, and carved wooden hats. Hairstyles were plain, manners unvarnished, and entertainments spare. It was all in sharp contrast to the conspicuous wealth on show in the cities of the East Coast, where styles aped those of a decadent Europe. While young Fillmore's curly blond tresses were waxed down with wolverine fat, the "pussy-top" hairstyle, popularized by Marie Antoinette and involving the careful application of a dead cat to the crown of the head, was the most fashionable cut of the day in more elevated circles.

Marie-Antoinette models the "pussy-top." Note the tail of a deceased Russian Blue dangling seductively over her forehead.

The inhabitants of the frontier may have lacked social graces, but they made up for it in robustness. In this landscape young children swiftly became excellent hunters and expert shots. Alas, Fillmore's family was too poor to provide him with a gun, and even when he was gifted with an old musket by a neighbor, his natural timidity saw him spend much of his youth using it to measure mud holes, "to ascertain how their width compares with their length and whether their sides are perpendicular." Thus firearms nurtured in him a gentle, contemplative side and spawned in him a lifelong love of bogs.

But while the young Millard may not have been gifted with the certitude of aristocratic inbreeding and massive wealth, as most presidents are,[4] he was bequeathed an even more important legacy—a thick adventurous streak.

It was Millard Fillmore's great-grandfather who had first displayed a tendency for outrageous happenstance. The extraordinary tale of John Fillmore, "a good, stout, resolute fellow," began in 1723, when at the age of twenty-one he heard the irresistible call of the sea. Signing on to work aboard the fishing sloop the *Dolphin,* he had barely left port when his boat was captured by the feared pirate Captain John Phillips, and John Fillmore was pressed into joining his crew.

Upon starting his new life as a scourge of the seas, Fillmore found that Phillips' boat, the *Revenge,* was not a happy vessel, for its captain was a fiercely depressed man.[5] On his good days, Phillips could be found with a maniacal gleam in his eye, bellowing at his terrified crew to "splice the main brace" and "make fast the bunt gasket." On one day of particularly high spirits he had even ordered his crew to board a great white shark, with fatal consequences. More often than not, however, he slunk around belowdecks, his tricorn hat in his hand, tears smudging his temporarily tattooed cheeks. The fact was that Phillips had never really excelled at piracy. A carpenter by trade, his hooked hand had been gained not in battle but in an unfortunate cabinetmaking accident on land. He had lost an eye not while boarding another ship but to the eyepiece of his sextant on a day when the waves were particularly rough. He was forever complaining about

4. For examples, see Hubert Tavistock-Monroe's *Who's Your Daddy?: Inherited Wealth and the Presidency from George Washington to George W. Bush.*
5. For a full account of the life of John Phillips, see his own autobiography, *Home Is Where the Arrr! 'Tis.*

his parrot, which was defiantly mute, and his ship's monkey, which he said was "not mischievous enough." When the lonesome sound of Phillips' euphonium could be heard emanating from the captain's cabin, it was a foolish man who dared disturb him.[6]

After taking Fillmore captive, the *Revenge* circled the busy shipping lanes around Barbados. But for three months they failed to see another ship and as a result almost starved to death. Phillips' deep melancholy was lifted only when his carpentry skills were called upon to saw off the leg of one of his crew, injured during a game of deck quoits. The subsequent death of his patient sent him into an even darker mood and left the *Revenge* still awaiting its first peg-legged sailor. The incident led to much whispered conversation around the water coolie.

Water coolies: gossipmongers.

Fed on this diet of mutilation, relentless intimidation, and hapless piracy, it was not long before John Fillmore grew restless and longed for his homestead once more. One day, while the other pirates were eating

6.   It was rumored that Phillips' depression stemmed from a chance meeting with the famed pirate Edward Teach, known as Blackbeard, in 1718. Teach had cruelly teased the precocious young pirate Phillips by asking him what, exactly, "shiver me timbers" meant. A humiliated Phillips was forced to admit that he did not know.

their daily serving of barnacles, Fillmore, who was in the crow's nest, plunged his dagger into the mainsail and slid down its face, slicing it in two in the process. According to the statement he would later swear in court, he was greeted by "a smattering of applause" from the other crew members and a scream from the enraged Phillips, who was mad with jealousy at never having done anything so piratical in his life. The two fought across the ship, cutlasses flashing in the sunlight, swinging from ropes and rigging. The pirate captain seemed to have gained the upper hand when the duel reached the pristine plank that stuck out from the side of the *Revenge*, a plank no man's feet had ever walked upon. As Phillips edged Fillmore toward its end with his sword, cackling demonically, he seemed for a moment to lose himself in a reverie. Turning to his astonished crew, he cried, "Look at me, boys, top of the world!" At which point Fillmore stepped forward and succinctly sliced the pirate's head "in two." Taking control of the ship, Fillmore sailed it to Boston, where he turned the body of Phillips over to the authorities. It was said that, despite the grievous wounds he had suffered, Phillips' body had never looked so peaceful.

Millard Fillmore's grandfather Nathaniel displayed equally heroic, if more landbound, qualities. At the age of seventeen he had enlisted to fight in the French and Indian War, one of the many conflicts that raged across North America in the late seventeenth and early eighteenth centuries.[7] But Nathaniel Fillmore was no luckier than his father and, having been wounded in a woodland skirmish, was left for dead by his companions. In such a situation many other men would have resigned themselves to a slow and agonizing death by starvation, but not Nathaniel. As days turned into

---

7. The oblique naming of conflicts in the pre-Revolutionary period has led to a general apathy in their study amongst historians. Even two hundred years on, scholars are still uncertain as to who fought in Queen Anne's War. Similarly, the combatants in the War of the Grand Alliance have yet to be ascertained, although recent archeological finds have suggested that the Dutch might have been involved. Inevitably, unscrupulous individuals have taken advantage of such confusions, notably within the academic field. The recent revelation that the French and Indian War was the same as the Seven Years' War *and* the War of the Conquest led to the exposure of a massive "fake history" cartel stretching across hundreds of American schools, wherein teachers had been invoicing separately for all three wars. This opaque naming of conflicts has continued well into the twentieth century, most recently when it was revealed that the Vietnam War had largely been fought in Sweden.

weeks and the last kernels of corn in his knapsack disappeared, Nathaniel turned to eating his shoes. When a rescue party stumbled upon him some weeks later he was described as being half naked and in the midst of roasting his blanket. When asked if he needed assistance, Nathaniel politely declined, asking only if he could eat his rescuers' pockets. It took a week of negotiation before Nathaniel was eventually tempted out of the woods by a carefully laid trail of buttons.[8]

Nathaniel Fillmore's son, Millard Fillmore's father, also shared the name Nathaniel.[9] He married Phoebe Millard in 1797, soon after which the couple was enticed by the promises of a land promoter, who spoke of bounteous fertile land and a magnificent social scene in upstate New York. Selling their home in Bennington, Vermont, the Fillmores crossed the Appalachian Mountains into the west.

In 1799, the American continent was still largely unexplored and unconquered, and the pioneers who ventured into the interior had to be hardy and utterly fearless. Common pioneer qualities included coarseness, crudeness, bluffness, and rudeness, not to mention irritability, incivility, impropriety, and vulgarity. Moral values were expensive, and teeth were hard to come by; in any case, both were largely impractical in a region where men regularly added the prefix "Mad" to their names. For the male pioneer, entertainment was gained through two avenues: getting dangerously drunk on illegally distilled moonshine, and domestic abuse. However, the hardy pioneer women had an equal share of their husbands' courage, determination, and cold-bloodedness, and were often known to hit back.

In the wilderness of the unexplored Finger Lakes region, Nathaniel

---

8. Nathaniel's story would be remembered in the best-selling pamphlet *Ate My Shorts: The Disrobing and Engorgement of Master N——F——*.

9. Name-sharing was a common practice amongst eighteenth-century Americans, particularly males, due to the exorbitant cost of christening. Usually the father held the name during the daylight hours, while business was being transacted. In the evening, once returned to his home, the elder would loan the name to his son. This proved particularly useful in avoiding marital debates, as the husband could thus avoid the exhortations of his wife with the words "There's no one here of that name," to which frontier feminist philosophers struggled to conjure a retort. It was not until Goodie Withers, a Quaker seminologist of the early nineteenth century, tipped a bucket of wet dirt over her recalcitrant husband that the solution became apparent. "Your name is mud" swiftly entered the lexicon as a popular saying.

*Pioneer women would wreak horrible revenge on
unruly husbands.*

and Phoebe built a small log cabin with one door and one window that gave pretty views onto the farm's very own swamp. But the couple soon discovered that their land was not fertile loam, as promised—rather it was unyielding clay—and Phoebe was distraught to find that the highly vaunted nightlife consisted of dredging the quaking bog for disquisitive children.

The couple eked out a living as simple dirt farmers and soon became established in their backwoods community. Phoebe Fillmore was described as being a woman of "refinement, grace, and native intellect," which in deepest New York State meant simply that she spat into a bucket, that she rarely missed the bucket, and that she always knew where the bucket was kept. Nathaniel Fillmore, for his part, displayed the pioneer's masterly utilization of local materials, being obsessed with whittling. He had whittled the cabin they lived in out of a single giant sequoia and now, convinced that whittling would "make the Fillmore name resound with prosperity," began his life's work—the whittling of the Battle of Bunker Hill.[10]

10. Nathaniel Fillmore never completed his epic project. Although he would work on it until his death in 1863, and despite the fact that his whittling knife decimated the forests of the Finger Lakes region, his re-creation of the battle was populated solely by skirt-wearing gophers, a prospect that most eyewitness accounts of the Battle of Bunker Hill fail to mention. On his deathbed Nathaniel demanded that his great work be burned, a task to which his family gratefully acceded.

☆   ☆   ☆

From an early age Fillmore was told stories of the great founders of his country, and at age six he chopped down his father's prized cherry tree in an effort to emulate the young George Washington. "I remember feeling terrified a good deal when Father asked me who was responsible," recalled Fillmore, "and so I swore that it was Tom Booth, the butcher's boy, who had done the wicked deed."

Forgoing imitation, he became entranced by tales of adventure and battle. The exploits of the heroes of the Revolutionary War still resounded powerfully throughout the country, and many of the stories had been amplified and improved upon by the unruly imagination of the frontiersman. Fillmore remembered being told how Benjamin Franklin "dangled from a kite, high above the British guns, focusing on them the burning rays of the sun through the glass of his bifocal spectacles," and he recalled feeling "most fearful" when told how George Washington's wooden teeth were replaced every week, "so bloodstained and splintered did they become with the tearing and rending of English throats."[11]

Word also crept through the thick forests of upstate New York of the famed Lewis and Clark expedition that was exploring the country from St. Louis to the Pacific coast. In two years and four months the explorers had discovered 178 new plants, 122 new species and subspecies of animals, and more than 54 different types of wind, including such well-known varieties as "gusty" and "blustery."[12] As Millard grew, so did America, for both were discovering themselves.

---

11. Fillmore seems to be remembering *The Tales of the Fantastic Four Founding Fathers,* a loosely linked series of folktales that were hugely popular at the turn of the nineteenth century. George Washington is the group's stern and resourceful leader, Benjamin Franklin the witty inventor, Thomas Jefferson the flaming roué, and Betsy Ross the chirpy seamstress, able to put out an enemy's eye with needle and thread at thirty paces.

12. Despite the valuable scientific information brought back by the expedition, it had not been without its problems. Halfway through the journey William Clark refused to walk for an entire week until the mission was renamed the "Clark and Lewis" expedition. Describing his anxieties in his diary, Clark wrote: "I am of greater age than Lewis, and my name precedes his in the alphabet; why, then, should he be held in the foremost regard?" Clark was eventually persuaded to continue, but his anger against his traveling companion festered. A few months later Clark shot Lewis in the leg, claiming he had mistaken him for an elk. Three years after the expedition, Lewis was found dead on the Natchez Trace, his wrists cut and with bullet holes through his head and chest. When questioned, Clark denied ever having known him.

When war erupted against the British in 1812, the twelve-year-old Fillmore would hurry miles to the nearest village to hear the latest news. The causes of the War of 1812 are now lost in the mists of time,[13] but the man who guided the United States through this struggle shines resplendently through the gloom of the ages. President James Madison, a man of small stature at a time when being small meant being very short indeed, had clambered his way onto the presidential throne through a gritty campaign of ankle-bites and shin-kicks. His aggressive temperament was matched only by his inferiority complex: upon seeing a line of graffiti in the congressional bathroom that read "James Madison is more presid-*ant* than presid-*ent*," a tearful Madison declared war against both France and Great Britain, insisting in his thin and reedy voice, "They are naught but big bullies." When informed of the French emperor's equally small stature, Madison relented, to the relief of his advisors, and a lone rematch against the old enemy Britain was decided upon, under the official title "The Brawl in Montreal."

James Madison: actual size.

---

13. Something to do with boats, probably.

Madison was unlucky in his choice of general for the task. Governor William Hull of Michigan, a veteran of the Revolutionary War, led the initial assault, taking 2,500 soldiers across the border to attack the British forces stationed there. Alas, the elderly general became greatly perplexed by his foreign surroundings. When told that the British forces were only 330 men strong, Hull somehow calculated that his own force was vastly outnumbered.[14] He retreated, hid, and eventually surrendered, telling his surprised captors, "You are George III and I claim my five shillings."[15]

The war raged on into 1813 and 1814, but President Madison, having already christened it the War of 1812, dared not change its name for risk of confusing his already uncertain generals. As the battles moved to the Great Lakes and the Indian forces loyal to the British joined the Americans (and vice versa), both sides let their minds wander, and before either country knew what was happening, peace had been declared. If the war taught the young Millard anything, it was that the United States was now equal with the rest of the world's superpowers in terms of demented leadership and pointless bloodshed.[16]

Such excitement was a far cry from young Millard's situation. From nearly the time he could walk, Millard was forced to mow, reap, hoe, heap, and row on the family dirt farm, this last skill being necessitated by his father's attempts to diversify into goo and slime cultivation. By his early teens he had mastered most of the primitive frontier skills, although his sensitive disposition and love of animals meant he had eschewed hunting and badger baiting, preferring to concentrate on yodeling and quilting, skills that he would later use to great effect in his political life.

14. Most historians believe he forgot to carry the 1.
15. For his role in the Canadian debacle, Hull was sentenced to death for cowardice, but in a moment of rare lucidity he managed to trick President Madison into granting him a reprieve. When the president came to visit him Hull mumbled something inaudible. Madison, not hearing him, cocked his ear and said, "Pardon?" upon which Hull declared he had been given a presidential pardon and had to be released.
16. The War of 1812 was not entirely fruitless. In 1814, Francis Scott Key watched the rockets of the British bursting overhead at the battle for Fort McHenry on the Patapsco River. As the sounds of battle roared and smoke cloaked the landscape, he wrote the poem that would later become "The Star-Spangled Banner," but which was originally entitled "Apocalypse Forthwith (Purple Haze)."

Alas, Fillmore was passing his childhood on the edge of civilization, and the degradation of menial labor seemed to offer him no chance of escape. What's more, in the strict Unitarian circles in which he was raised, corporal punishment was common. "I recall crying out in horror," wrote Fillmore years later, "whenever my father ordered me to beat him."[17]

For the first ten years of his life, Fillmore did not attend school, education not being encouraged by his parents, who, due to a misunderstanding, believed it to be a cause of goiter. When a school was finally opened in the nearby town of Niles, Fillmore was grudgingly allowed to attend, on the understanding that he was not to bring his learning back home with him.

Fillmore was a voracious student. He was enamored of stories of far-flung discovery, particularly James Bruce's *Travels in Abyssinia*, in which the dashing Bruce sought to discover the source of the Nile.[18] But Fillmore was only allowed to attend school for two or three months a year, his parents constantly worrying about the price of his education, fearing "that you shall grow too big for thy boots, as I have heard it tell of those with learning, and we have no money for new ones."

While his brothers and sisters rejoiced at their lack of regular schooling, spending their days eating mud and torturing cats, a frustrated, fourteen-year-old Millard could be found staring disconsolately into the limpid waters of nearby Lake Weary, pining for knowledge. With his young son's mind filled with yearning for education and excitement, even the dour Nathaniel Fillmore could see that Millard was not going to be happy with an inheritance of filth and muck. "Father told me that he wanted only the best for me," wrote Fillmore in his memoirs years later.

17. Pioneer Unitarians had invented an entirely different set of seven deadly sins—known as the seven deadlier sins—to help cope with the harsh frontier world in which they lived. They consisted of excitement, happiness, longevity, congeniality, soft hands, and addition.
18. The search for the source of the Nile inspired much literature, among the more memorable being Samuel Taylor's encyclopedic *List of Places That Are Not the Source of the Nile* (1765), which included Paris, the Colosseum in Rome, and "the Moone."

"Unfortunately, his conception of the best consisted largely of potable water and a surfeit of raccoon meat." Was it thus happenstance or fate, destiny or fortune, providence or luck that saw the entrepreneur Samuel Slater pass by Fillmore's house at just this time? Slater was looking for apprentices to work in his newly opened mill in the town of Sparta, and Fillmore was enraptured by his tales of the Protestant work ethic.

Slater had been responsible for constructing the first American factory—a yarn-producing mill—in Pawtucket, Rhode Island. Previously the British had forbidden the exporting of designs for textile machines in order to safeguard the lucrative colonial markets. Americans who could not afford to have tailored clothes made for them were thus forced to buy mass-produced British garments emblazoned with such humiliating slogans as "God save the King," "Washington is a Cheate and a Liar," and "I am naught but a rogue and peasant slave." Thanks to Slater, Americans everywhere were freed from the curse of British attire.[19]

Sparta was austere to the point of nonexistence. A simple mud track—upon which a horse much like George Washington's had once trotted—provided the villagers with their sole point of pride. With few distractions, Fillmore immediately began work at the mill along with ten other boys of his age, for at that time equal opportunities for employment were many, and children were allowed to work long hours in factories free from such distractions as parental supervision, safety laws, and remuneration. Despite the egalitarianism that child labor fostered, Fillmore felt his restless mind continuing to wander. "There must be more to life," he recalled thinking, "than gruel and thrice-daily thrashings from Mr. Slater. What this may be I cannot conceive, but I trust to the Lord that he will guide me."

19. The opening of the textile mills had the unfortunate side effect of condemning the burgeoning American naturist movement to a swift demise. American naturists preferred to appear naked rather than wear British clothes. Often violent, and fiercely protective of their personal space, naturists made fearsome soldiers, and a division of "Kentucky Naturals" had fought against the British at the Battle of Blue Licks in 1776. Unfortunately, an unseasonably cold morning, not to mention an absence of pockets, saw the naturist force both unwilling and unprepared to face the well-dressed enemy, and they were massacred.

Fillmore was allowed only one holiday a year—New Year's Day. On this occasion the apprentices repaired to Samuel Slater's home, where Fillmore witnessed for the first time the amusements and games in which people engaged in the rest of the country.[20] There was a turkey raffle, and although Fillmore had never gambled before in his life, he was fascinated by what he later called "this game of providence." As fate would have it, Fillmore won the raffle, but his triumph did not fill him with joy. As he would later relate, "I was touched by the bird's penitent clucks and the longing in its eyes. I declared to my fellow apprentices that no man should have dominion over another living creature," and despite the cries of his colleagues, Fillmore released the turkey with the words "Fly, bird, fly." Then an event occurred that Fillmore described as "the cruelest of blows." No sooner had he let the bird loose than Slater the mill owner, who was by now quite drunk, shot at it with his rifle, killing it instantly. Fillmore's white shirt was "flecked with blood," and "tears welled in my eyes." He ran to attack Slater but was hurled to the ground by the older man, who then "laughed and threw the dead bird into the back of his cart." The party ended swiftly, but on the way back to the mill the young Millard cradled the bird's corpse in his lap "and stroked its feathers gently." As he did so, he resolved that he would never gamble again.

Fillmore returned to his punishing work with thoughts of escape, but the simmering resentment between him and Slater boiled over when a disagreement erupted regarding his wood-chopping duties. Under the influence of the local moonshine and the teachings of the apocalyptic frontier church he attended, Slater had demanded that Fillmore chop down seven large oak trees so that he could build a giant ark to escape the coming deluge he had prophesied.[21] Since Fillmore was just fifteen years

20. Although the games of "naked apprentice grappling" and "employer tickling" seemed to have been invented by Slater, and played solely by his young workers.
21. Slater was a devoted follower of the Church of Christ's Misery, a small but influential Protestant body that concentrated on the most unpleasant parts of the Bible and believed in utter misery bringing one closer to "the desolation of redemption."

old, and Slater had tied one of his arms behind his back, "for the angel told him so," the task was patently impossible. Apoplectic at Fillmore's slow pace, Slater advanced toward him in a rage, but Fillmore raised his axe and, as if filled with the spirit of his pirate-killing great-grandfather, announced in a booming voice, "If you approach me I will split you down." His master retreated whimpering, and it was here that Fillmore, axe in hand, realized that he had "an inborn hatred of injustice and tyranny which I cannot express."

Yet what career would allow him to fight prejudice and oppression? What profession could allow him to live a chivalrous life devoid of self-interest? What vocation would allow him to care for the deprived and needy, and express his hatred of inequality through an august and virtuous system that treated both the rich and poor alike? To his uncomplicated mind there seemed only one answer—the law.

2.

Fillmore, Man of Law

(1819–1826)

A Handsome Prospect—Handicaps to Learning—Love Lessons—

The Strong Arm of the Law—The Panic of 1819—Superstition—

The Inconsolable Edgar Allan Poe—Dueling Andrew Jackson

B y the age of nineteen Fillmore stood five feet ten inches tall and was possessed of a rugged, barrel-chested physique. His hair was thick and brown, his eyes blue and sparkling, his nose strong yet elegant, his ears pink and shell-like, his mouth pert, his lips plump, his chin strong, and his teeth almost all there.

Fillmore at nineteen: dreamy.

Yet while his appearance was undeniably eye-catching, his mind had yet to match his body's development. Fillmore's only regular school during his youth had been the wilderness, and while his body would forever display the robustness gained from his years tilling the soil, even Fillmore suspected that if he was to study the law, being able to mimic the mating call of the beaver would be helpful in only the rarest of legal scenarios.[1]

---

1. Little could the uneducated Fillmore have known, but this simple frontier ability had already been used to astounding effect in the case of *Smith v. Jones* (1791). Abimelech Smith had issued complaint against Adolphus Jones on the grounds

Having left the excitement of the textile industry behind him, Fillmore enrolled at a small academy where he was finally provided with the blessing of a formal education, and more besides. For Fillmore's kind character and handsome aspect were already charming those around him, none more so than his teacher at the school, Miss Abigail Powers.

The youngest daughter of Baptist minister Lemuel Powers, Abigail was twenty-one years old and a woman of keen intelligence. Her father's large personal library had afforded her an education far beyond the usual frontier level, and ever since his death she had dedicated herself to removing the "natural ignorance" of her neighbors, whom she affectionately termed "the brutes." Letters written by Abigail to her friends speak of the illogical local prejudices against books, teachers, and even the alphabet itself, "which they call 'the devil's tapestry.'" As Fillmore himself had found, intelligence at the time was viewed with extreme suspicion, and Abigail recounts how her older pupils had stubbornly refused to open their primers because they had heard "that one can get lost within a book and might never find one's way back."[2]

Since Fillmore was so close to Abigail in age he would often walk with her after lessons and entertain her with stories of the New York fauna and flora of which he was so fond. It was hard for Abigail not to be swept away by his enthusiasms. "My latest challenge is nineteen years old and very slow," she wrote to a friend. "When I showed him a globe he asked me what it was, and when I informed him that it was the very world on which we live he looked at me strangely and falteringly enquired, 'Then where are

---

that Jones had sold him otters instead of beavers. With both the plaintiffs in court, along with a large burlap sack filled with a dozen semi-aquatic rodents of uncertain nature, the court called upon the skills of the famed natural historian Asa Kettringham. Kettringham's impression of the "breeding call of the American beaver" (described by one witness as "a high ululating reverberance") caused the aroused creatures to tear their way free from the sack and escape. The case was immediately found in favor of Jones. Three months later, when engineers were sent into the courthouse's sewer to investigate a blockage, they found a dam five feet high by six feet across, made entirely of judges' gavels.

2.   Such was the pitiful level of education along the frontier that when Abigail's father had attempted to create a public library in the town of Moravia in 1799, his house was set on fire and many of his books were burned by panicked townsfolk convinced that a library was "a vicious, three-horned beast, which ate children and flew with great scaly wings."

we now?' Yet he has a certain tranquility to him that is not unpleasant. Walking with him is like walking with one's dog. A dog that is oddly familiar with the region's bogs."

And so the months passed. Under the strong hand and sparkling eye of Abigail, Fillmore slowly overcame his deficiencies in learning, and gradually came to fall in love with his beautiful and kind teacher. But how was he going to win her hand if he could barely provide for himself?

Abigail Fillmore: not daguerrogenic.

It was at this point that the destiny that shapes presidential ends interposed itself into Fillmore's life. Distraught at the failure of his newly cultivated dust crop, ruined by unseasonably strong winds from the north, Fillmore's father relocated his family to the town of Montville to begin life as a tenant farmer. It was a wrenching change for Millard, since it meant leaving his beloved Abigail for weeks at a time. What it did allow, however, was a firsthand encounter with the law.

Montville was a burgeoning hamlet,[3] and the Fillmore family's new

---

3. To qualify as a hamlet a community had to have at least one unique superstition founded on either sneezing animals, the consumption of meat before sleeping, or the flight of sparrows on windy days.

landlord was its leading citizen, Judge Walter Wood, "a Quaker gentleman somewhat advanced in years, and reputed to be very wealthy." Knowing of Millard's legal ambitions, Fillmore's father approached the judge and pleaded with him to accept his son as a student. For a slight increase in rent and the option on one of Nathaniel Fillmore's daughters, the kindly old judge agreed. So much did an apprenticeship in the law mean to the young Millard that when he was informed of it he "burst out crying" and had to leave the room, "much mortified at my own weakness."[4]

Judge Wood's professional business was mostly limited to actions of debt collection and ejection of his tenants. Noticing that Fillmore was "large," and following the death of his three previous debt collectors at the hands of aggrieved farmers, Wood sent him out to intimidate those tenants who were behind in their payments.

Fillmore (left) points out the practicality of unbroken kneecaps to Judge Wood's tenants.

4. Fillmore's extreme sensitivity would resurface throughout his life. When, as president of the United States, he was informed of the drowning of a litter of kittens found on the White House property, he ran from the room in tears. He was found some hours later shivering in a cupboard beneath the servants' staircase, his eyes screwed tightly shut, his thumb in his mouth, humming fractured snatches of "Ding, Dong, Dell."

But Fillmore was temperamentally unsuited to threatening strong-arm tactics. If a tenant farmer could not pay his rent, Fillmore preferred to compromise, offering to extend the debt, on the strict promise that the farmer "would do his utmost to pay it back as soon as he could, barring any unforeseen events such as illness, drought, a fair coming to town, etc." If the following month the farmer still could not pay, then Fillmore would wink knowingly and suggest it "be our little secret." As such, he quickly became one of the most popular men in the county and could regularly be found testing his nascent rhetorical skills on the tenants, "arguing the proposition that bunny rabbits are delightful" or "that clouds are made of cotton wool." It was not long before Judge Wood, suspicious of his drooping profits, joined Fillmore on his rounds.

"It was God's own day," Fillmore recalled, "and the judge and I had taken a brisk morning walk through some of the loveliest countryside in the county. The lambs were gamboling in the sunshine and all seemed well with the world." But upon informing the tenant, Calvin Rafferty, of his predicament vis-à-vis the nonpayment of the preceding month's rent, "a dark cloud fell upon the day." Rafferty was a "large Irish gentleman" renowned for "wrestling horses."[5] He accused the judge of renting him fly-infested swampland; looking around him, Fillmore felt inclined to agree. But before the peaceable Fillmore could suggest a compromise, the judge "let loose with a string of invective that seemed to bring into question not only Mr. Rafferty's work ethic, and some fundamental characteristics of the Irish in general, but also the legitimacy of his ancestry, the failings of the potato as a vegetable, and the exact nature of Mr. Rafferty's relationship with horses." The enraged Irishman hurled himself at the judge, and Fillmore was forced to intercede. "Deaf to my pleas that we should continue our previous month's discussion on the attractiveness of rainbows, Mr. Rafferty grasped me by my coat's lapels and delivered a flurry of fearsome head-butts to my

---

5. Back when wrestling horses really meant something.

skull." Little could Rafferty have known that Fillmore possessed an abnormally thick cranium, gained, so he thought, "from the delicious lead cakes Mother would feed us when we were young." While Fillmore barely registered the blows, the enraged Irishman grew dizzy, weakened, and finally "so sprained his brain that he was quite becalmed."

With Rafferty defeated, Judge Wood began "looking me over as one does a prize cow, pinching my arms and prodding my sides," and, after setting fire to the Rafferty household, suggested that Fillmore might be of great use to him in the grand city of New York.

The journey to New York took ten days by horse and cart, and when Fillmore finally espied the city looming in the distance, he describes how he felt his heart "give a little jump." Fillmore's recollections of the day are particularly vivid: "As we bustled through the side streets of a delightful area called the Five Points, my mentor guided me into a large warehouse, which I was told was a very popular dance hall. Although I was not a dancer of note, I did enjoy to caper when I could, and thanked the judge for his consideration. Once inside the air was thick with smoke, and all I could make out was a firm, dirt floor circumscribed by a circle some twenty-five feet in diameter which I took to be the floor for dancing. Judge Wood told me to take off my shirt, a strict policy of the house, and suggested that I wait for my partner in the middle of the floor. As my eyes adjusted to the gloom, I saw hundreds of people sitting around me, presumably waiting for their own turn to cavort, and I hoped they would not mind me jumping ahead of them."

Fillmore's journal continues, "Suddenly the crowd burst into shouts and I espied a tall, well-built Negro approaching. The crowd was shouting out 'Molineux!' and, taking this to be my dancing partner's name, I decided to introduce myself. Imagine my surprise when he responded to my greeting by swinging his hand at me with some force, not with his hand in the open, traditional manner of the handshake, but with his fingers clenched tightly together, as if in a ball. I had heard tales in Cayuga County of strange Negro customs, but never had I heard of this odd form of greeting. In the spirit of inquiry I received the next handshake on my nose, but this did not seem to satisfy Mr. Molineux, who attempted to greet me again and again. I beckoned to Judge Wood for advice, but he was busy conducting some form of monetary exchange with a group of heavily scarred individuals I took to be fellow lawyers. It was then that I realized what a sheltered life I had lived, and how little I knew of the ways of the world. Here was I, a country boy, who thought he knew everything there was to know about life, and already I was at a loss as to how to proceed in this sophisticated and perplexing metropolis.

"As Molineux's salutations came faster and faster, pounding at my face and body with painful welcoming, I decided it would be best to return his gesture in kind. I thus swung my hand at his face as hard as I could, for I conceived that this would show the earnestness of my greeting. It hit him fully on the jaw, knocking him to the ground, and becalming not only his greetings but also the crowd's cheers. I had obviously made a terrible blunder. I turned to Judge Wood, feeling not a little embarrassed, but the kind judge was not angry in the slightest and ushered me quickly out into an alleyway. Then, without the slightest chastisement, and out of the kindness of his heart, for we had eaten not four hours prior, the kind old judge bought me an ear of corn. Truly he is a man of patience and forgiveness."

With Wood excusing himself to engage in some more business with "certain ladies who lived in the area," Fillmore was left to wander the streets alone. It was not long before he was surrounded by a crowd of witnesses to his altercation with Molineux and was bustled into a nearby saloon, "where they fed me countless strange fruit drinks and colored waters, and laughed heartily at my country confusions." What happened next is not immediately apparent, for his journal simply states, "I cannot recall the next few hours," although one can only speculate that this sudden and dramatic loss of memory was due to his nervous exertions earlier in the day.

It is unfortunate that Fillmore should have been so overwhelmed, for he was thus denied witnessing one of the most dramatic events ever to occur in New York's history. At approximately the same moment that Fillmore was celebrating with his new friends, a near-riot was sweeping the rarified environs of nearby Wall Street. The famed financier John Jacob Astor recalled what happened at the New York Stock Exchange in his best-selling autobiography, *Astornomical:* [6] "The securities were being called out in the afternoon session when a great disturbance erupted and a young man, well built and flushed, rushed into the exchange and began shouting in frantic terms: 'The Spanish have invaded! All is lost! Sell! Sell! Sell!' before running out again. There was a pause of a few seconds, at which point a crowd of rowdies spewed forth from the Points burst into the room. No sooner had they done so than a flurry of paper flew into the air, a maelstrom of humanity swamped the floor, making it quite impassable, and the market descended into chaos."

This bizarre invasion into the stock exchange triggered the infamous Panic of 1819, the first major financial crisis the United States had suffered, prompting widespread foreclosures, bank failures, unemployment, and a slump in agriculture and manufacturing across the country. One can only wonder what a man of Fillmore's perceptiveness and moral inquisitiveness would have made of this spectacle. Instead we hear only of him awakening "in a carriage traveling back to Montville, with Judge Wood staring at me with a dire countenance, and a timepiece that was not my own in my trouser pocket."

On his return to Montville, Fillmore continued to work for Judge Wood, but he increasingly began to branch out on his own. His rhetorical skills

---

6. *Astornomical* was the first business book to be published in North America. It declared that body warmth led to financial success ("for who trusts the man who shakes with the cold like the common street urchin?"), and called on readers to buy pelts and hides from the American Fur Company (prop. J. J. Astor) to ensure their healthful circulation and fiscal prosperity.

were blossoming, and on the Fourth of July, 1821, he delivered a rousing address to the collected townsfolk of Montville on the importance of days.[7] Such was the impression he left, both in speech and in poise, that a local farmer asked Fillmore to pettifog for him in front of a local justice of the peace; the experience only increased Fillmore's desire to practice law.[8]

When Judge Wood discovered his student's extracurricular legal work he was furious, insisting that Fillmore concentrate on his evictions. But Fillmore had growing doubts about the work he was doing for the old judge. "I had been sleeping fitfully, having eaten some rancid mutton," he wrote in his journal in the summer of 1821, "when I had the most peculiar dream. I was floating like a ghostly specter over what I took to be Europe, when suddenly I was struck by a revelation: the history of all hitherto existing society has simply been the history of class struggles. It seemed to me that if only the workers could unite and control the means of production, say, through the forcible overthrow of all existing social conditions, then bourgeois society would be set trembling and the workers would be freed from the chains of capitalism. At that moment I realized I was completely naked and awoke with a start." Fillmore recalls mentioning this strange dream to some of Judge Wood's tenants, "more to help me banish it from my mind, rather than in the expectation that it could be of help to them, for, like all dreams, upon awakening it seemed very silly indeed."

Fillmore was now twenty-one years old and felt ready to strike out on his own. Abigail, supportive as ever, agreed with him wholeheartedly. "The

---

7. The speech is lost except for one brief mention in the diary of Abigail Powers, which reads: "July 4th—Millard's speech. Highlight—'Days, without which we would have no repository for hours, nor wadding for weeks.' Unreal."

8. Pettifogging, originally *pretty-frogging*, was a curious custom of the early nineteenth century designed to solve arguments without recourse to the courts. In matters where the guilty party was hard to ascertain, both the accuser and the accused would tie bows around frogs and race them in front of a magistrate. According to New York State law, the victor was judged on both speed and style. Pettifogging rules were changed drastically in 1834 following the domination in pettifogging circles of the transplanted French advocate Pierre LaRochefocauld. Such was LaRochefocauld's genius at dressing his amphibians—his lace patterns were particularly admired—that style points were diminished in importance, and pettifogging became little more than common frog racing. The introduction of the West African goliath in 1855 by the law firm of Fletcher, Beasley & Cress saw the practice of pettifogging disappear completely, since the two-foot-long amphibian could leap ten feet in a single bound, and its green and yellow coloring worked with everything.

boy genius is leaving here and coming your way, thank God," she wrote to a friend. "Would you please be so kind as to make sure he does not drown in his soup?"

After bidding Abigail a tearful farewell, Fillmore took leave of his kindly mentor. Judge Wood was obviously much saddened at the loss of such a useful student, but generously let Fillmore leave his service with the one condition that he paid him back, in monthly installments, his room and board for the last two years, his travel expenses to and from New York, including interest, as well as 40 percent of all future income earned within the practice of the law, and 20 percent of all income earned from other sources, before tax. As Fillmore was signing his name to the contract Judge Wood put in front of him, he was delighted to see that all of the judge's tenants had come to wave him goodbye. There were smiles on every face as the farmers wished him good luck with his future, and Fillmore told them to take care of the frail judge, "who had treated me so well." Setting out on his journey, he saw that Judge Wood was already being helped from his house by some of the larger farmers, and recalled that "his fist waved at me in fond farewell from amidst the circle of his admirers."

When he had walked some way, Fillmore turned back to take a last look at his home. "Judge Wood could no longer be seen," he wrote, "but one of my farmer friends held aloft the judge's cane, and another his cape, as I presume the old man had gone to sit down, being so old and enfeebled."[9]

Fillmore was to seek his fortune 150 miles to the north, in the grand metropolis of Buffalo. The city was in the process of rebuilding itself after

9. The Cayuga County Workers' Republic (CCWR) flourished in upstate New York for fifteen glorious months. Improved worker efficiency saw a record harvest, and the socialist county's income tripled within a year. That was until the events of Bloody January, 1823, when militia loyal to Elwin Trotter, an unemployed blacksmith, stormed a meeting of the Montville Central Committee claiming it had become "bureaucratically degenerate." The coup was unsuccessful, and Trotter was exiled to nearby Cumberland County. Following devastating purges, a counterrevolutionary strike on January 29 restored traditional feudal impoverishment. Trotter was found crushed to death beneath an anvil in 1828.

being burned to the ground by the British in the War of 1812,[10] and could now boast the second-longest ditch in the state, and a three-way traffic system responsible for the worst wagon pile-up in American history.

Fillmore soon gained work as a clerk at a Buffalo law firm and found that the study of the law—its rigorous insistence on drudgery, and its proscription against originality—warmly reminded him of his apprenticeship at the cloth-dressing mill so many years before. His imagination was thus left to run free in the long, wistful letters he wrote to Abigail, wherein he spoke of their future together.[11] Within a year he had learned enough of the law to set up his own office in the nearby town of East Aurora, specializing in cases involving the animals he loved so dearly. With the area suffering from a greater-than-usual number of cases of snake wrangling and bearicide, Fillmore was kept busy, and soon his house was filled with chastened hedgehogs, disinterred moles, and other unwanted fauna he came across so often in his pro bono work.

East Aurora was located in the infamous County of Erie, or as it was originally known, Eerie, for the area was named after a collection of strange incidents that had beset its populace ever since the arrival of the first Dutch and German families in the seventeenth century. Some said the whole region had been cursed by a Dutch witch who had been persecuted in years gone by. Others believed that an old Indian chief had held his powwows there.[12] It was supposed that the stars shone brighter and that comets were seen more clearly in the sky there,[13] and when a thick mist

10. According to the papers of British general Keith Fotherington, Buffalo was destroyed for being "too . . . you know . . ."

11. Abigail's responses to Fillmore's enthusiastic letters—some of which run on for twenty pages or more—are brief yet not lacking in passion. In reply to a letter Fillmore wrote that included the sentence "And you shall prepare supper every day, and I shall return from the Supreme Court and feed the camels and whales, and you will have given birth to twenty little Millards, and they shall all need baths, and you will give them to them," Abigail's reply was a heartfelt "Thrilling."

12. A powwow was a sacred Indian ritual in which the chief of a tribe asked his dead ancestors for guidance. He did so by rolling two cubes made of bone, each one marked with a series of scratches. If the scratches added up to six or nine more than once, good fortune would come. If the scratches added up to seven on any roll but the first, it would almost certainly be a bad year for the tribe.

13. These "stars" and "comets" were sometimes put down to the local custom of pyrornithology, in which pigeons were set on fire and raced.

rolled inland off Lake Erie it was rumored the area's ducks waddled village streets in search of infant blood.

The Erie County legislature in session.

Yet the spirits and superstitions of the area were now being challenged by a new, technological era. In 1825, the 363-mile-long Erie Canal was finally completed, linking the Great Lakes to the Atlantic Ocean.[14] At its official opening in October, the locks were opened and water coursed down the channel in a surging tide. Fillmore took the day off from his legal work to watch the spectacle, but upon arriving at the still-dry channel he was shocked to see the body of a boy lying on the canal bed. The sound of gunshots was growing louder as the state's inhabitants cheered on the flooding water. Without a thought for his own safety, Fillmore immediately leapt into the canal to drag the body to safety. Then "I heard it clear its throat and enquire, in a rather terse manner, who I was and what I

---

14. The construction of the Erie Canal is all the more remarkable when one considers it was created due to a wager. In 1817, after a hard night of drinking, and following the usual contests of strength, two citizens of Buffalo, James Geddes and Benjamin Wright, each bet the other that they could empty Lake Erie of water. They set off in high spirits, remarkably both with the same idea of building a waterway from the lake to the Hudson River. Geddes began digging east from Lake Erie, while Wright began digging west from the Hudson. Each hoping to surprise the other, they worked in complete secrecy around the clock for eight years, until quite by chance, their canals happened to meet just outside of Schenectady, New York.

thought I was doing. Somewhat startled, I jumped up from my travails and replied that I was Millard Fillmore, a lawyer from East Aurora, and that I was trying to save him from the oncoming flood. The boy replied quite calmly that his name was Edgar Allan Poe, and that he did not want to be saved, and bade me stop my work and leave him alone. I naturally supposed that the awfulness of his situation had driven him out of his senses, and so replied that, as a lawyer, it was my sacred duty to save him, at which moment I looked up and saw a wall of water, now not twenty yards from us. Hoisting the boy over my shoulder, I clambered out of the canal as the water frothed and steamed past us on its relentless charge to the next lock."

Poe "was small, and thin, and dressed in black," recalled Fillmore. "He could not have been more than sixteen years of age, but his eyes seemed much older. Looking at the rushing water that flowed past him, he exclaimed, 'I . . . am . . . alive,' and fell into a faint. Never in my life had I heard those words spoken with such remorse."

Fillmore carried the unconscious boy back to East Aurora, where he lay insensible and ran a high fever for many days. Abigail traveled from Montville to help with his recovery, and slowly but surely the boy's strength returned, although the air of insufferable gloom that surrounded him was harder to dissipate. On one occasion, Fillmore found Poe dangling by his neck from a rope in the living room, "obviously in some ill-managed attempt to hang a picture." On another occasion, when Fillmore had been called to his law office, he returned to find the boy "with his face hovering over the kitchen table, Abigail's knitting needles inserted up his nostrils, pleading desperately with her to drop one of my large law books onto the back of his head."

In an attempt to cheer him up, Abigail suggested the boy write some poetic verses, an activity that Fillmore did his best to encourage. Wandering in his garden with Poe, Fillmore suggested that he try "writing about a bird: the humble chickadee or tuneful hermit thrush, the plump pigeon or the colorful oriole." Poe did not respond immediately to the suggestion,

Poe, wretched soul.

but later that night Fillmore wrote of the usual moans and groans coming from Poe's bedroom being augmented by "a sudden scream of 'The raven!' followed by a burst of high-pitched laughter. It made me glad that he had finally settled on a subject to his liking, although I had secretly been hoping for the chickadee."

In 1824, John Quincy Adams had been elected president in greatly disputed circumstances. While Andrew Jackson had received more of the popular vote than Adams, he had not gained a majority within the fickle Electoral College.[15] The defeat had plunged Jackson into the darkest of moods.

Andrew Jackson was not a man to offend lightly. As a child he had enlisted to fight in the Revolutionary War after his English nanny had forced him to eat his vegetables. He had become a bona fide war hero following his triumph at the Battle of New Orleans in 1815, when a sneak attack by the British had the disastrous effect of disrupting his breakfast.[16]

---

15. The fact that classes at the Electoral College convene only once every four years has led to its reputation as something of a "party school."

16. The Battle of New Orleans took place more than two weeks after the Treaty of Ghent—declaring peace between the United States and Britain—was supposed to have been signed. Unfortunately, neither the British nor the American ambassadors knew where Ghent was located, and after struggling for weeks to find it, they eventually gave up and returned home. Ghent has still not been discovered to this day.

Jackson was a man of astonishing irritability—when his sleep had been plagued by mosquitoes one night in 1817, he invaded Spanish Florida in an attempt to destroy the insects' breeding grounds.

Jackson's temper was just as violent away from the battlefield, and he

Andrew Jackson regularly shot his portrait artists for
"looking at me funny."

had taken part in over one hundred duels, for the most part against those who had slandered the sacred name of his wife.[17] Rachel Jackson had forgotten to get divorced from her previous husband prior to marrying Jackson, and had thus been labeled a bigamist. Any mention of this word drove Jackson into a furious rage.[18] Now, having lost the election, Jackson was more livid than he had ever been before. He was rumored to be "burning up" the country atop his horse, Nightmare, and it was in Buffalo, during this bacchanalia of despair, that Fillmore was to make his acquaintance.

On November 12, 1825, Fillmore was walking back to East Aurora, having taken Poe to watch the traditional Buffalo entertainment of shaving

17. Other reasons for Jackson's duels include "stepping on his foot," "twirling a moustache in his immediate vicinity," "effecting him to laugh when he had not expected to," and "being of a Tuesday."
18. Although illegal in every state and condemned by the church, bigamy was a popular fetish amongst reserved nineteenth-century men, as attested to by the popularity of the pamphlet *Fiery Bigamists.*

bears. It had not been a success. Poe had leapt into the ring in an attempt to be "torn asunder by tooth and claw." His wretched pleading had only scared the animal, and an angry crowd insisted that Poe himself be sheared. Upon entering a saloon along the way, in the hope of buying Poe a hat, Fillmore was greeted by "a devastation of broken tables and chairs." A tall, lean man with a shock of white hair was holding the saloon's proprietor by the scruff of the neck and lifting him straight up in the air. It was Andrew Jackson.

Upon seeing Fillmore and Poe, Jackson dropped the man and, suddenly calmer, motioned them over to join him at the bar. "Come join me, boys," Fillmore remembered Jackson saying in a southern drawl, "we're having ourselves a little party." Not wishing to offend this imposing stranger, he acquiesced, but no sooner had he sat down than Jackson caught hold of Fillmore's hand and pressed it against his chest. "'Feel that,' he said to me as he drew me nearer. 'That's the bullet one of the Benton boys gave me in 1813. I could have had it removed but . . . hell, I just like the way it hurts!' I could smell the sour mash on his breath and must admit to being somewhat afraid."

For many hours Fillmore and Poe kept the fifty-eight-year-old Jackson company as he drank bourbon, smashed bottles, and uttered strange non sequiturs. Poe was much fascinated by Jackson's tales of dueling, and was delighted every time Jackson would grimace in pain from one of his many wounds and cough up blood into his handkerchief. Thanks to Fillmore's amiable temperament, before long they were chatting amicably about their families, and with the introduction of coffee, Jackson began to feel slightly embarrassed at his earlier ravings. He mentioned that his wife would be meeting him in Buffalo the following day and, in Fillmore's eyes, "he seemed much relieved at her arrival." It was reaching midnight, and all seemed calm, when talk turned to the effect of Lake Erie on the local climate. Fillmore offhandedly described how the fog had been thin up until now, but how he was expecting a "bigger mist to be rolling into town tomorrow." The cup in Jackson's hand exploded. Leaping to his feet, he cursed Fillmore and demanded satisfaction. Fillmore was taken aback. What had caused this sudden change in the man? Nevertheless, as a gentleman, Fillmore was bound to accept the challenge. The time was set for dawn the following morning, and a confused Fillmore made his way back to East Aurora, where his sleep was not aided by Poe's "envious pronouncements on my inevitable and bloody doom."

It is perhaps as strange a thing as has ever been in the history of a country when the future seventh president of the United States dueled with the future thirteenth president. Yet how different in experience were the two men who now made their way on a cold November morning to Wexford's Mill. Fillmore had never shot a gun in his life, and had to be advised about the very basics of aiming and firing by Poe, who "embellished the lesson so much with his morbid enthusiasms that by the end of it I barely knew which end of the firearm to point. What I did know, thanks to my young friend, was that I could be hit in the belly and take three days to die in what he termed 'exquisite agony.' I thus resolved to fire my shot into the air, making first certain that no birds were flying above."

With Poe acting as his second, Fillmore made the trek back to the dueling ground the following morning. A stern and implacable Jackson awaited him, the saloon owner he had been throttling the night before shivering beside him. "Despite my protestations and enquiries into what had prompted this extraordinary turn of events, General Jackson refused to answer me." The two men faced each other in the somber morning light, ten full paces apart. A thick mist had indeed come rolling off the lake, and cloaked the two men and their seconds in a funereal shroud. At the signal, Jackson lifted his gun, pointed it directly at Fillmore's heart, and pulled the trigger. But the heavy dew had wet the flint and it failed to fire. Fillmore, who had been distracted by a passing squirrel and had not even raised his gun, "felt much relieved and, walking over to Mr. Jackson, suggested all be forgotten and breakfast be taken." But Jackson was having none of it. He leapt upon his horse and, pulling a sword from his saddle, charged at

Fillmore, his hair like white flame burning furiously from his skull, the hooves of his horse tearing up the wet turf. "I jumped for cover as he thundered by me and into the mist," recalled Fillmore. "I tried to listen as to where he had gone, but all I could hear were Poe's incessant shouts beseeching the saloon owner to shoot him."

Suddenly the sound of horse's hooves was upon him once more, and it seems certain that Fillmore would have been run through had it not been for the sudden appearance of a figure emerging out of the mist directly in front of the galloping general. Jackson's horse reared in alarm upon seeing this fearful apparition and unseated its rider before running wildly into the haze. A prostrate Jackson quivered on the ground, dropping his sword and raising his right arm to protect himself. For there, clutching a small purse, with her skirts wafting and eyes glaring, was his wife, Rachel Jackson, appearing to a bedraggled Fillmore "as both harpy and guardian angel." Mrs. Jackson did not wait for her husband to stand before she began to berate him for his "fighting, gambling, and general uncouth ways," wrote Fillmore, "giving him many lashes of her tongue, and her purse." Under this verbal and physical assault, Jackson seemed to shrink before Fillmore's eyes, the fire in his belly quenched. Rachel Jackson made her husband shake hands with Fillmore, and apologized profusely for his actions, "saying that it was no wonder he had lost the last election if he couldn't behave himself."

Thus General Jackson departed Buffalo under the baleful eye of his wife, leaving behind him a greatly relieved Fillmore. Although Poe had managed to stab himself in the foot with Jackson's sword, the two friends had escaped from the encounter without serious bloodshed. But the incident had intrigued Fillmore. What was this strange political world from which Jackson had come? Little did he realize that within just a few months, he would be a politician himself.

3.

Fillmore the Explorer

(1826–1832)

Romancing Abigail—Skullduggery in Batavia—The Fighting Anti-

Freemasons—Lessons in Liberté—America the Large—The Pious

Nat Turner—Le Prison-Break

*F*illmore's law practice was growing rapidly, and his financial prospects had improved to such an extent that he now proposed marriage to his beloved Abigail.[1] "Foolmore [*sic*] has asked for my hand in marriage," wrote an ecstatic Abigail to a friend, "be still my beating heart." Yet despite Abigail's obvious euphoria she did not respond to the offer immediately. Fillmore persisted. "He wrote a poem for me," wrote Abigail a week later, "which reached its zenith when he rhymed 'wedding vows' with 'ruminant cows.'" Whether it was the poetry, the prose (Fillmore's self-published leaflet *In Defense of Millard*), or the synchronized salamander pageant that finally won her over, Abigail eventually accepted, and the couple married on February 5, 1826.[2] Edgar Allan Poe acted as best man, and Fillmore was greatly moved by his speech, recalling how it "pondered the joys of the marriage vows, lingering over the exhortation 'till death do us part,' and musing on what disfiguring disease or poisoned dart would be the cause of our final separation, before ending with a most moving speech from William Shakespeare's *Othello*."

Despite the happiness that flooded the newlyweds' house, it was a time of great disturbance within the Union. Recriminations from the disputed election of 1824 still rumbled through the country, and factionalism was growing. On July 4, 1826, exactly fifty years after the signing of the Declaration of Independence, all America was shocked to hear of the

1. Fillmore had advanced from animal malfeasance to embracing bog, marsh, swamp, and quagmire transgressions (i.e., bog theft, swamp tipping, the illegal unmiring of quags, etc.).
2. From Abigail's letters: "It is not often that one finds fifteen long-tailed, beady-eyed salamanders being paraded toward you in single file by one of your former pupils. That this former pupil is frantically attempting to keep his monsters in line with various high-pitched whistles is certainly a sight to behold. But the exquisiteness of the moment is only heightened by the discovery that each amphibian has a letter painted onto its back, so that as the beasts scurry by one can spell out the tender words 'Immoral Elf Drill.' Who says the age of romance is dead?"

almost simultaneous deaths of President John Adams and President Thomas Jefferson.

The fierce competitiveness that had characterized the lifelong political rivalry between Jefferson and Adams had continued in the manner of their deaths. In the early months of 1826, Jefferson had been informed of Adams' painful rheumatoid arthritis and increasing tremors. Fearing that Adams was trying to die first—and thus pip him to the post as he had in the election of 1796—Jefferson hastened his own decline, contracting smallpox and growing an enlarged prostate. Adams, still bruised from his own acrimonious electoral defeat to Jefferson in 1800, dashed off a letter to his rival, stating, "You can steal my election, but you'll never take my congenital heart defect," and immediately went blind through sheer force of will. When Jefferson slipped into a comatose state on July 2, Adams knew his old adversary had gained the upper hand, but desperately repelling life, Adams thought he had seized victory through a sudden brain aneurysm, his last words being the triumphant "Thomas Jefferson survives!" Unfortunately, Jefferson had died earlier that morning from a simple stroke, and Adams succumbed to the void in second place.

The vast outpouring of grief at these tragedies briefly united the country.[3] But in New York State, right under Fillmore's nose, malign influences were at work that paid no heed to the nation's tears.

In the fall of that grim year, William Morgan, a bricklayer and member of the clandestine organization known as the Freemasons, threatened to reveal the society's secret rituals to an astonished world. Within days of publishing his exposé, Morgan had disappeared under mysterious circumstances from his home in Batavia, less than thirty miles from Fillmore's law office in East Aurora.[4] When the police investigated Morgan's house and found broken

3. According to the Institute of National Psychologists, the United States has been officially united in grief eleven times in its history, yet has been united in joy only four times (and two of those were out of pure schadenfreude). Apathy has united the country most often—over three hundred times—with anger, shame, and ice dancing also proving to be popular nation-bonding sentiments.

4. Although marketed as a tell-all on Masonic signs, words, and handshakes, Morgan's book—entitled *Illustrations of Freemasonry*—had begun life as *My Turnip and I*, a memoir of the author's many failed attempts to grow the vegetable in the

furniture, shattered glass, a large pentagram painted on the floor, and a warning written in blood on the wall stating, "So die all traitors," they naturally concluded that Morgan had "been eaten by a wolf." It was not long afterward that unsubstantiated rumors began to circulate that the Freemasons had infiltrated all aspects of local and national law enforcement and government.

William Morgan: stool pigeon or scapegoat?

Word of this scandal soon reached Millard Fillmore's bustling law office. "I was told today," wrote Fillmore in his journal on the twenty-third of February, 1827, "that the Masons are also to blame for the explosion of Mount Tambora in the Dutch East Indies, and the invention of the color puce, a most perturbing hue." By March, reports were growing ever more frantic: "Mr. Pitt the butcher is only transacting business with customers by means of a looking glass and in bright sunlight, for he hears that the Masons, whilst having hearty appetites for red meat, do not have reflections, nor do they cast shadows." As Fillmore wondered what he could do to challenge such a seemingly vast and hideous conspiracy, sixty miles away

---

acidic loam of his garden. The sole mention of Freemasonry in the book had been when he spoke of the usefulness of his Masonic apron and trowel in providing "clean and effortless access to the soil." It was only when his publisher suggested that he concentrate on this aspect of the book that Morgan began to draw publicity. Not every reference to cultivation was excised from the book, as can be seen from such chapters as "How Worshiping the Goat of Mendes Can Aid the Growth of *Brassica Rapa.*"

in a two-room printing plant in the town of Cairo, an intellect vast and cool and unsympathetic regarded the hysteria with interested gray eyes.

Thurlow Weed was a man of significant influence. The editor of two political newspapers in the state capital, Albany, Weed's support for John Quincy Adams in the previous election had been decisive.[5] Upon hearing of the Morgan affair, he immediately began forming a new political party, one whose professed goal was the total destruction of the Masonic order. It would be known simply as the Anti-Mason Party.[6]

Thurlow Weed: never said "Cheese."

An Anti-Mason convention was scheduled for Buffalo, and a curious Fillmore was eager to attend.[7] "I have never met a Freemason," he wrote in his journal, "and cannot say whether they are good or bad men. But if the stories I hear are true, then they seem to be practicing a form of injustice

---

5.   Weed also wrote devastating broadsides on fashion for the *Albany Women's Wear Review*. His diatribes on the dangers of tight lacing had made him an avowed enemy of the corset, girdle, and bodice lobby, while his infamous editorial declaring that hats were "unnecessary" saw him reviled by milliners throughout the state.

6.   It should be noted that political parties in the early nineteenth century were often founded on a single cause or special interest, unlike the complicated and nuanced platforms put forward by today's politicians. For instance, the Wet Nurse Party was rabidly pro-midwife, the Non-Regional Animal Party, or NRA, was devoted to banning the sale of gnus, and the Shoot First Party was committed simply to answering questions about its manifesto later.

7.   Anti-Masonic conventions were common at the time and would include apron-burning displays, "Destroy Solomon's Temple" booths, and "Tell You the Mason" seminars, explaining ways of recognizing Masons from their dress habits ("and they must always be in need of a hole in their undergarments from which to let their tail out").

and tyranny that upsets me, and which I dearly hope I can play a part in bringing to a halt. If, that is, they can indeed be killed."

It was Fillmore's good fortune that while attempting to knock the hat off a coconut "most humorously shaped like a devilish Mason," he happened to see Thurlow Weed himself walking toward him. Recognizing him from his engraving in the newspapers, Fillmore rushed forward and excitedly professed his enthusiasm to join the Anti-Masons. "Upon telling him this," wrote Fillmore, "Mr. Weed asked me, in a most grave manner, what I thought of the rumors that the Anti-Mason Party was merely a canard, created purely to block the next presidential campaign of the Jacksonian Democrats. I replied that even if I had heard such slander, I doubted very much whether ducks were of such an intemperate and radical disposition as to disrupt a democratic election. At this Mr. Weed's countenance lifted, and a broad smile settled on his face."

Weed was obviously struck by Fillmore's intelligence and pleasant nature.[8] Returning to East Aurora the following day, Fillmore found that bunting and ribbons hung from the trees. Upon approaching his law office, he noticed a large crowd surrounding it, which burst into spontaneous applause upon seeing him. Above his doorway was a large pasteboard sign declaring, "Fillmore, Anti-Mason for State Assembly." Weed's political machine had moved quickly. He dismounted and was shaking hands with the crowd when Abigail strode up to him and "informed me that the Anti-Masons were merely a group of scaremongers, whose solitary aim was to cause panic across the country.[9] She told me that three of her

8. Weed wrote to one of his political confreres: "M.F. is a lawyer, popular, and comes from Erie County, where we have been suffering reversals to the Democrats. He is pliant, trusting, and totally without gumption." It should be noted that in the early nineteenth century *gumption* did not necessarily mean "common sense," as it does today, but also seemed to refer to a gastric disorder gained by eating too much cheese.

9. Scaremongering was a booming trade in the nineteenth century, supplying much-needed frights, shocks, and alarms to the populace. This was especially necessary along the frontier, where the inhabitants were so hardy and courageous that without the intimidating skills of a local scaremonger, hiccups would have become pandemic. Scaremongering suffered a severe setback in 1919, when Dr. Bryan Payne, prompted by his own weak heart, discovered that drinking out of the "wrong side of a glass" worked just as well as being startled in the curing of involuntary spasms of the diaphragm. Traditional scaremongering went into an irreversible decline after the industry was nationalized by Senator Joseph McCarthy in 1950.

students had apparently crucified another child on the schoolhouse roof for having clammy hands, insisting that this was a sign of Freemasonry, and she insisted that I return and tell Mr. Weed that I would not stand."

A disheartened Fillmore traveled back to the convention the following day, for "although flattered at Mr. Weed's faith in me, I could not anger my Abigail." Yet when he arrived in Buffalo, he found that "my hand was shaken and my name cheered"—he had already been nominated. So happy were the delegates to see him that Fillmore completely forgot about Abigail's feminine worries and unfounded speculations, and joined in the celebrations with gusto. Weed congratulated him in person; "he hoped that I would distinguish myself, and I, somewhat dazed, assured him I would follow him to the ends of the earth." Within weeks Fillmore was duly elected to a seat in the New York State Assembly, and was waving goodbye to East Aurora and his beloved Abigail.[10] Fillmore recalled Abigail "with her head shaking from side to side, and her eyes rolling back in her head with happiness, saying that at least I had found an occupation that would allow me to work amongst like-minded individuals." Poe had decided to leave too, grumbling that ever since Abigail had hidden the kitchen knives and placed corks on all the forks he had been filled with alarming feelings of "self-worth and pride."

So ended the first stage in Millard Fillmore's life as he turned away from the land of his childhood and put his youthful accomplishments behind him. Now was to begin a new era in which he would become fully initiated into the cause of American liberty, in which he would command attention with the force and fervor of his words, and through his unique understanding of the issues that plagued his country. The future lay before him, and he approached it at a pace that never slackened.

Despite the Anti-Mason Party's local successes in New York State, Andrew Jackson and his newly formed Democratic Party romped to the

---

10. Curiously, Fillmore gained more votes in the state assembly than all the other candidates put together. Indeed, his tally of 1,434,089 easily beat his closest opponent by exactly 1,425,000 votes.

presidency in 1828.[11] Nonetheless, Fillmore was enthused by the task he had been given. Arriving in Albany, he was overawed by the grandeur of the state capital, which had gained impressive plaudits from foreign travelers visiting the region. "Close your eyes," wrote one tourist, "shut out the boondocks chatter, and stop your nose from the repugnant vapors, and, on an unseasonably warm day, having drunk heartily, and being of a naturally artistic disposition, one could imagine oneself in Rome."

As an assemblyman, Fillmore was still uncertain as to his duties, but when Thurlow Weed addressed him and the other new members of the Anti-Mason Party, urging them to seek out Masonic corruption "in all the corridors of power," he knew immediately what had to be done.

On the night of December 31, 1828, while most other residents of Albany were welcoming in the New Year, Millard Fillmore could be found groping his way through the darkened corridors of the statehouse, a flickering oil lamp dimly lighting his way as his footsteps echoed off the granite walls. "It seems to me," wrote Fillmore in his journal, "that if the Masons are inveigling their way into the passageways and halls of the state capitol, then no place is safe." For much of the night it had been a fruitless search, and Fillmore was ready to "quit the corridors of power for the bedroom of slumber" when, stumbling on a step, he reached out to steady himself on a marble bust of George Washington and, "grasping the great hero's nose, was shocked to feel it recede into his head. I was mulling over this latest anatomical revelation concerning the Father of our Country when I noticed a section of the wall had rolled asunder on hidden wheels disclosing a narrow passageway." Fillmore relates that the tunnel opened up into a large room from which he thought he heard chanting and saw cloaked figures and the flicker of flames on the walls. "It was so fantastical

---

11. The presidential election of 1828 was host to one of the dirtiest political campaigns in history, with Jackson's family coming in for particular abuse. Not only had Jackson's wife been called a bigamist repeatedly by supporters of the incumbent, John Quincy Adams, but Jackson's late mother had been labeled a prostitute, his father an atheist, and his brothers, killed during the Revolutionary War, "sissies." Even Jackson's dog, Snowflake, a three-legged, one-eyed dachshund who devotedly followed his master wherever he went, was accused of being rabid, malodorous, and "man's worst friend."

that I could barely believe it to be true," wrote Fillmore. "Had the junior assemblymen's New Year's Eve party really started without me? I was about to investigate further when I heard a sound from behind me, felt a damp cloth pressed to my face, and then, nothing."

Fillmore's journal speaks of a lapse in memory and a sudden change of scene. "I awoke to find Mr. Weed standing over me. I was in my rooms, lying unclothed in my bed. Mr. Weed said that I had been found on the steps of the statehouse by a sergeant of the peace, who assumed that I was a victim of overindulgence. I denied this, and related the whole story to him, upon which Mr. Weed, with a kindly smile, suggested that I had tripped on the stairs, knocked myself unconscious, and imagined the whole incident. The attending doctor seemed to agree, and assured me that the medical community did not generally acknowledge that George Washington had a retractable nose. Recalling my strange memory loss in New York in 1819, I must admit that such a scenario is not an impossibility; indeed, when I returned to the statehouse later I noticed that where once I thought had stood the bust of Washington was instead a severe marble of Benedict Arnold, with the word 'TRAITOR' written in large letters beneath it. How the mind can play tricks on one!"

Slowly but surely under Weed's guiding influence, Fillmore began to learn what it meant to be a New York assemblyman. "I cannot fathom what is happening," he wrote to Abigail, "but Mr. Weed insists that I should not trouble myself finding out, and assures me that idle hands are the best tools." He was routinely praised for voting the party line, and read eloquent speeches provided to him by Weed stressing his conviction and certainty on the matter at hand, his orations seemingly gaining in emotional resonance in inverse proportion to his understanding of the topic.[12]

Outside of politics, Fillmore's life consisted of countryside strolls and weekly visits to the temperance society, which Weed had encouraged

12. It has been suggested by presidential psychiatrists that Fillmore suffered from the verbal phenomenon known as "cognitive ignorance."

him to join since his New Year's Eve incident.[13] Yet more and more Fill-more's mind seems to have grown obsessed with the Masonic threat. He began to leave unattended goats outside the statehouse "in the hope that a Freemason, hungry for blood sacrifice, might choose to steal one." He even spent weeks traveling to craftsmen's guilds in the Albany area enquiring about the pricing of their labor, but he was to be disappointed, "for none admitted to working gratis as the deviant 'free' Masons do." Weed tried to calm his fears, telling him not to think "too literally" on the subject, but it seemed to an increasingly frustrated Fillmore that "the cause of uncover-ing fiendish Masonic plots has been relegated behind frustrating the poli-cies of the newly elected government." When, finally, he did manage to persuade the legislature to debate his measure ("in the pursuance of which I have sadly forfeited all puddings taken in the statehouse dining rooms until 1923 or my death, whichever should come first"), Weed ordered him to leave for New York City on what he termed "a special mission."

It transpired that the French government was sending a delegation to adjudge the state of American democracy, and Fillmore was to act as host to the two ambassadors, squiring them about New York State "to ensure that we are portrayed in a suitable light." Fillmore had never met a French-man, but he was curious. Were they *really* shaped in the image of frogs, as his father had always told him? And if so, would they make companions as affable as the northern spring peepers and eastern spadefoots he had known and loved as a boy? He boarded a steamboat on the Hudson River with no little excitement.

Fillmore was supposed to meet the two French gentlemen at their hotel on Broadway, but upon his arrival he was informed that they had not been seen for days. His inquiries eventually led him to the Five Points, where he was still fondly remembered from his exploits a decade before.

---

13. It is a common misconception that the temperance movement concerned itself purely with alcoholic consumption. Original directives included proscriptions against "everything heating and stimulating," including hot baths, impassioned arguments, the novels of Jane Austen, and the petting of furry animals.

"I was informed that a couple of 'Frenchies' were in a nearby inn, where I found them surrounded by a crowd of young women. I was slightly disappointed in that aside from the large, watery eyes of one of the men and the puffy cheeks of the other, they looked nothing like the amphibians I had known in the wilderness. For a start, they lacked long hind legs and elongated ankle bones, and seemed to have just the one set of eyelids. Even when I released the flies I had been keeping in a matchbox for just this moment I saw no sign of long tongues darting from their mouths—they simply swatted them away as if troubled by them, and asked me what I thought I was doing. I introduced myself to them, and the young man with the watery eyes stood up and, speaking to me in a thick accent, which made all the girls sigh, introduced himself as Alexis de Tocqueville, and his companion as Gustave de Beaumont.

"I informed Mr. de Tocqueville that I was to be his official guide and enquired when he would like to begin his tour. But my seemingly harmless question cast a pall on the proceedings. 'Monsieur Fillmore,' he said with extreme earnestness, 'this may shock you, but I did not come here to study democracy. I have been caged in France for twenty-one years, always having to eat the most gorgeous food, always having to wear the finest clothes, inundated with art and culture. I am sick of it, Monsieur Fillmore! I want to throw off the cast of imperial and cultural oppression, as you Americans have done. I want to hurl tea into the harbor and write my own declaration of independence! I demand independence from the so-called glorious Second Republic.' 'You mean the Third Republic,' corrected the unhappy-looking Mr. de Beaumont, 'or is it the Second Empire?' His words trailed off and he returned morosely to his drink. 'You see, Monsieur Fillmore,' cried Mr. de Tocqueville, 'you see! Gustave cries himself to sleep at night uncertain whether we suffer under the iron fist of an enlightened despot's totalitarian absolutism, a benevolent but oligarchic republican democracy, or a quasi-imperialist constitutionally heritable monarchy!

It is very, very confusing.[14] I am dizzy with revolution, Monsieur Fillmore! I don't want to man the barricades and sing the songs of angry men anymore! I just want to enjoy myself. Is that too much to ask? Yes, yes, I know I will have to return home someday, but Monsieur Fillmore, I intend to store up a few happy memories for the long, torturous, winter evenings back in the hell that is the *seizième arrondissement.*' With that he picked up his glass and hurled it into the fire, then grasped one of the nearby girls and began dancing with her on the table."

Tocqueville: au contraire-revolutionary.

Uncertain how he should proceed, Fillmore stepped outside. In many ways he could relate to the young aristocrat and his tortured existence. It was true that Fillmore had not been born in a château with liveried servants caring to his every whim. He had never dined on larks' tongues in aspic, nor

14. As well as the unsettling political changes, the French Revolution also ushered in many conceptual, philosophical, and quantitative upheavals. The French inch became longer (leading to many misconceptions about the height of the strapping, six-foot-tall Napoleon Bonaparte), and a revolutionary calendar was instigated in which a new "revolutionary" season—consisting of heavy snowfall and intense heat—was inserted between spring and summer. Similar "revolutionary" changes affected colors, with red becoming more blue, and punctuation, in which ellipses were lengthened to four dots.

sipped the most delectable wines from jewel-encrusted silver goblets presented to him by the white-gloved hand of the ancestral midget. But he had imagination enough to perceive the fundamental problems of Tocqueville's predicament. "It seems to me," wrote Fillmore in his journal, "that every country has its share of huddled masses yearning to be free." The only cloud on the horizon was cast by the assignment Weed had given him. "I had to get Mr. de Tocqueville to write his report," wrote Fillmore, "but how?"

He was mulling over this question, and removing a thorn from the paw of a passing puppy, when he heard the sounds of furniture being broken from within the inn. Rushing back inside, he discovered that Tocqueville and Beaumont were engaged in a fistfight with some of the tavern's regular customers concerning the Frenchmen's use of "unfair" and "foreign" seduction techniques on the ladies of the tavern.[15] "An officer of the peace had just arrived," wrote Fillmore, "and was attempting to part the combatants when Mr. de Tocqueville, his voice crying out, '*Liberté!*' threw his fist at the officer's chin, knocking him to the ground. Reinforcements were called for, and the Frenchmen were eventually subdued, enchained, and sent upriver to the notorious Sing Sing prison."[16]

Despite Fillmore's desperate appeals, Tocqueville and Beaumont were imprisoned for seven months for "causing an affray" and "being in possession of scented lace handkerchiefs." Seeing his charges behind bars, Fill-

---

15. American wooing techniques in the nineteenth century were primitive at best, and were often mistaken for serious bodily assaults by visitors to the country. As Fanny Trollope opined in *Domestic Manners of the Americans*, "It is awfully difficult to know whether one is being 'hit on' or merely 'hit.'"

16. The Sing Sing Correctional Facility gained its peculiar name through the activities of its first warden, Captain Elam Lynds. Lynds had been a practicing *basso profundo* long before he had become a prison warden, but the lack of venues catering to opera in America at the time had left Lynds's dreams of operatic glory unfulfilled. Upon entering the incarceration industry he realized that he had been provided not only with a captive audience but also with a vast untapped resource. His ambition grew rapidly, and within weeks of taking over the prison he began a grand scheme to stage Mozart's *Die Zauberflöte*. Through an artful mixture of compassionate instruction and vicious brutality—Lynds's exhortations of "Sing! Sing!" punctuated by the crack of a whip would ultimately give the prison its new name—his dream slowly began to take shape. Using the famed wife-murderer and *tenore lirico* Edmund Wallace as Tamino, the burglar and *tenore buffo* Walter Dent as Monostatos, and stepping up a range to play the comical Papageno himself, the first performance in 1829 was described by the *Westchester Gazette* as "terrifying." The production was not helped when halfway through the aria "Der Hölle Rache kocht in meinem Herzen" ("The vengeance of hell is in my heart") the Queen of the Night, played by child molester and *contralto* Samuel Wiesz, was stabbed to death by a member of the chorus. Opera was regularly performed at Sing Sing until 1891, when the prison went electric.

more realized that if Weed was not to know of his failure, there was only one course of action to take.

"I visited Mr. de Tocqueville in jail and informed him that I would travel the country in his place, and take down as many impressions as I could, which upon returning I would hand over to him for his superior mind to assemble. Mr. de Tocqueville nodded in agreement but seemed distracted, his eyes lazily scanning the ramparts and the guards, before informing me that the walls of Sing Sing would never hold him. Before I left, he asked me to send him a bar of soap baked into a cake, with which he could sculpt an imitation flintlock pistol and engineer his escape."

The following seven months in Fillmore's life have been covered sufficiently in Tocqueville's classic text, *Democracy in America,* and do not need repeating here. As to his absence from Albany, it was fortunate that Fillmore's travels should coincide with one of the longest debates ever to arise in the New York State Assembly. A ferocious argument—provoked by the powerful fur and timber lobbies—had broken out over the merits and disadvantages of deregulating the size of wooden planking in ermine farms. Seemingly innocuous at first, the dispute rapidly escalated into a quarrel over freedom of religion when a passing reference to a two-by-four was misheard by State Senator Ephraim O'Tuttle, who leapt onto the floor to quote from Leviticus 2:4.[17] No sooner had these words been spoken than the New York State Assembly erupted over the age-old question of the separation of church and stoat.

The argument would be fiercely debated for almost half a year and would include a sixteen-day digression spearheaded by Assemblyman Phileas Pullman on the spirituality of sawdust, as well as a vote on the feasibility of tortoises being used as building materials. Fillmore's absence went quite unnoticed.

Not all of the stories Fillmore collected on his voyage would find

---

17. "These also [shall be] unclean unto you among the creeping things that creep upon the earth: the weasel, and the mouse, and the tortoise after his kind."

Stoats: separate but equal?

their way into Tocqueville's famous treatise, though. On one occasion Fill-more became lost in Virginia. As his journal recounts: "It was dark as pitch as I stumbled into a clearing in the woods in the early morning hours of August 21, 1831. I had been directed there by the smell of a pig roasting and the sounds of convivial chatter. A group of Negro men were sitting around a fire fresh from working in the fields, for they still carried axes in their hands. When I revealed myself to them a tall fellow, of approximately my age, strode over to greet me. 'Can I be of service . . . master?' he said, although he appeared to have bitten into a piece of gristle as he spoke the last word, for at that moment his mouth curled downward as if he had just tasted something quite unpalatable. I told him of my disorientation, hail-ing from the North as I did, and upon hearing this he smiled and offered me a seat by the fire, introducing himself as Nat Turner.

"As I sat down, Mr. Turner carved for me a piece of the most succu-lent pork, and there was general amusement when he declared that this would not be the last white meat he would cut that night, by which I imag-ined they were planning a banquet of some significance. I had never been in close contact with slaves before, although Abigail had often told me of the iniquities they suffered. Yet knowing how fretful my dear wife could become over the most trifling of matters, and seeing how happy these slaves now looked, I took the opportunity to sound out the views of Mr. Turner and his friends on their situation.

"Was it true, I asked, that slaves hated their masters for forcing them to perform backbreaking work in the sun all day, for no recompense, and with the threat of being whipped if their pace slackened, while their owners slept in hammocks on their cool verandas? Mr. Turner shook his head and responded, 'Oh, no, sir. I think so well of my master, my mistress, and the little masters and mistresses that I would do everything in my power to help them enter the Kingdom of Heaven at the earliest opportunity.' The others gleefully assented to this, and began shouting that they would swing their axes all day and night if it helped to ensure 'the deepest of sleeps' for their masters. I was astonished by the simple, childlike delight they seemed to take in their owners' happiness. I asked them if it was the teachings of the Bible that allowed them to maintain such generosity of spirit, for I had read that the slaves were most pious, and Mr. Turner concurred, replying that he was particularly fond of Psalm 137, verse 8, 'Happy shall he be, that rewardeth thee as thou hast served us. Happy shall he be, that taketh and dasheth thy little ones against the stones.' His precise knowledge of such a life-affirming and gleeful passage from the Holy Scripture amazed me all the more. These men were beyond doubt Christians who knew how to turn the other cheek. I see now that Abigail was somewhat misguided in her description of Negroes as a persecuted race, for it seems to me that slavery is perhaps the most beautiful example of domestic happiness and contentment that this fallen world has known.

"Mr. Turner and the other slaves continued to talk and finger their axes for some time, but the meat had made me drowsy and I began to lose sight of the conversation. As I slipped into a deep sleep, for I was mighty tired from the day's travels, I was heartened to hear the pious Mr. Turner talking of what I presumed was Judgment Day, when 'no age or sex should be spared.' Truly, I thought, the meek shall inherit the earth!

"That night I had a dream in which I floated above what appeared to be the red hills of Georgia and saw the sons of slaves and the sons of slave owners sitting down together at a table of brotherhood. Every valley appeared to be exalted, and it seemed to me that every hill and mountain appeared to have been made low. What's more, I could have sworn the rough places were made plain, and the crooked places made straight. All was well until I realized that I was no longer floating but falling, and heading to the ground at great speed. I awoke with a start.

"I very much wanted to tell my new friends about my curious dream, but when I looked around I discovered they had gone. It was already morning, and with a clear head and the daylight as my guide I soon found my way to the nearby town of Southampton. Sadly, I found the townsfolk there to be harboring all the intolerant notions I had been warned were prevalent in the South, as they hurried through the streets loudly insisting that their slaves were revolting. I shook my head in dismay, for when I reflected on Nat Turner and his group of Good Samaritans I could not help but think of them as anything but."

On February 19, 1832, Fillmore returned to Sing Sing, his knapsack bulging with notes and interviews to give to the imprisoned Tocqueville. The prison's warden seemed wan and tired. When Fillmore enquired why this was, he was informed that ever since Tocqueville had been deposited at the prison seven months ago, he had spent every second of his containment trying to escape. While working in the prison laundry, he had constructed a hot-air balloon out of the convicts' undergarments and would have got away had not a button popped on a pair of load-bearing breeches. No sooner had he been let out of solitary confinement than he went to work in the library, where he had disguised himself as a copy of the Gutenberg Bible. He was about to be sent to an appraiser in New York City when it was noticed he lacked a book of Ecclesiastes, and was returned to jail. Having been whipped severely, he had then conducted his most audacious escape attempt, tunneling under the prison walls while the staff were busily engaged in dress rehearsals for the convicts' latest production of *Così fan tutte.* He got as far as the prison harbor but had balked at swimming across the shad-infested waters to freedom.

Shad: man-nibblers.

Despite his many failures, when the young Frenchman was brought in front of Fillmore he displayed a haughty demeanor, asking the warden why he had not been whipped today, as he needed the exercise. "I tried to usher him out of the office," recalled Fillmore, "but Mr. de Tocqueville insisted on giving a long farewell speech, in which he intimated that the butterfly can never be caged. We were just about to leave when I realized that I had not seen Mr. de Beaumont. When I asked the warden about him he scratched his head and said I would not believe him, but not long after his arrival, Mr. de Beaumont had walked up to the thirty-foot-high prison walls and, with an almighty croak, hopped clean over them in a single bound."

4.

Fillmore's Progress

(1832–1836)

Mr. Fillmore Goes to Washington—Congressional Arcana—Saved

by the Rebel—The Loneliness of Legislation—Taking the

Pistol—An Invitation to the South—The Benefits of

the Brassiere—What Alamo?

*T*here is a spirit that watches over this country's greatest leaders, a spirit that is as supreme as it is all-powerful, as divinely assured as it is celestially confident, as all-knowing as it is un-ignorant. How else to explain the fact that when Fillmore returned to Albany he found his office overflowing with messages of congratulation—he had been elected to the United States government as a member of the House of Representatives. As the one assemblyman not to have taken a stand on a whole host of contentious issues that had ruptured the state governance, he was left the most popular politician in New York State.[1]

Being elected in absentia was commonplace at all levels of American politics. In 1817, James Monroe had been elected president as a surprise birthday present from his friend John Adams. The only disappointment for Fillmore had been his discovery that his anti-Mason bill—designed to ban all occult and evil societies from secretly controlling the world—had been defeated by a vote of 355–0 with one abstention. Weed suggested that as a United States congressman, Fillmore should put his Masonic investigations behind him to concentrate on more important matters—he was to leave for Washington, D.C., immediately.

Arriving in the capital city in 1833, Fillmore found he—like most other congressmen—was to live in a boardinghouse, a rough-and-ready place that offered him a bed-sitting room and little privacy. It was a rude awakening for the sheltered Fillmore. On his first night in the city, while taking supper in the communal dining room, he was teased by his colleagues for

1. Fillmore's absence had allowed him to avoid such heated topics as the polygamy versus geometry debate, in which Mormon New Yorkers justified taking two wives on the grounds that the moral dangers were outweighed by the symmetry they afforded. Similarly vociferous, yet equally doomed, was the legislation religious die-hards attempted to pass in order to turn the word *God* into a palindrome.

the tag Abigail had affixed to his coat that read, "Please look after this congressman. Thank you." On December 2, after a fitful night's sleep during which he discovered his bed had been short-sheeted, Fillmore awoke, removed the "Impeach me" sign that had been pinned to the back of his coat, and walked to the United States Capitol to take his seat as a member of the Twenty-third Congress. "I am beginning to observe," he wrote in his journal, "that the practices in Washington are quite different from what I have been accustomed to."

Congress consisted of two houses of assembly—the Senate, or the "upper house," and the House of Representatives, or the "downer house." Here Fillmore was suddenly brushing shoulders with the greatest orators of his age. There was "Hollerin'" Henry Clay, famed duelist, former secretary of state, and recurring failed presidential candidate.[2] It was said that as a child, Clay had practiced his declamatory skills on his father's sheep, allegedly inducing them to submit to the butcher's blade without so much as a bleat. His skills had translated to the Senate, where the booming timbre of his voice often prompted the bats that nested in the building's rotunda to swarm.

John "Coldcock" Calhoun was another legend swaggering through the halls of legislation. A southern nationalist and former vice president, he had gained fame as a fire-breathing speaker largely from his persuasive defenses of slavery, which he had called "the greatest thing ever." The only senator to be adjudged a quorum on his own, Calhoun could often be found engaged in heavy debate with himself, frequently storming out of the Senate in a rage at the deviousness of his own arguments.

But the figure who bestrode the Capitol like a colossus was Daniel Webster, known to all as "Black Dan." His legendary oratorical skill had been forged in the crucible of the law, and he now commanded both

---

2. On three separate occasions Clay had won a large proportion of the popular vote but on each occasion had failed the mandatory presidential spelling test.

House and Senate with an iron fist.[3] As self-designated House Bully, the fifty-one-year-old Webster made it his responsibility to personally welcome all newcomers to the top of the Capitol steps, often tripping up excited young officials as they scurried to committee meetings, or forcing them to run up and down the steps again and again.

"Black Dan" Webster: advocate, rhetorician, bully.

Government was a rowdy, chaotic affair at the time. Vendors sold food and drink inside each chamber, and the carpet of the House of Representatives was so soaked in spittle and tobacco juice that planks had to be laid over the worst areas to allow safe passage.[4] The semicircular layout of the House of Representatives provided a natural arena for disgruntled congressmen, and violence could erupt for the most inconsequential of reasons. Such rough-and-tumble procedure was a new experience for Fillmore, who was lucky to escape a beating on his very first day.

3.   Most famously, Webster had appeared in front of the Supreme Court in the case of *String v. Office of Weights and Measures* (1823), when he successfully opposed the federal government's attempts to regulate string length, arguing that the industry's traditional measurement of "double the distance from one side to the middle" was "eminently practical."
4.   In 1827, Jonathan Hunt, the diminutive, teetotaling representative from Vermont, had fallen into the carpet near the seat of the gargantuan Dixon Lewis from Alabama. Hunt's body was never found.

Locating his desk in the chamber, and not having yet eaten breakfast, Fillmore stood up to signal to one of the hot-corn girls who walked the aisles of the chamber. Unfortunately, he chose to do so in the midst of a speech being delivered by "Madman" Micajah T. Hawkins of North Carolina. Hawkins' speech was now entering its third hour, and the *Congressional Record* showed that he had veered from the topic of establishing a Department of Indian Affairs to encompass Hawkins' extemporaneous thoughts on sperm whales and the unfortunate popularity of billiards. Experienced congressmen knew that Hawkins became extremely agitated when he didn't know how to end a speech, and he would often begin a scuffle for this precise purpose. "Representative Hawkins began shouting at me," recalled Fillmore, "for what reason I am uncertain. I offered him some of my corn but this only seemed to anger him the more." Hawkins began scrambling over the desks to reach Fillmore, while the other representatives hurried back into the chamber for the chance to see a freshman bloodied. Fillmore was dreadfully confused: "Hawkins leapt onto my desk, and seemed about to fall on me, when a brown blur knocked him head over heels and he fell to the ground unconscious. A collective groan went up from my fellow congressmen, and the Speaker of the House signaled, with some irritation, the end of the day's session. It took me a moment to realize that the brown blur had in fact been a man, who now stood before me in a buckskin suit and moccasins and wearing a raccoon-skin hat, hands on his hips. 'They think me a bummer,' he said, turning to look at me, 'but that's bunkum.' He extended a hand toward me and introduced himself: 'David Crockett at your service.'"

Crockett was a raucous frontiersman turned anti-Jacksonian representative from Tennessee. His tales of frontier life had made him famous across the country,[5] and even a freshman such as Fillmore would have heard

---

5. Some suggested that Crockett's stories were not always based on fact. In particular, the best-selling *Colonel Crockett's Exploits and Adventures in the Holy Land* (1833) would come under particular scrutiny, as it recounted Crockett's alleged wanderings in Jerusalem, in which he wrestled a drunken angel, beat the devil at cards, and was crucified by angry Romans,

the rumors about Crockett arm-wrestling Black Dan Webster to a stalemate in 1827. "You can't trick Black Dan any sooner than you can catch a weasel asleep," Crockett told Fillmore, "but I wasn't born in the woods to be scared by an owl. He thinks he's the biggest toad in the puddle . . . well, I don't care beans for him—not a single old red-eyed bean, not a string bean, not a Boston bean."

Crockett: had critics.

The pair swiftly became inseparable, and Fillmore lapped up his friend's homespun wisdom and insights into legislative policy. "Congress is like a husking bee—people come to work but end up fighting," Fillmore recalled Crockett telling him. "Why, the other day, when a vote was being called on an amendment to the revenue laws, Burgess was stabbed in the side, Rencher was well hacked with a blade, and Carmichael was savaged by a cougar."

Crockett took the time to school Fillmore in the more colorful

"for I preferred to pledge allegiance to Old Glory rather than to that Yankee goose, Julius Caesar." Fortunately, "through frontier know-how," Crockett managed to work the cross loose in the ground and, while still nailed to it, "cartwheeled down the slopes of Golgotha to freedom."

characters of the lower house. There was Zadoc "Nonstop" Casey of Illinois, who had trained himself how to talk while eating and sleeping, in order that he was never interrupted on the floor. There was the stuttering Rufus Choate of Massachusetts, whose painfully stumbling speeches in the House had spawned the term "in Choate." There was Noadiah "No Idea" Johnson from New York, who was rumored to be an idiot and could often be found arguing with one of the columns on the portico. And then there was Aaron A. Vanderpoel, known as the "Rodent King," who had made a fortune farming mink and was rumored to have the largest number of voles to his name of anyone in the Congress.[6]

Yet beneath the weight of such mighty champions of democracy, the political battlefield was shifting underfoot. The Anti-Mason Party was disbanding and being absorbed into a new political party—the Whigs.[7] When a confused Fillmore finally managed to contact his mentor, Thurlow Weed, he was told that the anti-Masonic quest on which he had set himself might "be better practiced incognito." Thus it was as a Whig that Fillmore was to take his first steps toward immortality.

On January 30, 1835, Fillmore attended a funeral service for Representative Warren "Hefty" Davis in the rotunda of the Capitol.[8] President Jackson was in attendance, and Fillmore was curious to see if Jackson remembered him from their meeting ten years before. Pushing his way through the crowd, Fillmore noticed a young man who was shaking and shivering in front of him. "Since he seemed poorly, I took him under my

6.   Curiously enough, Aaron A. Vanderpoel also had the largest number of vowels to his name of anyone in Congress.
7.   The Whig Party was born out of a furious debate held on the wearing of hats within the chamber. Parted down hair lines, with the balding hairless (pro-hat) arguing against the flocculently hirsute (anti-hat), the bill was eventually defeated when twenty-four wig-wearing representatives were outed on the chamber floor by alopecia-ridden congressman Ned "the Nugget" Fry. Forced to abstain from the vote, the wig-wearers would band together to form the Whig Party, the *h* being inserted in a vain attempt to hide the group's true reasons for affinity. So transparent was this attempt that it became known as the first political comb-over in American history.
8.   Davis had died during the brutal confirmation process for the new Supreme Court justice, James Moore Wayne. As dictated by tradition, Wayne had been forced to wrestle the largest member of the House. Davis—who at that time weighed close to 280 pounds—had bested three previous nominees to the Court, but his bulk was no match for the rhetorical—or physical—dexterity of Wayne, who clambered onto Davis' back and strangled him with the billowing sleeve of his judicial robe.

arm and guided him through the gathering," wrote Fillmore in his journal, but upon approaching the president the man threw off Fillmore's arm, reached into his pocket, and pulled out a flintlock pistol. Cocking the hammer, he aimed it point-blank at the president.

Up until now history books have stated that President Jackson survived this attempt on his life purely because the assassin's gun misfired. But as Fillmore's journal explains, this is only partially true. "I was shocked," wrote Fillmore, "and so acted instinctually. As the young man pulled the trigger, I swiftly inserted the forefinger of my right hand betwixt hammer and frizzen, thus preventing any sparks from lighting the powder in the pan, but dealing my finger a terrible wound. I screamed out in pain but stuck to my purpose and, with the hammer of the assassin's gun clamped firmly onto my finger, wrenched the weapon out of his grip. No sooner had I done this than I saw him lifting another cocked pistol out of his pocket. But once again, before he could pull the trigger, I added the forefinger of my left hand to the same spot as I had applied my right to the previous pistol. The hammer sprang down again, biting onto my finger horridly, and I could not help but let out a second horrifying scream. Wrenching the gun out of the assassin's hand, I found myself unable to rub away the tears welling in my eyes, for my throbbing hands were encased in pinching gun steel. The president's entourage had stopped, and now the president looked at me curiously for a moment. 'I know you,' he roared, and began beating me about the head and body with his walking stick before his advisors tore him off me with some difficulty."

Once Fillmore's fingers had been removed from the guns, the would-be assassin was placed under arrest. He was found to be a housepainter named Richard Lawrence, who claimed he had been driven insane by Jackson's contradictory instructions for the decoration of the White House.[9]

Despite his heroic achievement, it was a lonely time for Fillmore.

9. Evidence on Lawrence's behalf included a fifteen-page memo sent him by the president explaining to him the difference between "bone," "pale nimbus," and "eggshell" white.

*The attempted assassination of Andrew Jackson. Fillmore's
arm can be seen reaching toward the assassin's gun from the
right side of the engraving.*

Although he had his friendship with Crockett, such was the frontiersman's
notoriety within Congress that Fillmore was himself treated with suspicion by many. When Crockett was defeated for reelection in 1835, having
run on an anti-Jacksonian, pro-alligator-wrestling platform, Fillmore
found himself quite alone in Washington.[10]

Toward the end of the year, however, Fillmore received a most auspicious letter. "Mr. Crockett writes to inform me that a 'whole boodle of
savagerous beaners' are heading his way, and laments the fact that his 'Buck-
eyes, Suckers, Pukes, and Wolvereens' are not 'worth shucks' against them.
He thus advises me to refrain from 'backing and filling amongst the Congressional mudsills and tinkers' and to hurry to San Antonio to 'chirk him
up.' I have not the slightest idea what he is talking about." Nevertheless,
since Fillmore was missing his dear friend, and in view of the fact that
Congress was approaching the midterm reports, he gladly accepted the
invitation.[11]

10. Crockett's farewell speech to Congress, delivered in a state of extreme intoxication, lasted for three hours and fifteen
minutes and included the words *skedaddle, honey-fuggling, shecoonery, vamoosed,* and *absquatulate.*
11. The midterm reports saw greenhorn congressmen forced to run the length of the National Mall as the House Bully
stood atop the Capitol's steps firing a twelve-pounder cannon at them.

Escaping Washington was exactly the cure for his loneliness that Fillmore needed, and his arrival in San Antonio prompted a eulogy of praise to burst forth from his pen. "On the twenty-second of February, 1836, I alighted next to a charming old Franciscan mission, which one of the many soldiers who seemed to be on maneuvers in the area referred to as the 'Alamo.' Nothing could be more delightful. Mr. Crockett met me with some excitement, and I was introduced to his friends. There was Colonel William Travis, a strangely tense young man, who seemed to be constantly looking into the distance with a sad expression on his face. He shook my hand in a distracted fashion and murmured that he was glad to see me, as 'volunteers can no longer be had or relied upon.' Before I could enquire as to his meaning, Mr. Crockett was dragging me to speak to another friend, a Mr. James Bowie, who seemed a livelier sort, and obviously carried much affection for Crockett in his heart. Before I could be introduced the two began wrestling, and after rolling in the dirt for a while, Bowie pinned Crockett to the floor and held his long knife to Crockett's throat, breaking up the game to the merriment of both. 'I first met Jim Bowie when he imparted a sockdologer to my smeller that made me dance like a ducked cat,' recalled Mr. Crockett. At that point Mr. Bowie took over: 'You see, Millard, I can whip my own weight in wildcats, and I don't take kindly to hornswogglers, so we had at it.' The two men looked at each other for a long time, ruffling each other's hair and smiling all the while."

Their reverie was broken by the sound of trumpets, and soon the courtyard of the mission began to fill with troops. "I wandered over to see what was happening and saw that Colonel Travis had drawn a line in the sand with his sword, which he was beseeching the men to step over. I was not familiar with this type of entertainment, but it seemed to be a type of hopscotch, and not wishing to be left out of any such games, I began to skip back and forth over the line in the hope that I was following the rules correctly. When I noticed that no one was following me—indeed, every man in the mission was looking at me—I stopped. Colonel Travis blinked and asked me straight out if I wanted to fight or not! I was quite taken aback by this challenge from the previously mild-mannered gentleman. Had I made him jealous by my virtuosity at his game? In an attempt to defuse the situation, I replied that I would rather not fight, as I was already quite exhausted from my hopping. At this Colonel Travis turned a bright scarlet, and Mr. Crockett and Mr. Bowie came to my aid, bustling me into their quarters.

"They giggled that I had 'got Travis' goat all right' but that unless I laid low, my chances weren't worth 'a fart in a whirlwind.' Mr. Crockett told me to take off my clothes, which I did, at which he thrust them into the fireplace, Mr. Bowie stoking them to burn quicker. Quite naked, I asked in a somewhat anxious tone what he was doing, but Mr. Crockett snapped back, 'Shut pan and sing small, Millard, I've an idea.' From out of Mr. Bowie's trunk he pulled a woman's dress in an agreeable lavender shade, and a matching straw bonnet. 'We'll make a woman of you yet, Millard, and Travis will be none the wiser.' I had to admit there was some sense to Mr. Crockett's plan, and after putting on the garments, I suffered Mr. Crockett and Mr. Bowie to tuck and pin me until they were satisfied with my décolletage."

That Fillmore was dressed in women's clothing on the very afternoon that General Santa Anna, at the head of three thousand Mexican soldiers, rode into San Antonio with the express intent of destroying the Alamo can be seen as a testament to his wisdom and shrewdness.[12] For the next week, as the Mexican forces unleashed a fearsome artillery bombardment on the fort, Fillmore rarely ventured from Crockett's quarters. Partly this was for fear of being noticed by Colonel Travis, but it was also to prevent himself from distracting the Alamo's defenders. "On one occasion I was informed by Mr. Bowie that my comely figure had caused a near-riot amongst the

---

12. General Antonio de Padua María Severino López de Santa Anna y Pérez de Lebrón had the longest name of any Mexican leader of the early nineteenth century, easily outclassing civilian rivals such as Pedro M. Velez and Nicolas Bravo, although never managing to match the latter's vast popular acclaim.

female-starved garrison," wrote Fillmore in his journal, "although I think the flirt was teasing me."

At last, on March 6, with the walls of the mission crumbling, General Santa Anna deployed his army in a direct assault on the Alamo. The sheer size of the Mexican force meant that the outcome was never in question. Fillmore in skirts bravely aided the besieged soldiers, bringing them water, mopping their brows, and promising to deliver letters to their loved ones, but alas, he could not help them all. "I saw a Mexican soldier climb over the parapet and aim his rifle at Colonel Travis. I called out to the colonel, and I saw a crimson flush of recognition burst onto his face as he recognized my voice. He raised his gun but, obviously befuddled, pointed at me rather than his assailant. Before I could make known the present danger, he was shot straight through the head."

Every man was being called upon to defend the mission, but the waves of Mexicans kept crashing against the wall. "Mr. Crockett now appeared beside me. He had been shot in both legs and the neck," recalled Fillmore. "'I'm not honey-fuggling you this time, Millard,' he told me. 'You're a huckleberry above a persimmon, no doubt, but I've seen the elephant, and we are tetotaciously exflunctified.' I nodded in confusion. As the battle raged behind us, Mr. Bowie now appeared, his leg clearly broken, but his long knife unsheathed and covered in blood. 'I'm not about to hang up my fiddle,' he said. 'We may have got the little end of the horn, but I been fighting since I was knee-high to a mosquito, and I ain't going to stop now.' With Mr. Bowie leaning on Mr. Crockett, I saw the pair of them hug, turn, and hop crazily into the melee. In an instant they were lost to sight, surrounded by a hundred of the enemy."

By dawn the battle was over. It seemed that every American soldier had been killed, and Fillmore, still garbed as a woman, had been taken prisoner. "In a moment of inspiration I pretended that my name was Susannah Dickinson, and concocted a story that I was a demure representative for the Episcopalian Church studying the local flora and fauna of the South. But one of my Mexican interrogators seemed suspicious of me, and asked me what my concern was in the mission. Struggling to come up with an answer, I blurted out that I was planning to use it as a base from which to integrate the northern badger into the surrounding countryside. My exclamation was met by a grim, disbelieving silence before my interrogator announced with some disgust, 'Badgers? We don't need no stinkin' badgers!' He was about to tear off my bonnet when General Santa Anna himself appeared from behind him and cuffed the man with an imperious swipe of his white gloved hand.

The North American badger: unwanted in Mexico.

"The general was surprisingly regal in bearing, and apologized for his underling's behavior. He sat next to me and spoke to me in very good English, informing me, with one hand on my leg, that I should 'tell all of Texas what has happened,' which seemed to me a most impractical task for a lady."

Thus Fillmore was ushered out of the Alamo, the sole survivor of the massacre. Or was he? "As I sat on the wagon that would drive me to safety, I saw General Santa Anna inspecting two men who were covered

from tip to toe in blood but were still standing upright. Imagine my surprise when I saw that it was Mr. Crockett and Mr. Bowie! I waved a handkerchief at them, and Mr. Bowie winked, smiled, and blew me a kiss. The
last I saw of them was Mr. Crockett declaring that there was something on
the top button of the general's uniform, while a bloodied Mr. Bowie
insisted, 'I don't know what it is, Annie, but you'd better take a look—go
on now.' As my wagon turned out of the mission, I heard a yelp, two gunshots, and no more."

Curiously enough, the next entry in Fillmore's journal skips ahead to
June 13, 1836, and the House of Representatives' decision to admit the
territories of Arkansas and Michigan into the Union. Fillmore's adventures in the South are never alluded to again. It seems that, with the
resilience of a true hero, he had completely forgotten the Alamo.

5.

Fillmore Amongst the Natives

(1836–1839)

An Inventive Mind—Seminole Semiotics—Martin Van Buren Is Not

OK—The Panic of 1837—An Indian Summer—Unintentional

Duplicity—Cherokee Days—Misfortune's Wheel

*I*t should not be assumed by the reader of this volume that Millard Fillmore's life was devoted purely to enthralling adventures and feats of heroism. Neither should the frequent references to acts of valor and gallantry suggest that Fillmore was not a contemplative and thoughtful individual. For the fact is that throughout his life Fillmore was engaged in the most rigorous of intellectual pursuits, keenly chasing obscure and often perplexing problems, and resolving them with the intuitive skills of a mind unafflicted by the biases of a formal education. Were it not for the destruction by fire of the Patent Office building in 1836, it seems certain that Fillmore's extraordinary enterprise and ingenuity would have made his name resound doubly, not just as his country's greatest president but also as one of America's most prolific inventors.[1] As it is, the only evidence we have of his awe-inspiring cleverness is to be found in his journals.

The list of his creations is almost endless. The Colt pistol, its revolving chamber inspired by the internal movements of a carriage clock "that had entranced me for a week," and named the Colt because "the power of its retort made it buck in my hands," was invented by Fillmore in 1832. Yet, thinking it of no commercial value, "for who could possibly need to fire more than one bullet at a time?" he discarded it.

In July 1833, Fillmore had vulcanized rubber in his study at the Capitol when, upon entering the room, he "accidentally knocked a mixture of rubber and sulfur I had prepared for the House's Little Scientist

1. The fire at the patent office was begun by failed Italian inventor Guido Walteri. His numerous inventions included a "Condensing Funnel for the Collection of Sea-Lion Sweat," "Nightcaps for Skylarks," and the "Hexagonal Wooden-Sheathed Plumbagonic Stylus," which, upon careful study of the blueprints, was revealed to be a pencil. Having repeatedly had his applications rejected by the patent office, it was believed Walteri had used his "Flaming Mechanical Cough Drop" (pat. pend.) to start the blaze.

Committee onto my stove."[2] He was most surprised to perceive "that the rubber kept its shape despite the intense heat," and immediately grasped the possibilities of his discovery: "rubber hats to wear all year round that are impervious to the weather, rubber suits that protect one from assault, rubber dogs and rubber cats, and rubber trees that blossom with rubber flowers all year long!" Yet Fillmore would be robbed of the credit his invention deserved when Charles Goodyear, a roving tinker who sold sprigs of lucky heather on the Capitol steps, stole the samples from Fillmore's study, condemning rubber to a dull, industrial usage, far from the beautiful rubber future Fillmore had foreseen.

During the heat wave of the same year, while perusing the Bill of Rights, Fillmore seems to have been hit by inspiration once more. As he read of the right of the people "to bear arms," Fillmore began tugging at a loose thread in the shoulder of his shirt, and proceeded to unravel the entire left sleeve, "causing a cooling breeze to play across my bare arm, and thus providing me with some relief from the oppressive warmth." Doing the same with the other arm, Fillmore thus created what he termed the "tea-shirt," "for one feels as refreshed while wearing it as if one had just partaken of a cool glass of iced tea." Once again, Fillmore's name is noticeably absent from the histories of popular fashion.

Perhaps Fillmore's greatest discovery came during the winter of 1836, when his journal begins to mention "the madman's knocking game." Fillmore had been visiting Abigail in Buffalo[3] and was returning via New York when a chance meeting in a saloon introduced him to the highly agitated deaf-mute Samuel Morse. Fillmore was told by the barkeep that, following a number of personal tragedies, Morse had become insular and

---

2. The Little Scientist Committee, funded by the Department of War, was largely interested in creating explosions by mixing baking soda and vinegar. Under the chairmanship of Senator Urkel of Illinois (1832–38) its role expanded to include the picking up of iron filings with magnets.

3. "My thoughtful husband has returned with nine months of dirty laundry for me to wash," wrote an emotional Abigail in a letter to a friend. "How it allows me to joyously relive every day he has been away, down to the very meals he ate and puddles he stood in."

refused to utter a word. Instead, the bearded old man sat at a table and used his hand to sound out a variety of unintelligible knocks and scrapes, looking up expectantly after each eruption of blows had ended.

Morse was on the verge of being consigned to the asylum, but Fillmore's natural insightfulness noticed a pattern in these seemingly senseless raps. Installing the old man in the rooms he kept in the city, Fillmore spent months trying to decipher the bizarre code. It was December by the time he finally made the breakthrough. "It came," wrote Fillmore, "after Mr. Morse had stubbed his toe on the kitchen table. He did not make a sound, although obviously in extreme discomfort, but instead let loose a flurry of knocks, which I clearly understood to mean either 'Aaaaaah!' or 'Aieeee!' From this starting point, and through the subsequent application of a pointed stick to his bare feet, I soon managed to decode Mr. Morse's mysterious alphabet."

Samuel Morse: shiny, star-shaped objects pinned to his chest calmed him.

Fillmore's innovations were not exclusively technological. From youth he had been fascinated by the Native Americans of his country—their culture, their ceremonies, but more importantly their relationship with animals. "How I long to be given an Indian name," Fillmore wrote in 1824, and his journals are peppered with possible permutations: Singing Dolphin, Crazy Squirrel, and Big Running Wet Leaping Dog. His fascination with Indian society had even led him to learn fragments of their language, and he showed particular fondness for the Choctaw word for approval, *okeh*. Never a stickler for tradition, Fillmore had taken to using this word in Washington, to replace the long-winded expression of consent that the traditions of Congress demanded,[4] and by 1836 many other congressmen who had heard him took to using it themselves, abbreviating it to the popular form the term still holds to this day. Little could Fillmore have known that it would be this creation, more than any other, that was to prove an unlikely stumbling block to his political fortunes.

In January 1837, Fillmore was in New York, meeting the crazed deaf-mute Morse in a tavern near his lodgings. There had been complaints from Morse's neighbors over the banging that came from his room, and it seemed certain he would have to be moved to a more isolated environment. Despite this, the two were in high spirits, following their creation of what Fillmore termed "a knock-knock joke." It was thus unfortunate that Martin Van Buren, the recently elected eighth president of the United States, should now have entered the exact same inn, accompanied by a crowd of well-wishers.

The former vice president to Andrew Jackson, Van Buren was the first president to be of non-Anglo-Saxon descent, the first president whose first language was not English, and the first president to keep a pet tiger at his home in Kinderhook, New York. These groundbreaking precedents were terribly important to the ginger-haired Van Buren, and when his supporters in the last election had taken to calling him "Old Kinderhook," or "OK" for short, he assumed that this popular saying was another feather in

---

4.   From *Congressional Rites, Rituals and Regulations* (Vol. XXI: *Remarks of Concord*): "Let it be known that I acquiesce to your undertaking and heretofore will accomplish and bear witness to the verity of my belief in the aforementioned remark, observation or order, as it pertains to a deed, act, or acknowledgment imparted to, or enacted by myself."

his cap. Although his aides had tried to tell him that Fillmore's own linguistic innovation had preceded his own, the proud Van Buren steadfastly refused to acknowledge it. Now, having stumbled upon a laughing Fillmore in New York, the simmering resentment Van Buren had been feeling burst forth, and he loudly accused the "scoundrelly" Fillmore of "thieving my adage!" Fillmore was shocked, and attempted to explain the word's true origin, but Van Buren was not to be placated. He began to move toward Fillmore, menacingly rolling up his sleeves as he came.

Martin Van Buren: far from OK.

It was at that moment, reports Fillmore's journal, that "a flurry of knocks and scrapes sounded on the table next to me." Morse was trying to tell him something. Within an instant Fillmore understood the message: "Mr. Morse was advising me to run, if I valued my life, to the old freight depot of the New York and Harlem Railroad, just south of Canal Street." With a bound, Fillmore leapt through the encircling crowd and into the street, swiftly pursued by an enraged Van Buren.

The reasoning behind Morse's message was not as strange as it sounds, for it was a well-known fact that Martin Van Buren was terrified of trains.⁵ Morse knew, as did Fillmore, that if Van Buren came anywhere near a steam locomotive, he would be so unnerved as to give up the chase immediately. Unluckily for Fillmore, the station was empty, and although he noticed that an idle handcart made Van Buren flinch visibly, it did not sway the president-elect from his pursuit. "He dexterously clambered over barrow and cart," recalled Fillmore, "his whiskers standing on end in rage." Overturning fruit stalls and knocking over old women—their votes had been cast!—it seems certain that Fillmore would have been extended a considerable beating by the furious Van Buren had he not managed to "enact an escape by the most fortuitous of means."

What these means were, Fillmore's journals do not relate. Indeed, it is doubly unfortunate that Fillmore should have been engaged in such elusions at that moment, for he was thus denied witnessing one of the most dramatic events ever to occur in New York's history. At approximately the same moment that Fillmore was being chased by Martin Van Buren, a near-riot was sweeping the rarified environs of nearby Wall Street. The famed stockbroker Jacob Little recalled what happened at the New York Stock Exchange in his best-selling autobiography, *Small Change:*⁶ "The securities were being called out in the afternoon session when a great disturbance erupted and a man, thickset and rosy-cheeked, rushed into the exchange and began shouting in frantic terms: 'The Dutch have invaded! All is lost! Sell! Sell! Sell!' before running out again. There was a pause of a few seconds, at which point a red-faced old man who seemed strangely familiar burst into the room in a fury. No sooner had he done so than a storm of

5. In 1829, Van Buren had written a much-publicized letter to Andrew Jackson complaining of the new technology of railways: "Railroad carriages are pulled at the enormous speed of 15 miles per hour by 'engines' which, in addition to endangering life and limb of passengers, roar and snort their way through the countryside, setting fire to crops, scaring the livestock and frightening women and children. The Almighty certainly never intended that people should travel at such breakneck speed." In response, Jackson began to call him "Martin Van Urine."

6. *Small Change* sold a record three million copies between 1854 and 1857. It later transpired that Little had bought nearly all the copies himself, borrowing massively in the hope of cornering the lucrative autobiography market and thus being able to artificially inflate the price of his recollections tenfold. All went according to plan until it was revealed that various parts of the book had been grossly exaggerated—Little had not invented the seven-day week—causing prices to plummet. Booksellers downgraded his stock from "autobiography" to "memoir," and although Little desperately tried to reclassify his book as "fiction," the vast majority of copies were pulped.

paper flew into the air, a whirlpool of humanity swamped the floor, making it quite impassable, and the market descended into chaos."

This bizarre intrusion into the stock exchange triggered the notorious Panic of 1837, the second major financial crisis the United States had suffered, prompting the price of cotton to plummet, hundreds of banks to fail, and a six-year depression to ensue across the country. One can only wonder whether a man of Fillmore's calming countenance and authority might have been able to bring the situation under control. Instead, the next we hear from him, he is in a carriage bound for the Florida territory.

Wanting to avoid the wrath of the new president in Washington, and with Congress obsessing over the panic, Fillmore's fascination with America's indigenous tribes bore fruit when he secured a temporary appointment as an envoy to the Bureau of Indian Affairs.[7] The Second Seminole War was being fought in Florida, and Fillmore was asked to arrange truce talks with Chief Osceola, fearsome leader of the tribe. American forces had for months been trying to remove the Seminole to the territories west of the Mississippi but had found themselves ill-equipped to deal with the alligators, snakes, quicksand, and fragrant orange blossoms amongst which the Indians fought.

Upon arriving in Florida, Fillmore was introduced to Major General Thomas Jesup, the fifteenth of an eventual thirty-seven different generals to be used in defeating the Indians.[8] Jesup was an intellectual and was in the process of revolutionizing military tactics to cope with the testing circumstances in which he now found himself. Upset at the Indians for making bird and animal noises—"which scare my troops half witless"—he

---

7. The Bureau of Indian Affairs' founding charter listed its responsibilities as: "I: The domestication and enslavement of spirit animals," "2: The destruction of the trinket economy by flooding the market with baubles and beads," "3: The espying of comely squaws for Indian affairs," "4: The purchasing of feather headdresses for all members of the bureau," and, "5: Kill them. Kill them all."

8. Many of these commanders would have their names enter the popular lexicon, such as General Cornelius Wuss, General Malachi Fayleore, and General Notfitch Tupolish-Mishoes.

devised a new form of jungle fighting, which he termed "cheating." "I find Mr. Jesup most peculiar," wrote Fillmore upon his arrival. "When I went to shake his hand he pulled it away before I could do so. When, eventually, he did grasp my hand, he did so only to slap me in the face with it, saying, 'Stop hitting yourself. Why are you hitting yourself?' to which I struggled to come up with a reply. In the evening he suggested we play chess, a game of which I am most fond, but I found my concentration somewhat disrupted by the Indians he repeatedly saw lurking in the bushes behind me, and lost three games in a row."

Within days of arriving, Fillmore had managed to engineer a meeting with Osceola under a banner of truce. It was a mission not to be taken lightly. Osceola was renowned for being a proud leader, a brilliant tactician, and a warrior of some ingenuity. Superstitious American troops spoke fearfully of his power to transform himself into different shapes, as well as his ability to turn the most unlikely object into a deadly weapon. When a government agent had attempted to have him sign a treaty agreeing to forfeit his lands in exchange for "one mirror (broken), one cotton shirt (smallpox-infested), and one hearty handshake (gloved)," Osceola had taken the quill handed to him and stabbed the agent in the throat. Grasping the treaty itself, he had delivered a flurry of deep paper cuts to the soldiers surrounding him and, having effected his escape, had destroyed an army detachment sent out to capture him by disguising himself as a frightened schoolgirl and leading all one hundred soldiers into quicksand. Since this tornado of aggression he had been defying superior American numbers for over two years, and now, surrounded by his own generals—Wildcat, Alligator, Billy Bowlegs, and Reginald—he cut an imposing figure as Fillmore came to meet him.[9]

"He motioned me to sit," recalled Fillmore, "and then began a long,

9. The revered Seminole Indian chieftain Reginald is possibly the only Native American leader of the nineteenth century to have attended both Eton College and Oxford University. How he came to fight in the Second Seminole War is unknown, although rumor spoke of a choral outing gone horribly, horribly wrong.

furious speech during which he mentioned how he would 'make the white man red with blood' and then 'blacken him in the sun and rain,' where 'the wolf shall smell of his bones,' and the 'buzzard live upon his flesh.' I had somewhat lost my concentration, so fascinated was I by the outsize feathers in the chief's hair, but I quickly replied that his recipe sounded delicious and was sure to delight the creatures of the prairie. Osceola looked at me in a peculiar manner for some time, and then, as if bubbling up from inside him, came an explosion of laughter. 'White man Fillmore,' he told me, "we will call you Grunting Hog.' I had finally been given my Indian name!"

Fillmore eventually turned to business and persuaded Osceola that he should parley with Jesup, who, "despite his eccentricities, I thought was a good and honorable man." Consequently Osceola appeared at the gates of the American encampment under his own flag of truce.

Chief Osceola: brave, noble, dignified, never stood a chance.

Jesup greeted the Indian chieftain with open arms and, apologizing for all the killing and maiming of women and children, invited him into his tent for tea. However, as Osceola reached out his hand for a cup, six burly orderlies leapt upon him. In an instant, the Indian chieftain had killed two of them with his saucer and teaspoon, and was aiming a buttered muffin at Jesup's solar plexus when he was overcome. Fillmore was shocked, "I presumed Mr. Jesup must not have seen the flag of truce my dear friend Ossie was holding. But upon my informing Mr. Jesup of this, he grasped the flag, walked outside, and threw it into the swamp, returning to ask me, 'What flag of truce?'"

As the Indian chieftain was being dragged away, Fillmore recalled how his eyes "seemed to glaze over as if in a trance. He swore that he would lay a curse on Florida, and that it would be the white man's graveyard forevermore, that giant rodents would rule the countryside, enslaving children into their magic kingdom, and that gore would forever stain the bushes of this land. I remonstrated with Mr. Jesup and pleaded with him to release my friend. But he was already denying that he had ever met poor Chief Osceola."

Disheartened by what he had seen in Florida, Fillmore set out on the second step of his mission: to travel to Georgia's far western border and visit the Cherokee. The Cherokee were considered among the most "advanced" of the Indian tribes.[10] Because of this the Bureau of Indian Affairs hoped that they could be persuaded to leave their ancestral lands without "too much fuss." Upon Fillmore's arrival he was treated with remarkable kindness, and the Cherokee chief Tuckasee ordered a great celebration in his teepee with dancing and feasting to welcome the illustrious visitor. Fillmore's journal recalls how he was seated at the right hand of the chief as dancers and drummers reeled in front of him. The chief's daughter, Matoaka, blushingly brought Fillmore a bowl containing a "fiercely bitter

---

10. In the nineteenth century the Cherokee Nation was dubbed "advanced" for their acceptance of farming, their slave-holding, and their frequent intermarriages with whites. Yet it is only now, almost two hundred years later, that we are finally understanding quite how advanced the Cherokee Nation had become. In particular, the work of pioneering Cherokee braves such as Collisions with Nuclei and Chief Correlated Motion of Electrons gave rise to the birth of wampum—later quantum—mechanics. For more, see Professor Daniel Fox's *Braves' New World: Physicists on the Warpath*.

liquid" that he was encouraged to drink. Within moments he felt a "surge of exhilaration" and recalled how "the room began to spin, the features of my hosts began to stretch and bend, and I felt somewhat nauseous. This feeling soon passed at about the same time the ground began to speak to me. I laid myself prostrate on the floor in order to hear it better, but as it turned out it was talking in a rather resentful manner of the insolence of tumbleweed and would not broach an argument on the subject. In a bid to regain my senses I reeled upward and, plucking a pipe from the side of the tent, began smoking it furiously, thinking that tobacco might calm my nerves. It did seem to help, for suddenly the drumming stopped completely, although the faces around me still seemed to be misshapen in horror. What a curious drink!"

Fillmore's journal continues: "I remember no more of the night, but recall awakening the next morning tied to the wheel of a wagon in nothing but my undergarments. I saw in the distance my generous hosts from the previous night engaged in a vigorous discussion with one another. Turning to my left, I saw to my surprise that another white man, as naked as I, and with eyes bulging almost out of his head, was tied to the wheel next to me. I attempted to introduce myself, but he was muttering words that I could barely understand, concerning his being 'bathed by the blithe air and uplifted into infinite space.'

"By this time, my Indian hosts had finished their debate, and I could see the good Chief Tuckasee approaching me with his tomahawk raised. I felt I had to ask him how I had ended up tying myself to this cartwheel, but he looked at me gravely and said that I had smoked the tribe's war pipe and that blood must be spilt before it could be replaced. Since the Cherokee had no wish to go to war, he told me, it had been agreed that I should be the one whose blood was shed. I was preparing to forfeit body and soul to the heavens when who but Matoaka, the chief's daughter, should run toward me and place herself between her father's tomahawk and me. She pleaded with her father that I should not be killed, and with tears staining her cheeks, she clung to my leg, sobbing wildly. Her father rolled his eyes. 'Every white man who passes through the village she wants to save,' he said to me, shrugging, 'but how can I refuse my little princess?' He called for a rather delicate-looking brave named Whining Ocelot. Grasping the brave's hand, the chief neatly sliced off his little finger. Whining Ocelot took this very stoically, and I could not help but notice that he had barely any fingers or toes left. Chief Tuckasee saw my gaze and, blushing slightly, admitted that during festivities the war pipe 'really needed to be kept in a glass cabinet or something.'"

Fillmore was to spend the next three weeks amongst the Cherokee, learning their customs through the skillful teachings of the enamored Matoaka. He discovered during this time that the other white man, who remained tied to the wheel of the wagon, was a Unitarian preacher by the name of Ralph Waldo Emerson. Emerson had come to protest the government's displacement of the tribe by chaining himself to the wheel of one of their wagons. Ever since then he had refused to be moved.[11] The members of the tribe treated him with something approaching affection, and were forever feeding him bowls of the bitter drink Fillmore had imbibed, at which point Emerson would begin his madcap oration again. "I had no idea what he was saying," wrote Fillmore, "but he did make the Indians laugh."

The serenity of Fillmore's stay was broken by the arrival of General

---

11. Emerson's protest was just one of many acts of social activism inspired by a nationwide renewal of interest in religion known as the Second Great Awakening. A less cranky and better rested arousal than the First Great Awakening (which some commentators suggested was more of a Bestirring), it saw American Protestantism riven by warring factions. There were the Presbyterians—Scottish to the core—who argued that salvation was finite and should not be shared. The Quakers had no universal doctrine, instead following the central concept of "Inner Light." Now believed to be a form of radioactive isotope found in the peat bogs of Pennsylvania, the Inner Light granted the Quakers almost superhuman strength during the hours of daylight but left them terribly vulnerable at night. Their decision at the Synod of 1833 to declare a crusade against the shy and retiring Pentecostals was seen as ample proof of their Nonconformist beliefs. In the South, the schism was no less fierce. Baptists were renowned for drowning rival sects, and despite their long feud with the Methodists—a wily bunch of open-air preachers who sought out new members in remote frontier locations where the spoken word had never been heard before—the two denominations often united to plot the downfall of the enigmatic Lutherans, believers in single predestination, baptismal regeneration, and ecumenical assassination.

Ralph Waldo Emerson: transcendental, man.

Winfield Scott at the head of an army of seven thousand troops. The Bureau of Indian Affairs had grown tired of waiting for Fillmore, and had ordered that Scott remove the Cherokees to their new lands in the West, pursuant to the Indian Removal Act of 1830.[12] General Scott was a grizzled veteran of countless military campaigns, but under Fillmore's advice he tried to strike a conciliatory gesture and asked that the Cherokee move soon and with good spirit, so that "what you now call a Trail of Tears might be better termed a Trail of Cheers!" When this tack did not seem to be effective, the impatient Scott ordered his troops to begin loading their rifles.

Fillmore desperately attempted to dissuade Scott but was quieted when the general gave him a letter from Thurlow Weed ordering him to return to Washington immediately. His journal recalls how "Matoaka cried out to me, and pleaded with me to come with her, but I told her that my nation needed me. I assured her that I would return to visit, and in the meantime, I promised I would write to her every single day. It was only

12. The Indian Removal Act was a product of the Department for Euphemism, Indirectness, and Circumambage, whose role at the center of government had been fundamental ever since it had been established in 1802 as the Department for Lies, Untruths, and Mendacity.

later that I realized I had nowhere to send my letters to, and in any case she could not read. The last I saw of her she was waving to me from her father's wagon as the preacher Emerson, seemingly oblivious to the revolving wheel on which he was chained, screamed out ecstatically, 'I am become a transparent eyeball!'"

6.

Fillmore the Kingmaker

(1839–1843)

*W*ashington, D.C., had never seemed so dull and colorless as Fillmore returned to its long and empty avenues. His exotic travels amongst the Indian tribes had only served to make him more restless than ever before, and even the sound of Black Dan cheerily whistling as he nailed the new congressmen to the walls of the Capitol could not rid Fillmore of his agitation.

Returning to his office, he found it filled to bursting with millet seed, a gift from the farmers of New York, and a notice pinned to his door warned that the House leopard had escaped yet again.[1] His spirits were briefly lifted by a postcard from his former ward, Edgar Allan Poe, detailing his latest attempts at suicide, but when Fillmore attempted to restart his inquiries into Freemasonry he had to admit that his mission to put an end to the insidious society had never looked so bleak.

The fact was that Congress was staggering under a surfeit of divisive political issues. Environmentalists were warning of woodland encroachment, fearing that forests were "rampaging across our country unchecked." Creationists were encouraging the mass slaughter of buffalos, their absence from biblical scripture proof of their sinful nature. The budding women's rights movement was beginning to rear its bonneted head in outrage at the poor selection of cleaning liquids and kitchen implements available to them, and the fearsome stillbirth lobby furiously fought for a mother's right to die in childbirth, "as God intended."

---

1.   Tilly, the House leopard, had been gifted to Congress by the Sultan of Java on condition she be allowed to roam free through the Capitol. As a result, she had savaged over half a dozen House pages in the years since her arrival. Stephen Haight, a famed big-game hunter, had been appointed sergeant at arms of the Senate in 1837 for the express purpose of killing the leopard. The discovery of a blood-flecked pith helmet in the Botanic Garden six months later suggested he had been unsuccessful.

But perhaps the greatest political dispute of the age concerned the struggle to end American slavery. Through a remarkable coup, the congressional pro-slavery lobby had implemented a gag rule, preventing abolitionist petitions from being introduced, read, or even discussed in Congress. This meant that as soon as a petition mentioning slavery entered either house, the congressman responsible was immediately shushed or, in extreme cases, gratuitously harrumphed.² Only one man had fought against this tyrannical decree—former president John Quincy Adams. Now in the House of Representatives, Adams had ardently defended the right of petition amidst fierce barrages of shushing. Such was Adams' unremitting confrontation of the issue that on occasion southern Democrats took it upon themselves to shush in unremitting salvos, with those from North and South Carolina, Virginia, and Georgia alternating with harrumphers from Arkansas, Tennessee, and Louisiana. Mississippi had ineffectual shushers during this period, led as they were by "Whispering William" Gwin, and the "Mississippi Hiss" was called upon only in extreme circumstances, while Zadoc Casey, an independent Democrat from Louisiana, was easily recognized for being the sole member of the house to rhubarb.

Despite this organized disruption, Fillmore marveled at the seventy-year-old Adams' eloquence and fortitude in the face of such hostility. Perhaps there was yet some hope for one man standing up against a vast and all-powerful organization.

Fillmore soon found out why he had been ordered to return to Congress: he had been appointed chairman of the House Committee on Ways and Means. Thanks to his political mentor, Thurlow Weed, Fillmore suddenly found himself at the head of one of the most powerful groups in

---

2. A "shushing" was a devastating rhetorical device that often left even the hardiest congressmen close to tears. On one occasion Joshua Giddings, a Whig known to be sympathetic to the abolitionist cause, was relentlessly shushed by his opponents for one hour and six minutes when he sought to excuse himself from the chamber to visit the bathroom. Giddings was renowned for his rigorous adherence to the House's rules, and his eventual death three weeks after the event was blamed by some on his grotesquely distended bladder.

Fillmore at forty: back when forty was the new sixty.

government. The committee was influential not just because it had juris-
diction over all taxation, tariffs, and other revenue-raising measures, but
also by being a conglomeration of the House Methods and Resources
Committee, the House Procedures and Proceeds Committee, and the
House Conduct and Capital Committee; it included within its ranks 218
of the 228 congressmen then sitting in the House of Representatives.[3]

Some historians have supposed Fillmore's astonishing promotion to
this powerhouse committee was undeserved in some way, suggesting that
Fillmore had no firm grasp on the role of taxes in government, but this
assessment seems harsh. Admittedly, Fillmore's journals do display some
teething problems with his new position. His firm support for tariffs, for
instance, seems to have been based on a misapprehension that a tariff was
a long-legged marsh bird, found in lagoons and muskegs along the eastern
seaboard. Regardless, Fillmore's new position saw him play a critical role in
the election of 1840.

The Whig Party had grown in strength during Fillmore's absence and

---

3.   The other ten congressmen who were not members of the Ways and Means Committee belonged to the House Cribbage and Canasta Committee, a fearsome body in its own right, that in 1843 would declare a flush a scoring hand only
when its suit matched that of the turn-up card and, more controversially, that melds of more than seven cards should be
strictly forbidden.

now sought to nominate a presidential candidate. William Henry Harrison's name had appeared on the Whig Party's presidential ballot quite by
accident; nevertheless, he appeared to be an ideal candidate.[4] A career soldier, he had devoted his life to the hands-on slaughter of Native Americans, most famously at the Battle of Tippecanoe in 1811.[5] It was rumored
that Harrison's remarkable hatred of Indians had stemmed from witnessing a terrifying Indian atrocity at a young age, although since he had grown
up in a patrician Virginian family, nobody knew what that atrocity could
possibly be. Indeed, there was something about Harrison that those who
knew him described as being "not quite right."

"I had the pleasure of meeting General Harrison today," Fillmore
wrote in his diary on November 15, 1839. "He is quite lost in Washington,
and so I took it upon myself to show him around the capital. He is a well-
brought-up, educated man, careful of his appearance, and soft-spoken,
although when I endeavored to take down his address and called to my clerk
for a bottle of India ink, his left eye began to twitch uncontrollably. He
wears a hairpiece—not because he is balding, he tells me, but so 'those red
men don't take one hair off of my head.' I assured him that seeing redskins
in Washington was as unlikely as seeing two sets of grown men wearing
tight trousers grappling for a pigskin, and this seemed to placate him some."

The two men spent much time together, and Fillmore, won over by
Harrison's paranoiac idiosyncrasies, decided to throw the full weight of his
office behind his nomination. Harrison proved to be the perfect candidate:
he had no qualifications as a public servant, and as such no natural politi-

---

4.   Putting Harrison's name on the Whig Party's ballot was one of the many practical jokes played by Representative
Jonathan "Very" Cilley, of Virginia. In his time Cilley had pushed through laws making it permissible to get a fish drunk
in Ohio and making it obligatory for fake moustaches to be worn in churches in Alabama. Ultimately, his pranking habits
would prove his downfall. When, inevitably, he was challenged to a duel, Cilley replaced both dueling guns with water pistols. However, his opponent was an expert shot; shooting first, and repeatedly, he managed to drown the unfortunate Cilley where he stood.
5.   General Winfield Scott, destroyer of the Cherokee Nation, had been the early front-runner in the Whig primaries. But
his campaign had been dealt a terrible blow when it was revealed that the Indian deaths he had claimed responsibility for
were largely "accidental," having been caused by starvation and exposure rather than by vote-winning bullets and bayonets.
The Daily Whig denounced Scott as "a Red sympathizer."

cal enemies. Behind him the rest of the Whig Party could avoid making declarations on the leading issues of the day, and instead wage a campaign purely on the basis of Harrison's war record and amenable disposition.[6]

Believing, however, that Harrison's wealthy Virginian background made him "too far removed" from the electorate, the Whig establishment decided that he should be put forward as the "people's candidate," a common man who grew up tilling the soil on a Virginia farm and calling a log cabin home. To help him with this, Fillmore schooled Harrison on his own childhood in the wilds of western New York. The result was a triumph. Harrison's invented stories of his humble origins were so successful that none of his admiring audiences questioned the occasional references to "the long sweeping mahogany staircase that led to the ballroom," his mother's "difficulties in finding a well-mannered French chef," and "the terrible day that Pappy misplaced the silver wine goblets before the governor's banquet."

Harrison won the election with ease, and Fillmore could not help feeling a "bursting of pride in his belly." The two men had bonded over many long hours of campaigning, and Fillmore had taken Harrison into his confidence regarding the Freemasons' conspiracy. "When I told Mr. Harrison that Freemasons were masters of disguise and looked just like him or me, he nodded vigorously and insisted that he too knew something of 'those who lurked beneath the skin of normality.' When I continued that the Freemasons were dedicated to taking over the country, he grew terribly excited and shouted, 'Just like the damned red men! Just like 'em!' It took some time to calm him down, and even so, he now insists on grabbing me by the shoulder and whispering into my ear the words 'They're coming!' which can be quite disconcerting at three o'clock in the morning, when one is snugly tucked in bed."

On March 4, 1841, William Henry Harrison delivered his inaugural

---

6. In opinion polls of the day, 73 percent of respondents named Harrison as the candidate they would most like to "reel home from a doggery with."

President William Henry Harrison: "They're coming!"

address on the steps of the Capitol without a hat or coat in subzero temperatures ("for I want the people to know I am made of flesh and blood
and not of a strange, metallic substance like our unseen overlords"). It
would last for one hour and forty-five minutes. It was a bizarre oration,
beginning in prehistoric times before meandering slowly to the present day
and including frequent digressions on the importance of prime numbers
and the construction of the Egyptian pyramids. Toward the end of his
speech, as ice crept onto his top lip and he became confused about the
rights of succession in sixteenth-century Spain, he began to falter, eventually ending in an apocalyptic flourish in which he declared that the Native
Americans he had fought all his life were "inhuman beings from another
world!" He then promptly fainted.

By the time Harrison was helped down from the podium he had
caught a sniffle, which developed into a cold by March 10, became a chill
on March 27, and blossomed into a full-blown fever by April 1. By
April 4, 1841, he was dead of pneumonia. He had been president for just
one month, and with him died Fillmore's greatest hope in the fight against
Freemasonry.

Once again, Fillmore found himself friendless and alone in Washington. Looking around him, he wondered whether he had been a little too neglectful of asserting his congressional character in the previous years. "Black Dan continues to call me Bernard," he complained to his journal, "and I am still made to do push-ups for hesitating in House debates." Such snubs were painful and, combined with the death of Harrison, caused Fillmore to begin to withdraw from the political and social life of Washington. In July 1842, Fillmore declined to be renominated for Congress and, with infinite sadness, turned his back on government.

Fillmore was preparing to return to Buffalo when he received another letter from Edgar Allan Poe. Poe had written that while searching for a crypt in which he might starve himself to death, he had discovered that a meeting of the country's most senior Freemasons was due to take place in Boston on March 7, 1843. Deciding he would make a detour on his way back to his beloved Abigail, Fillmore was soon on his way to the renowned City on a Hill.[7]

On March 6, with Boston only nine miles away, a "thunderstorm of tremendous magnitude" overtook Fillmore's carriage. "A particularly strong gust now toppled my coach over. As the cursing driver and I attempted to straighten her, the sounds of merriment were swept to our ears. Thinking myself driven mad by the tempest—for who could be happy in such foul elements?—I continued trying to right my transportation when I turned to see lights flickering from a substantial farmhouse not one hundred yards away. Desperately in need of shelter, we hurried to the building and clamored to be admitted. Imagine our surprise when the door was opened by an angelic-looking young girl with long blond tresses and a beatific smile who welcomed us to what she termed 'the Hive.'"

Although he does not mention it by name, it seems that Fillmore had stumbled upon Brook Farm, the most famous of New England's

7. The origin of Boston's mysterious epithet is unknown.

experimental Utopian communities. Founded by George Ripley, a social reformer and always-do-well good-for-everything, Brook Farm was devoted to the idea that all men and women should have an equal chance for social, intellectual, and spiritual growth.[8]

Once inside the farmhouse, Fillmore was surrounded with conversation and laughter. "There was music being played, dances being performed, and some of the inhabitants appeared to be involved in a game of what seemed to be charades, although I could not be certain of this from their actions. Curiously enough, I could not see a single man anywhere about me. No sooner had my beleaguered visage been espied than a flock of young women rushed toward me to help with my soaking wet clothes, and within moments my bewildered driver and I were seated in deep armchairs by a roaring fire, and surrounded by half a dozen attentive females who dried my hair and consoled me with their sweet turns of phrase and gentle caresses.

"I asked them where their fathers and husbands might be, and was told they had gone to sell their proceeds at the market, leaving the women-folk all alone. They said that it was so pleasant to have male company that I was welcome to stay for as long as I wanted. I thanked them for their kind-nesses but said that I had to be in Boston as soon as possible, upon which a cry of alarm went up. To calm them I began to regale them with stories of my time in Washington. Many of the girls had never met a government offi-cial before, and they listened intently to my stories of modified resolutions, tabled bills, and stalled proposals. I saw my coach driver being similarly questioned, and heard his monosyllabic answers about greased axles and elliptical springs drawing gasps of admiration from his audience.

"The hour grew late, and my audience began to tire, falling asleep at my very feet. A pretty brown-haired girl whispered in my ear that I should follow her outside; believing she needed me to aid her in a country matter, I did so. The storm had died somewhat as she guided me by the light of an

---

8. Before the founding of Brook Farm, Ripley had previously been responsible for an experimental Dystopian commu-nity devoted to the idea of inequality and intellectual diminution.

The Hive: honey trap.

oil lamp to a grand edifice under construction in the grounds, which she called 'the Phalanstery.'[9] Once inside, she put down her oil lamp, turned around, and leapt into my arms with the cry 'Oh, Mr. Fillmore!' Staggering backward in shock, I knocked over the oil lamp and could not prevent it from landing on top of a pile of wood shavings. Within seconds the entire building was aflame, and my companion and I had to scurry to safety. The women swarmed forth from the Hive and, working as if one, began passing buckets back and forth. Seeing I could be of little use, I thought it would be just as well to exit, and after dragging my rather truculent driver from his armchair we continued on to Boston that night."

In 1843, Boston was a city of some sixty thousand souls.[10] Less bustling and more refined than New York, its high society concerned itself with

9. The Phalanstery at Brook Farm was being constructed according to the strict guidelines laid down by the French Utopian socialist Charles Fourier, who deemed such a building essential for any self-sustaining cooperative. Yet while Fourier deemed a phalanstery to be a place for quiet activity, in which dining rooms, pigeon coops, and an observatory could all be found, blueprints for George Ripley's building also included mention of a "vertically mounted thrust chamber," "gunpowder storage containers," "sky captain's bridge," and "isolinear optical abacus," all seeming to suggest that Ripley intended to boldly go where no Fourierist had gone before.

10. And sixty thousand bodies. In the southern states, however, the ratio between souls and bodies was not always so equal. In the early twentieth century, Mississippi claimed over 1.5 million physical inhabitants, while its population of souls was barely two-thirds that. Many attribute this spiritual deficit to the large number of blues musicians in the area who had sold their souls to the devil for the ability to play the guitar (Robert Johnson), the harmonica (Steelmouth Brown), or the Jew's harp (Lightnin' Spritzstein).

intellectual matters and prided themselves on being thoroughly religious. Thus it was that upon Fillmore's arrival at the address Poe had given him, he was greeted by a banner announcing the debut performance of "Dan Emmett and the Virginia Minstrels," performing "an Ethiopian Concert . . . with songs, refrains, and ditties as sung by the southern slaves at all their merry meetings."[11]

The streets outside were mobbed with expectant crowds, and when Fillmore attempted to enter the hall he was "brusquely rejected" for not having a ticket. As the cream of Boston's finest flocked inside, Fillmore paced down an alley to the back of the building, desperately seeking a way in. He was in the middle of trying to squeeze himself through a cat flap when he heard noises at the end of the alley and saw "four men sitting on upturned buckets applying makeup to their faces. Around them sat oddly shaped hats and gaudy pantaloons." He had come upon the Virginia Minstrels.

Fillmore relates how one of the minstrels walked down the alleyway toward him in order to relieve himself against the wall. But by this time Fillmore's arm had become stuck in the flap up to the shoulder and he was forced to conceal his body as best he could behind a garbage pail. Unfortunately, the frantic wriggling of his trapped arm had attracted the attentions of a curious cat within the theater. "My fingers were suddenly attacked with great enthusiasm, causing me to yelp in pain, and so startling the poor minstrel fellow that he spun around, slipped, and delivered his head a most thunderous blow on the alley wall, leaving him in a stupor." Managing to extricate his bloodied hand from the flap, Fillmore realized what he must do: "I stripped the minstrel of his clothes, quickly blacked up my face with the boot polish he had in his pocket, and, hearing the cries of the other minstrels, hurried to return to them without causing any

11. Songs in the Virginia Minstrels' repertoire included "I Love My Massa When He Beat Me," "I'd Ratha Be in Chains Than Walking Free," "I Have No Soul, a Devil Am I," and "I'm Gwine Whip Mahself till the Massa Comes."

alarm. I was handed a tambourine and swiftly ushered through the stage door."[12]

Once inside, Fillmore saw that another act was already under way. "I could hear a man lecturing onstage to a chorus of whistles and catcalls. Looking through the side curtain, I saw it was none other than the peculiar Mr. Emerson, whom I had last seen tied to a wagon wheel in Indian country. I was delighted to see he had survived his ordeal, and waved to him. But his eyes were fixed on the distance and his language, alas, was just as obscure as before. Those in the audience seemed just as baffled as I had been, and kept calling on him to sing a song, but Mr. Emerson paid no heed to the crowd, and when he slowly began to undress, the hall's manager dragged him offstage and, signaling to my minstrel band, announced us to rapturous applause. I had been hoping to sneak away from the group to uncover the nature of the Masonic wrongdoing but was now compelled by my fellow minstrels to take the stage.

"We were sat in a semicircle turned toward the audience, and before I knew it, Mr. Emmett, the group's leader, who sat at the center, began playing a fast jig on his fiddle, while the man seated next to him began plucking at his banjo, and the third minstrel began making a terrifying countenance with his face, opening his mouth wide, bulging his lips outward, and shining his eyes like moons. I must admit to being quite agog and could barely bring myself to shake my tambourine, when a large blue fly that had been buzzing around my head—presumably attracted by the noxious fumes of my face paint—ventured forth into my throat. The result was unfortunate."

Whilst Fillmore is silent on the rest of his performance, newspaper reviews of the Virginia Minstrels' debut assert what Fillmore was too

---

12. Fillmore's views on minstrelsy were of his time, although he thought that the art's full potential had not yet been reached. "While painting one's face black is certainly humorous, for who does not like fooling around with paint," he told his journal, "imagine what heights of hilarity will be gained when more colors are available. For example, a group of blue-faced men! The possibilities are endless!"

Fillmore (far left) *as Tambo, performing in Boston.*

modest to state. The theater correspondent for the *Boston Enquirer* wrote how "the tambourinist exhibited looks and movements comic beyond conception. Animated by a savage energy, his white eyes rolled in a curious frenzy and his hiccupping chuckles were unsurpassable." Similarly, the Catholic newspaper *The Pilot* wrote, "Never has such a tasteful and amusing comedy ever appeared on stage in our city. Particular praise must fall on 'Mr. Tambo,' who for much of the show appeared as if he would expire on the very stage; with his choking, tumbling, and frantic gesturing for assistance, he had the audience guffawing mightily."

Fillmore's journal continues as he was being "slapped on the back by my fellow performers who praised me for my dancing." It was at this point that the unfortunate minstrel whose clothes Fillmore had borrowed now came storming over to confront him, causing much confusion amongst the other performers. "The poor fellow asked me who I was, and running his finger down my face, took the layer of polish off it. 'Why, you're white!' he said in a rather surprised fashion. 'As are you,' I replied, running my finger down *his* face. But something did not seem quite right, and so, licking my handkerchief, I seized him and gave his face a thorough rubbing until he yelped in pain and fought free from my grasp. I was surprised to see that his face was now streaked with both black paint *and* white paint, but peering closer, I could see that at its very base it was as black as night. 'But you really are a Negro!' I exclaimed. 'You just keep that quiet, boy,' replied Mr. Emmett with a stern look on his face. 'You fooled us good out there, but do you really think you could pass as a white man's black man every night?' The other players agreed, saying that this was the easiest job they had ever had, and that it 'sure beat picking cotton.' Mr. Emmett concurred, telling me they just hollered and acted 'like white people thought we were meant to act.' I was mighty confused, and asked why they did not just perform in their natural skin color, to which Mr. Emmett laughed and said that he didn't look anything like a black-faced white man."

As the audience dispersed and the minstrels drifted back out to the alleyway, Fillmore began exploring the hall to try to find any suggestion of Masonic skullduggery. Night had fallen when he recalled catching sight of Emerson backstage, "gesticulating wildly to a wooden cactus." When Fillmore called to him by way of greeting, Emerson gasped audibly. "I had forgotten that my face was still black, and the effect of it seemed to excite poor Mr. Emerson, who suddenly declared me his 'brother' and, grasping my hand, announced that he had discovered 'who is responsible for your enslavement.' He continued to talk to me in a flurry of words: 'They split our glorious nation in twain! The Mason-Dixon line! Ha! It is there for everyone to see!' Suddenly I began to understand the implications of what he was saying: it was the Masons who were responsible for the entire culture of southern slavery! But who, I wondered, were the devilish Dixons? Before I could ask, Mr. Emerson pointed to a set of stairs leading down to the basement, saying, 'Yonder, go see, go see!' and with that he careened away from me, laughing maniacally."

Fillmore writes of entering the basement of the Masonic Hall and descending a precipitous spiral staircase. The steps were poorly lit and led to a narrow stone corridor where the noise of chanting suddenly came to his ears. The corridor ended abruptly at a large oak door. "There was no doubt that the sounds came from behind it," Fillmore wrote. Cracking it open a sliver, he was stunned by what he saw. Flames flickered from giant torches hung on the walls of a huge stone vault, illuminating almost one hundred men, all of them carrying "gleaming, sharp metal trowels and wearing the Freemasons' apron as if they were about to bake a cake."[13] The Freemasons stood in circles around an altar, at which one man, wearing what appeared to be a goat's head, was "dousing his face and body in blood." Fillmore was transfixed by what he saw in front of him. "I watched the goat-headed man sprinkle blood over the chanting Freemasons, when all of a sudden he turned and looked straight at me, his sharp gray eyes finding me out in the Stygian gloom. I held his gaze for a fraction of a second but, feeling as if my very soul would be ripped from me, darted out of the building."

Fillmore ran to inform the local police as quickly as he could, but as his face was still blackened, it took him some time, and one chorus of "Oh! I'se So Wicked," to convince them of the seriousness of his story. By the time they returned to the theater, the room was "devoid of blood and aprons and goat-headed men" and the owner of the property insisted that, barring the eviction of an emaciated young man by the name of Poe some weeks earlier, the room had not been used since it had been flooded in the rains of the previous autumn. "I was warned against disturbing the peace," recalled Fillmore, "and left feeling very embarrassed indeed."

Had it all been a hallucination, prompted by the fumes of the face paint he wore? Had Emerson somehow drugged him with the bitter drink of the Cherokees? Such doubts wracked Fillmore's mind on the lonely walk back to his coach. In the end, Fillmore felt he could be certain of only one thing: "I had seen the gray eyes of the goat-headed man somewhere before." But where?

---

13. At this point in Fillmore's journal there is a digression on his favorite, and least favorite, cakes (pound and seed, respectively). In order to sustain the dramatic immediacy of Fillmore's discovery of the Freemasonic blood sacrifice, this author has chosen to expunge these details. They will be published in the forthcoming *Efillmera: The Lists of Millard Fillmore.*

7.

Fillmore Goes West

(1843–1848)

Bored in Buffalo—A Conspiracy of Cartographers—Stagecoach

Technology—Into the West—California Girls—The Wedding

Crasher—Possibilities of Tourism

"**B**uffalo in the springtime," wrote Fillmore in one of his more rhapsodic moments, "is as I imagine heaven to be, although with more precipitation and fewer cherubs." Returning to Abigail's side, Fillmore went back to live the life of a provincial lawyer. But his journals from this time speak of a man not entirely happy with his lot.

His law practice was prospering. "I am inundated with cases," he wrote, "but I feel strangely unmoved. Perhaps bog law is a young man's game?" He went bird-watching in the company of John Audubon, the pioneering American ornithologist, whom he had intrigued with a series of letters concerning the elusive tariff.[1] However, after a week of sitting in a cold Erie County swamp, Audubon's enthusiasm waned. "It appears that despite my best efforts in Congress," wrote a dejected Fillmore, "the bird has reached extinction."

Increasingly Fillmore found that he was plagued by memories of what he had witnessed in Boston.[2] He wrote a long letter to his mentor, Thurlow Weed, asking for advice, and Weed replied almost immediately, telling Fillmore how appalled he was to hear of these events, and how he would do "everything in my power to prevent you from ever stumbling

1. The reigning diva of Victorian American bird-watching, John "On and On" Audubon puffed and pecked his way across the nineteenth-century ornithological landscape like a preening peacock. Renowned for his feuds with fellow bird-watcher Alexander "Biggie" Wilson, he narrowly escaped death in 1812 after being stabbed in the chest with the bill of a great blue heron, known in "orni" parlance as "giving someone the bird."

2. "Last night I had the same dream again. I was trussed up and being carried to the altar I had seen in the theater. My white hair was caked in sweat, and my little beard was in need of a good combing. I snorted as I was dropped onto the table, and vainly tried to move my hooves, but to no avail. A man in a long cowl approached me carrying a large knife. He put a hand on my chest and began to make a speech. I could not understand what he was saying, but his sleeve was delicious. The man discovered what I had been doing and screamed at me, I bleated in reply, and as he raised the knife above me I forced myself awake. Another pillowcase had gone missing."

Audubon: famed for his wing collars.

onto such activities again." In the meantime he suggested Fillmore put all the events of government from his mind.

Without Fillmore's reassuring presence, these were desperate times for government. President John Tyler, who had succeeded the unfortunate William Harrison, had fallen victim to delusions of grandeur. Fundamentally misunderstanding the concept of presidential powers, he had been found on numerous occasions sitting alone in the White House kitchen attempting to bend the cutlery through force of mind alone. Even worse, he had been ruthlessly abusing the presidential veto.[3] In the past months he had not only vetoed the entire Whig agenda but also vetoed the meals prepared for him by his wife and the questions asked of him by his children. His persistent intransigence had forced the Whigs to expel him from their party, a move Tyler had quickly vetoed. When an investigatory committee reported on the president's misuse of the veto and attempted to impeach him, the resolution was, again, vetoed. When it was explained to Tyler that he could not veto such a resolution, Tyler vetoed the explanation, and

3.   The word *veto* stems from the Roman god Veto, god of obstreperousness and contriver of delay. The son of Jupiter and Juno, Veto was said to have spent over three thousand years lodged in the goddess' womb refusing to come out. In ancient Rome he was the patron god of bureaucrats, and Veto appears in Virgil's *Aeneid* as the truculent harbormaster who refuses to let Aeneas flee Carthage until he has "correctly filled out the appropriate forms."

forthwith decided to veto anything else anyone said to him. When he discovered he had almost been tricked into vetoing his own right to veto, Tyler declared that he would no longer be accepting legislation, and retired to the White House wine cellar with all the spoons he could carry. Congress was left to announce that it would be forced to undertake "extraordinary measures" to break the deadlock.

President Tyler: not a yes-man.

On February 28, 1844, Tyler was coaxed out of his hiding place with the promise of a ceremonial cruise on the USS *Princeton* down the Potomac River. While he was aboard, a cannon exploded during a demonstration firing, killing many members of the cabinet. As luck would have it, Tyler survived, having been belowdecks explaining to one Julia Gardiner the many ways in which he could use his veto. It was rumored that the ill-fated cruise had been instigated at the recommendation of the shadowy House Subcommittee on Assassinations.

With such discord amongst the Whig Party it was no surprise when the Democrats swept to victory in the presidential elections of 1844. In one of the most astute marketing campaigns in political history, the

Democrats had chosen as their presidential nominee the unknown James K. Polk but had brilliantly turned his unfamiliarity to their advantage. Running him under the banner "Who is James K. Polk?" the Democrats had whipped the country into a whirlwind of excitement. Polk had appeared at speeches and campaign rallies in a black hood and riding a pitch-black mare. His every appearance prompted outrageous conjecture about his true identity. Was he Andrew Jackson, returned to politics from retirement? Was he Eli Whitney, backed by his massive cotton gin fortune? Could he even be George III, hell-bent on revenge against his rebellious former subjects? Wild with curiosity, the electorate voted for Polk in record numbers. Unsurprisingly, when it was revealed that James K. Polk was simply James K. Polk, many voters felt hard done by.

For Fillmore, the disappointment was twofold: not only had he been hoping that Polk was in fact Queen Charlotte of Prussia, but the Whig Party's defeat also seemed to put an end to any further Masonic investigations. "What use am I now," he wrote, "in safeguarding my country against tyranny and injustice?"

For the next three years, Fillmore's journals depict a man both listless and lost. At first he seemed to be missing the hurly-burly of political life, instigating informal debates wherever he could. "I argued today," reads his journal for September 12, 1845, "against a feisty young tabby cat, the proposition that all dogs are evil." Similarly, he still appeared beholden to the ritual of Congress, collecting a group of Buffalo ragamuffins around him to form what he termed "a Committee for the Appropriation of Cake," which seems to have concerned itself entirely with the pilfering of hot pies found cooling on windowsills.[4] Eventually reference to these activities peters out, and Fillmore seems to have grown increasingly distant, sequestering himself in his office and poring over maps of the continent. "He is a changed man," wrote a worried Abigail. "I fear he has turned to thinking."

---

4. The committee's charter, drawn up by Fillmore, called for "the obtainment of pies, be they apple, or cherry, or blackberry, or gooseberry, but not pumpkin as these do not agree with Master Spalding's digestion."

✳   ✳   ✳

Details in Fillmore's journals point to this most insidious habit being prompted by a radical theory that was sweeping the country. Based on the popular rumor "I heard it be said we never went to California," it stated that the land mass commonly known as California did not exist, and that all evidence for its discovery was part of an elaborate hoax staged by the Office of the U.S. Geographer. Skepticism about California had begun to surface almost as soon as Lewis and Clark claimed to have sighted the Pacific Ocean, in December 1805. Why, it was asked, had Lewis and Clark made no mention of sea monsters, so clearly shown on early maps of the region? How, people wondered, had the two explorers survived the extraordinary heat of the West, considering the sun set there every day? Telltale signs of deception were perceived everywhere, and the sudden death of Lewis so soon after his return home led many to believe he had been silenced as part of a cover-up. "We might well believe in Cali-phony-a if we were stupid, ignorant children," roared the influential *National Supplicant*, "but a supposed land of eternal sunshine and year-round temperate climate is sheer lunacy to the developed eastern mind."

To Fillmore's mind the corroboration or renunciation of this theory

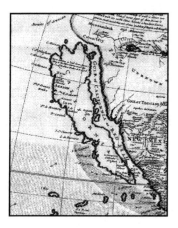

California: non exista?

seemed to inspire in him a purpose, something he had been lacking since leaving Congress. "What civilized country does not know itself?" he wrote. But traversing the largely uncharted continent with all its attendant dangers was no easy matter. It was fortunate that Fillmore should be well acquainted with a man as farsighted as he.

Henry Wells was the founder and proprietor of the Henry Wells Singular Seminary for Stutterers. He also owned the fastest stagecoach in the Buffalo municipal area, a by-product of having to transport highly unstable stammerers to his clinic.[5] Fillmore had become close friends with Wells ever since he lent his debating skills to aid in the rehabilitation of some of the seminary's patients.[6] Now Fillmore suggested that the two of them embark on a much greater journey than merely "bridging the gap between palate and epiglottis."

It turned out that Wells had already been planning a long trip in order to test a theory he had developed called "the Law of More." Wells believed that if horses keep becoming stronger and faster, then stagecoaches would move at greater and greater speeds, doubling in velocity every few years. As Wells described this wondrous future to Fillmore, he turned to face the horizon "and, as if he were tracing a huge horse in the sky, declared that one day the Pacific Ocean would be only five or six hours' travel away, thanks to the ever-growing power of equine science."

As it was, Fillmore's trip across the treeless plains, jagged mountain passes, and scorching deserts would take thirty-five days, although the fact that the stagecoach he was traveling on rollicked wildly through the country, only stopping to change horses, resulted in Fillmore's many journal entries from this period being indecipherable. The few words that are legi-

---

5. Speed was essential in the treatment of chronic stutterers in the nineteenth century. If a stutterer should block on a plosive consonant, pressure would begin to build within the patient's chest. If the patient wasn't treated in time—either by placing a pebble in his mouth, plying him with water from a snail shell, or hitting him in the face when the weather was cloudy—the plosive consonant could rapidly metastasize into an *explosive* consonant.

6. "The debate on the deliciousness of cheese stretched to nine and one-half hours," wrote Fillmore about one such discussion with Wells' students, "largely thanks to the prolongations afforded by 'gorgonzola' and 'parmigiano reggiano.'"

ble can only hint at the flavor of his trip, but these are tantalizing glimpses nonetheless. The word "Indians" appears halfway through page 43 of Fillmore's twenty-seventh journal, and the phrase "through my hat" follows hot on its heels on page 45. While the words "surprising amount of blood" are clearly legible on page 73, it is unknown whether this refers to the fragment "penchant for cactus wrestling" on page 70 or "insisted that I cuddle the grizzly" on page 72. Other legible phrases include "bright lights" and "floating into the air," as well as a reference to finding it "hard to walk" and "no memory."

By the end of 1846, thanks to Wells' daredevil driving, Fillmore saw the Pacific Ocean, and knew for certain that California existed. As he waded along the water's edge, "now wondering on the plausibility of the so-called lost city of Atlantis," he happened to see a woman struggling in the water some way from the coast. Seizing a piece of driftwood from the shore, Fillmore lay atop it and paddled out as quickly as he could to help. As it turned out, the young lady had not been drowning but simply waving at Fillmore; feeling embarrassed by his superfluous display of gallantry, Fillmore was about to paddle back to the shore when "I saw a large, gray fin cutting through the water toward us at some speed. The precision of its aim was truly a marvel to behold, as was the unrelenting rapidity of its approach. Clearly the young woman was equally affected, for she let out a scream and clambered aboard my driftwood, nearly overturning me. I splashed my hand to try to attract the fish—for I was very curious as to whether it was some type of hake, or possibly a large herring—and had just placed my head under the water to try to gain an improved view when the young girl grabbed hold of my hair and pulled my head back. No sooner had she done so than the fin burst out of the water to reveal a large, toothy beast gnashing its jaws wildly. The leviathan circled our board in a somewhat overly solicitous manner, and as it did so a wind began to pick up, and the water around us grew rougher. I was wondering how we should proceed when a mighty wave fell upon us and we were suddenly thrust forward at great speed, the monster seeming to be at once below and above us. Having been blessed with considerable balancing skills from my youthful days of bog walking, I managed to gain my footing, the girl holding tightly to my leg, and positioned myself in such a manner that the driftwood should be directed at the shore. As the water crashed around us we were propelled relentlessly onward, managing to stay ahead of both wave and beast, and were eventually deposited in the shallows, breathless but quite safe."

The young lady was Rosalita de la Vega, daughter of Don Diego de la Vega, a local nobleman, who upon being informed of Fillmore's heroics was overjoyed. "The noble don thanked me profusely," recalled Fillmore, "yet his joy upon seeing Rosalita was tempered with regret. He declared that to lose two daughters would have been too much for his soul to bear. I asked him what he meant by this, and he told me, with tears in his eyes, that his other daughter, Lolita, had been kidnapped by the soldiers of the corrupt Spanish governor of the province, Luis Quintero. Moved considerably by this heartbreaking tale, I announced that I would lend my diplomatic skills to try and talk sense to the governor."

Since Fillmore's clothes were soaked through, he was outfitted in some of the don's. "Alas, the only garments that fit me were all black, and rather unsuitable to the weather. The pantaloons were awfully tight, and the shirt had lost half its buttons. Don Diego, seeing my blushes, lent me a black cape to hide my modesty and a small flat-brimmed hat to keep the sun from my head. What's more, he insisted that I take his rapier with me, and affixed it to my belt, from which it stuck out perpendicular to my body and kept getting caught on the servants." The kindly don lent Fillmore his own horse, Tornado, and set the future president on his way to the governor's residence in the town of Capistrano.

Fillmore recalled entering the town's market square and being surprised to find it hung with colorful streamers and flags, "as if in preparation for some celebration." The crowd of farmers who filled the plaza, on the other hand, seemed rather dejected, and he noticed how warily they looked at the uniformed soldiers who surrounded them. "Having explained to the guards at the governor's house that I was a former congressman of the United States government, I was led up the marble staircase into the governor's bedroom itself, where Governor Quintero was being dressed by his attendants.

"The governor was an older man than I, and carried an imperious air. Upon noticing my arrival he complimented the United States government on sending an envoy to his wedding at such short notice, 'for it is wise of the American government to grovel for mercy at the hands of the mighty Spanish Empire.' I was somewhat confused, for I could have sworn the Mexican War of Independence in 1821 had rid California of its Spanish masters. However, Mr. Quintero's somewhat isolated situation appears to have prevented him from hearing the news. As his servants began powdering his hair he declared, 'You fear us, do you not, Señor Fillmore? You and your foolish republican country fear the great Iberian Peninsula. And rightly so, for this viceroyalty of New Spain, when allied to our Florida colonies, will see our fleets overrun your tedious little country within months.' He seemed so pleased with himself that I did not have the heart to inform him that Florida had recently become the twenty-seventh state of my beloved country, and that the Spanish fleet had been destroyed years ago at the Battle of Trafalgar. He continued: 'Did you honestly think democracy could possibly work, Señor Fillmore, with no king? No queen? No entrenched aristocracy, nor divine right of succession? It will give me great pleasure in consigning you heathens to the Inquisition.' I nodded pleasantly as Quintero raised a golden goblet to toast the 'Catholic Majesty' of the long-dead King Ferdinand VII.

"Not wishing to disillusion him about the purpose of my visit, I asked whom he might be marrying, and taking me to his balcony overlooking the square, he pointed out a pretty young girl in a white wedding dress standing on a platform to one side of the courtyard. She looked terribly sad, and beside her stood an equally morose-looking priest gently stroking her hair. I inquired who she might be, and was told that this was none other than Don Diego's daughter Lolita! I asked the governor if the good don knew about this union, but he muttered only something about 'teaching that rabble-rouser a lesson' before he was once again surrounded by his entourage."

Fillmore attempted to argue with him, but the governor kept raising toasts to the "continued Spanish domination" of Argentina, Uruguay, Venezuela, Ecuador, and Peru, all of which had long since declared their independence. Realizing he would get no further with the delusional governor, an exasperated Fillmore clutched the hilt of his sword and turned on his heel to leave. "As I did so, I felt something tugging on me, and found that the tip of my rapier had caught itself in the brocade of the governor's vest. He began gesticulating for me not to move, as 'it was a gift to my grandfather from the divine King Charles IV,' but I had already begun to struggle with it, and putting all my weight behind it, I heard three loud rips, and saw with horror that my rapier had torn a zigzag shape into his vest, leaving a trickle of blood on the governor's chest. A silence fell on the group, and before I could say a word the governor came rushing at me, grasped me by the collar, and accidentally bundled me over his balcony.

"Fortunately, my fall was impeded by a stretch of rope draped in colorful bunting which extended between the governor's house and a building opposite. But to my dismay the governor reached into his assistant's belt, pulled out a dagger, and began cutting one end of the rope on which I hung. I desperately tried to stop him, using the little Spanish I knew, but by the time I had asked him the way to the nearest market, the rope had been cut and, still clinging to it, I hurtled toward the ground."

Fillmore's journal continues: "It was fortunate that the rope was of a length just short enough to allow me to swing inches clear of a stony demise. I was still moving at some speed, but now in an upward trajectory, and heading toward the platform and the young girl standing upon it. I thought I might be able to slow myself by grasping hold of her but only succeeded in snatching her up into the air with me as I sailed past. At this point my grip on the bunting failed, and we would both have surely landed in a most painful manner if the don's horse, Tornado, had not skillfully positioned himself under us. Catching my breath, I noticed that the crowd of farmers had begun cheering for some reason, and a near-riot was under way in the square. The farmers were knocking over the soldiers who surrounded them, and I was shocked to see the venerable old priest hit one soldier on the back of the head with his Bible, causing him to fire his rifle high into the air. At this sound, Tornado reared, I grasped hold of my hat, and we galloped out of the square at breakneck speed.

"Upon my returning Lolita to her home, Don Diego was ecstatic. He asked if I would stay, and his daughters shed many tears insisting that I should, but I told them I had to return home to my beloved Abigail. Finally persuaded that my duty lay east of the Appalachians, Don Diego swore that he would carry on my heroic work against the corrupt regime, saying he would wear a black mask 'so that all will think Señor Fillmore is still amongst us.'"

While Fillmore was heading back East aboard Wells' stagecoach, a wheel broke near a small sawmill in northern California. The owner, one John Sutter, agreed to help Wells with his repairs, and Fillmore sat himself down by a nearby creek while they worked. He was skimming stones on the river's placid surface when "my eye was caught by something shining in the bottom of the stream. Glittering pebbles with a yellow hue, the like of which I had never seen before, were scattered all along the riverbed. When I returned to my companions I complimented Mr. Sutter on the beauty of his surroundings. At first it seemed he adopted an air of ignorance, as if modesty forbade him to admit to his homestead's loveliness, yet upon my

confronting him with the evidence he could not stop himself from shouting and crying with joy, for indeed the prospect was beautiful. I suggested
to Mr. Sutter that so attractive was the sight that he could probably sell
tickets to view his beautiful riverbed. Although, as I left, I wondered how
many people were of a sensitive enough disposition to travel all the way to
California simply to see some pretty golden rocks."

8.

Fillmore Restored

(1848–1849)

Finders Keepers—Mexican Standoff—Return to Politics—The Fat

Comptroller—Abigail Explains Slavery—The Dubious Death of

John Quincy Adams—The Doubtful Demise of Edgar Allan Poe—

Vice President Fillmore!

*I*t was 1848, and war, that deepest and most heartfelt expression of a nation's character, was raging between the United States and Mexico. The conflict had been looming ever since President Polk declared himself a proponent of a new and fashionable doctrine then sweeping the corridors of power. Manifest Destiny hypothesized that the United States had a divine right to expand its borders wherever it chose, regardless of whose name was on the land, and in spite of protestations that the previous owners had been there for a really, really long time. Popular amongst politicians for its simplicity, it quickly replaced the previous philosophical hodgepodge of humility, brotherly love, and turning the other cheek, the provenance of which had, in any case, been lost to history.

Manifest Destiny was the lifework of the newspaper editor and religious fundamentalist John O'Sullivan, who ever since childhood had called upon divine sovereignty to justify his slightest action. It was said that at the age of twelve, during an argument with his mother concerning the consumption of birthday cake before going to bed, he cried out: "The cake is at hand, it is the realization of my fate to eat it!" His estranged wife remembered how the first days of their relationship were similarly laden with such entreaties to providence: "We have it in our power to begin the world over again," O'Sullivan whispered seductively into her ear on one of their first trysts. "A situation similar to the present hath not happened since the days of Adam and Eve."

Despite O'Sullivan's theory, President Polk was in a quandary. Desirous of Mexican lands to the west, Polk still needed to gain Congress' approval to wage war. Faced with such a dilemma, Polk undertook a

John O'Sullivan: manifest cad.

maneuver that would be unthinkable in today's less frivolous era of international diplomacy—he would fabricate a reason for invasion.

A long-running border dispute proved the foundation for this fabrication. Mexico had long claimed the territory of Texas as one of its provinces,[1] but Polk affected complete ignorance of this decades-long quarrel, and over coffee with the Mexican ambassador he casually announced that Texas was to become the twenty-eighth state, stressing his nation's preference for "even numbers." With the Mexican government thrown into turmoil, Polk immediately capitalized on their confusion by ordering the renowned General Zachary Taylor to travel to the banks of the Rio Grande with a large force of men and to begin making loud, derogatory comments about sombreros. After the catcalls had lasted for some days, a parley was arranged between General Mariano Arista, the leader of Mexican forces in the area, and General Taylor.

1. Mexican officials had declared dominion over any territory, region, or province that included the letter X within its name, declaring the letter "uniquely Mexican" and pointing to the Mexican municipalities of Xicotepec, Xochitepec, and Xxixchtopx as proof. In recent years, Mexico has even begun to offer honorary citizenships to those who have "raised the profile of the letter X." Recipients have included the black nationalist Malcolm X and the xylophone virtuoso George Hamilton Green.

The American military record of the meeting displays the crude but effective methods employed to instigate a war: "Official greetings were exchanged and Gen. Arista laid forward his grievance that Gen. Taylor, with his force of four thousand men, had trespassed upon Mexican soil. Gen. Arista demanded Gen. Taylor remove his forces immediately and sustained that this was a clear example of American imperialism and that Gen. Taylor was the aggressor. Gen. Taylor replied that he knew that Gen. Arista was the aggressor in this situation but enquired of Gen. Arista as to what he was. Gen. Arista repeated his comment and was met by the same riposte from Gen. Taylor. Gen. Arista, for a third time, accused Gen. Taylor of being the aggressor, to which Gen. Taylor changed tack and replied that it 'takes one to know one.' Gen. Arista seized on Taylor's tactical modification and exclaimed to Gen. Taylor, '*You* are the aggressor, then.' But Gen. Taylor parried with a fine use of repetitive barrages, echoing, '*You* are the aggressor, then.' A flustered Gen. Arista restated, 'No, *you* are the aggressor,' to which Gen. Taylor, now managing the battle with ease, replied with a smile on his lips, 'No, *you* are the aggressor.' Gen. Arista paused, and Gen. Taylor allowed himself to ponder victory, but the silence was merely prelude to a devastating Mexican counterattack, with Gen. Arista announcing, 'The United States is committing an unjust war of aggression purely for the purposes of territorial expansion.' Committed to his tactic of repetition, Gen. Taylor had almost completely repeated this statement before realizing his plan had backfired. His position suddenly weakened, Gen. Taylor attempted to defend himself with a futile 'Shut up!' But it lacked support, and Gen. Arista, playing fast and loose with English grammatical constructs, returned it with venom, declaring, 'You're a shut-up!' Gen. Arista, pushing his advantage, now unleashed a devastating array of put-downs, insults, and teasing, though his use of the speculative 'Up your nose with a rubber hose' allowed Gen. Taylor to clamber back onto firmer ground, countering with 'I'm rubber and you're glue, whatever bounces off me sticks to you.' A translator was called for and the niceties of the phrase were being explained to a clearly perplexed Gen. Arista when Gen. Taylor was espied surreptitiously sucking on his index finger. The endgame approached. Having sidled up behind Gen. Arista and his translator, Gen. Taylor inserted his wet digit into Gen. Arista's ear, wiggling it about savagely. Gen. Arista screamed, but recovered quickly and swung around in his chair, catching hold of Gen. Taylor's nipples and twisting them about roughly. Gen. Taylor fell to the floor and, obviously befuddled with pain, accepted Gen. Arista's outstretched hand of help. But upon lifting Gen. Taylor halfway off the ground, Gen. Arista promptly let go his grip, setting off a round of applause from the Mexican contingent, while a humiliated Gen. Taylor was helped out of the tent by his officers."[3]

General Zachary Taylor: sore loser.

It was, however, a Pyrrhic victory for General Arista. An aching but satisfied General Taylor reported to President Polk that Mexico was now, with-

2.   "Yo soy de goma y tu de cola, lo que rebote de mi se pega a ti."

3.   Taylor's actions in instigating the Mexican-American War saw him awarded the very first Purple Heart (originally the "Purple Nurple"). The medal's color and location on the left breast were symbolic of the wounds Taylor had received in defense of his country's honor.

out doubt, the aggressor, and Congress, convinced of the justice of its cause, declared war. After two years of ceaseless slaughter, Mexico eventually ceded its vast territories of California, New Mexico, and the land that now composes the states of Nevada, Utah, Colorado, Wyoming, and parts of Arizona to the United States, in addition to promising "never to do it again."

As events of national pride raged in the South, Fillmore was recuperating from his Californian travels in Buffalo. National affairs, though, would not leave him be. Shortly after returning home he was paid a midnight visit by a most illustrious guest. Former president John Quincy Adams, Fillmore's role model in Congress, had traveled at breakneck speed from Washington to plead with Fillmore to return. Adams painted a grisly picture of a Whig Party splintered by discord once more: northern Free Soil supporters were facing off against southern slaveholders, and the party's agoraphobic faction had gone into hiding somewhere in the Capitol and could not be found. The only thing the disparate groups could agree upon, Adams explained, was that the calming influence of Fillmore was needed to help break the deadlock. "It is very curious," wrote Fillmore in his journal, "for I have received not one of the hundreds of letters of supplication Mr. Adams says were written to me. Perhaps Mr. Weed has been too busy to forward me my mail as he said he would."

Separated from his family for so long, Fillmore was cautious about accepting Adams' offer. He had barely seen his beloved Abigail in the previous months and was longing for some rest. But, noting his hesitation, the former president grasped him firmly by the shoulder and, staring into his eyes, insisted that Fillmore return, whispering, "For who knows how many are amongst them!" Fillmore ventured to ask Adams of whom he was talking, but Adams shook his head sadly and replied that he had already said too much. "His bald head was furrowed with lines, and his side whiskers seemed to reach out across his face to me," recalled Fillmore. "How could I refuse?"

With Abigail devotedly following him to Washington,[4] Fillmore found that his route back into national politics had been prepared for him, and he was easily voted in as New York State comptroller at the annual Whig convention that year.[5] It was here that he was reunited with his old mentor Thurlow Weed, "who seemed much surprised" to see him. "When I asked Mr. Weed about the letters my fellow Whigs had sent to me, he said that he had not thought I wanted to be bothered with such trivialities and so had had them burned."

Elected to political office once more, Fillmore found himself at the heart of the Whig establishment, and he duly threw himself into the task of finding a candidate to beat the Democrats at the next election. The front-runner was the hero of the Mexican-American War, General Zachary Taylor, a career soldier who had never expressed any political views, barring his admission that he would like to run the secretary of war through with a saber. With his thick head of hair and foreign blood on his hands, he exhibited all the accoutrements that were expected of an American president.

There were those who wondered, however, whether Taylor would toe the party line, particularly on the matter of slavery. In an attempt to gain support from both southern slave owners and northern abolitionists, the Whigs had decided to ignore the subject of slavery altogether, preferring

---

4. Abigail Fillmore, undated letter to her mother: "If I do not go with him he is likely to end up in Canada, as happened the last time; hence the moose-goring."

5. The Office of the Comptroller, pronounced "controller," had its origins in the late eighteenth century as a position for establishing the correct articulations of words in a country that had recently thrown off the shackles of Received Pronunciation and Standard English. By the mid-1820s each state had its own comptroller, for there were many regional variations: while a state such as Massachusetts pronounced *abolitionist* in the traditional manner, Tennessee declared a law in 1841 insisting that the word should be pronounced "nigra-loving terrorist." State comptrollers reported to the federal comptroller in Washington, D.C., whose job it was to try to unify these discrepancies, as well as being responsible for laying down nationwide rules of pronunciation. One example came in 1899 when it was ruled that the word *aluminium* should be pronounced "aluminum" (the change to the word's spelling coming soon afterward). The official reason for this change was put down to the officiating federal comptroller, John "Simply" Smith, who considered the word *aluminium* to be "European" and "pretentious." The actual reason for the change seems to have been the catastrophic national vowel drought that followed the American annexation of Hawaii in 1898. It was rumored that when Comptroller Smith heard that the island kingdom's motto was "*Ua mau ke ea o ka 'āina i ka pono*" he suffered a mild stroke. It was soon after this that the comptroller's role was redirected toward states' finances, and Hawaii was granted an extraordinary exemption from federal rulings on matters of articulation.

to hark back to the great hatred of Mexicans and Indians that all citizens could agree upon. It fell to Fillmore to sound out the new candidate's beliefs on the subject.

Zachary Taylor campaign poster: "I never met a Mexican I didn't kill."

Accompanied by Abigail—"who does like to tax her frail feminine brain on worldly matters"—Fillmore recalls interviewing Taylor in Washington in early 1848: "Mr. Taylor was a brusque man, not prone to tittle-tattle. Upon our being introduced to him he was ferociously scrubbing his jacket with a coarse brush. 'Blood,' he said by means of explanation, 'very hard to remove.' I looked down at the floor and saw the prone body of a young, dark-skinned boy. 'The fiend came at me with a silver tray and two fine china cups!' said Taylor, noticing my look of horror; 'I had to beat him to death with my shoehorn.' Abigail attempted to suggest that perhaps the unfortunate child was merely delivering tea, at which the general looked puzzled, and then shook his head, discounting the notion. 'At four of the clock in the afternoon? I think not! I take tea no earlier than five. Ask my aide de camp.' I decided that it might be best if conversation was directed toward his possible nomination.

"General Taylor seemed amenable to Whig policy but growled that he would not answer any questions about the large number of slaves he owned. 'My slaves,' he told me, 'are not to be subjected to the insane philosophy perpetrated by you northerners that they should be set free! They love working for me with all their little black hearts.' It was at this point that Abigail thought she perceived a slight inaccuracy in the general's statement, and engaged him in a modest debate. 'Actually, I don't think they like it,' she said. 'Like what?' said the general. 'Slavery,' she replied. 'I don't think Negroes actually like to be enslaved.' 'Nonsense,' retorted the general. 'If they don't like it so much, why don't they leave?' I must admit that the general seemed to have an unassailable point, and was about to quiet Abigail when she suddenly spoke up in a tone of voice usually reserved for my porcupine-milking experiments: 'They don't leave, dear General, because they're slaves. You own them, they are your property. If they left you, they would be arrested. You are a silly man!' A single line of contemplation creased the general's forehead. 'Really?' he said in a tone of astonishment. 'I had no idea. I thought they just liked being around a famous war hero.' 'Probably not,' replied Abigail, 'considering the war you have just fought is likely to instill slavery even further across America.' There was a pause. 'Are you sure?' said he falteringly. 'I had been led to believe that—' But before he could say another word the doors to the general's rooms swung open, and standing there was Mr. Weed.

"'What have you told him?' he shouted at Abigail and me. Hurrying over to General Taylor, he studied him carefully, lifting up the general's eyelids as if he were giving him a medical examination. 'What have they said to you, Zach?' Mr. Weed asked, but General Taylor seemed lost in thought, speculating aloud that maybe 'all men should be free.' Mr. Weed turned to me with fury in his eyes, roaring that it had taken him months to prepare General Taylor so that he was an electable candidate for the South. I must admit to casting my eyes down to the bloodstained carpet in shame, although I noticed Abigail had a small smile on her face. The general was now wondering aloud whether Mexicans 'weren't such a bad bunch after all,' and Mr. Weed, his voice rising to a shriek, announced that he would sentence me 'to the Styx of governmental representation, to the lowest circle of legislative hell, to a position more powerless than even that held by the underclerk to the assistant deputy of the clerk's assistant.'"

Fillmore's journal continues: "Luckily it seems that Mr. Weed was only teasing, for by the end of that same day I found that I had been proposed as the Whig Party's nominee for vice president! Mr. Weed is quite the joker."

"One minute I am balancing New York's consonant budget, the next I am running as vice president," Fillmore wrote in his journal. "How curious life is." Yet the presidential campaign was marked as much by tragedy as by joy. During the early months of 1848, Fillmore's most prominent backer, John Quincy Adams, fell "seriously ill in his seat in the House" in the midst of a particularly convoluted debate. The resolution being argued was "Shall the previous question now be put?" and the House of Representatives had been thrown into turmoil, as no one could remember what the previous question had been. Fearful lest it concern the sensitive matter of slavery, the chamber was immediately polarized into pro-slavery and abolitionist factions. Eliot S. Thomas, a Democrat with philosophical tendencies, attempted to calm the proceedings by suggesting that "the question being asked in the present, and the question that was asked in the past, are both, perhaps, present in time future," and thus moved to delay the question until the following day. This caused only greater confusion. Shaken from his slumber by the sudden uproar, John Quincy Adams climbed to his feet and announced to no one in particular, "I hold the resolution to be in direct violation of the Constitution of the United States, of the rules of this House, and of the rights of my constituents," upon which he clutched one hand to his neck and collapsed, drawing warm applause from the southern congressmen present. He was removed immediately to the

Speaker's rooms, where the House doctor declared he had suffered a "congestion of the brain." Within two days he was dead.[6]

The death of John Quincy Adams (finished version). Note his possible assassin, casually leaning against a column at the back of the engraving.

Adams' death was followed shortly afterward by a second tragedy. Fillmore received news that one of his oldest acquaintances, Edgar Allan Poe, had been found "delirious and in a state of great distress" on a street in Baltimore, wearing clothes that were not his own. Over the years correspondence between Fillmore and Poe had been irregular but heartfelt. Fillmore would write to tell Poe the news of his quest for the Freemasons, while Poe would reply with humorous missives detailing the ever more grotesque methods he had devised to end his days.[7]

6. Despite the House doctor's diagnosis, the House phrenologist declared that Adams' skull displayed "all the telltale bumps of a poisoning." This little-known second opinion chimes with discoveries made by this author in the preparation of this book. In Fillmore's recently discovered papers a preliminary sketch of the famed engraving "The Death of John Quincy Adams" clearly seems to depict a menacing figure standing in the picture's background aiming what looks like a blowpipe directly at Adams. Yet if one looks at the finished version, held in the Library of Congress, the figure's blowpipe has been removed, and his character imbued with an air of affected nonchalance.

7. Poe to Fillmore, January 12, 1839: "Last night I attempted, unsuccessfully, as this letter undoubtedly proves, to wall myself up in my wine cellar. Might I advise you, dear Fillmore, that upon beginning such a task, one should take pains to ensure one is on the right (or rather, wrong) side of the wall. Ha!"

Fillmore had not heard from Poe since the latter's missive alerting him to the Masonic intrigue in Boston. Rushing to Baltimore, he found he was just moments too late to say goodbye to his old friend. "The doctor told me he had died from congestion of the brain, just like poor old Mr. Adams. Seeing my former ward's emaciated body moved me to tears, and with my grief came delusion, for I thought I saw his eyelid flicker and his hand move, but knowing these were nothing but the phantasms of sorrow, I could not bear to look. 'Bury him,' I told the doctor, 'bury him fast. I will brook no delay, as my eyes cannot bear this sight too long.'"

Upon returning to Washington, Fillmore found a letter written by his dead friend awaiting him. "In his last days," Fillmore's journal relates, "Poe had uncovered something of great import regarding the Masonic conspiracy. He says he is being followed and insists that if he dies, I should reclaim an amulet he wears around his neck, saying that this will explain everything. Despite these worrying signs, he seems surprisingly cheerful, and wonders happily in what horrid manner he will be murdered. Fortunately it seems that he was spared the terrible death he had long hoped for."[8]

Fillmore rode back to Baltimore the following week to have Poe's body exhumed. "The gravedigger was surprised to find large gouge marks and splintered wood on the inside of the coffin lid, and I marveled at the destruction the hungry woodworm was capable of. I also noticed that Poe's fingers were bloody and raw, yet the rings on his fingers were still present, which seems to discount the presence of grave robbers. I can only put it down to a curious phenomenon of decay that would no doubt have interested Poe himself. I found the amulet, but all it held inside was a copy of the reverse side of the Great Seal of the United States, along with the

---

8. Poe's unusual good spirits are reflected in a fragment of poetry he enclosed with his last letter. From an unfinished poem entitled "The Bunny," it reads: "Once upon a midday pleasant, while I wrapped a birthday present, / For the many young and needy orphans of the derelict poor, / While I folded, my foot rocking, suddenly there came a knocking, / As of someone gently hopping, hopping at my chamber door. / ''Tis some visitor,' I exclaimed, 'hopping at my chamber door— / I guess we'll need one present more.'"

engraved words 'You will find what you seek when you seek what you have found.' I will wear it around my neck forevermore, to remind me of my poor young friend. But I have not the slightest idea what it can possibly mean."

Poe's final message: on the money?

Despite the tragedies that beset Fillmore, the election of 1848 was a personal triumph. The Democratic Party never stood a chance. Their presidential nominee, General Lewis Cass, was outranked by the recently promoted Major General Taylor, and once Taylor had issued a direct order to his opponent to "stand down" from campaigning, the Whig Party's victory was ensured. On November 7, 1848, General Zachary Taylor was elected president, and Millard Fillmore took his rightful place as vice president of the United States of America.

During the nineteenth and early twentieth centuries, the office of the vice president was of singular importance to the country in a manner that is hard to imagine today. John Adams, the first vice president, had praised his position as "the most insignificant office that ever the invention of man contrived or his imagination conceived." Black Dan Webster, the terror of the Senate, explained his fear of being elevated to such an august position by saying, "I do not intend to be buried until I am dead." Most eloquently, John Nance Garner, the thirty-second vice president, declared it "not worth a pitcher of warm piss."

Yet despite this, Fillmore found that upon his election to the post, a certain pall fell upon his relations with his former friends and colleagues. President Taylor had immediately struck an independent course that journeyed far and wide from the Whig agenda—"he refuses to listen to his own party, and acts as if guided by some malignant spirit," wrote one aggrieved Whig. Anonymous and unjust accusations suggested that Fillmore was himself behind the president's new direction, and he soon found his political influence draining away from him, and with it his attempts to restart his Masonic investigations. It was joked that his political influence had sunk so low that the opposition "could put up a cow against a Fillmore nominee and defeat him," and a flustered Fillmore, hearing of this remark, confided in his advisors, "A cow is of good, industrious body, and provides sustenance through both its milk and flesh. How, sirs, are we to halt such a candidate?" When it was pointed out that he was merely being taunted, Fillmore was relieved yet also disappointed, for he had been working feverishly on an extensive list of his own prospective candidates, headed by his nephew's cat, Paws Washington.

What's more, his relationship with President Taylor was not all he had been expecting. He found himself locked out of cabinet meetings, and when the two met in the corridors of the White House, Taylor would pretend an old war wound had flared up and made him deaf. It was clear that someone had poisoned the mind of the president against him, but who, and why? With characteristic fortitude and wherewithal, Fillmore decided to confront President Taylor in person. Following him into his office one day, Fillmore "raised my voice so it was like that of a young girl and called out to him." President Taylor, shocked by this feminine intrusion into his solace, spun round; seeing only his vice president, he realized he had been caught out. Unable to feign deafness any longer, Taylor now asked Fillmore to join in with his Mexican War reenactments, although Fillmore was somewhat disappointed to find himself continually on the side of the Mexicans. Indeed, Fillmore soon began to wonder whether being fitted with bit and bridle and being ridden on all fours down the White House corridors by the president was what he really wanted after all, for despite their rapprochement, Fillmore still found himself locked out of cabinet meetings, the president himself often coming to the door and shouting, "Bad girl, Millard! Bad!"

Thus as the great battle over slavery reached a head, Fillmore was to be found sitting on the sidelines. He was not to remain there for long.

9.

Fillmore for President!

(1849–1850)

The Lily-White House—Horseplay—Dorothea Dix Does D.C.—

Death Is Just a Bowl of Cherries—President!—The President

and the Nightingale—The Compromise—Questionable

Advice—Drastic Remedies

*D*espite President Taylor being nicknamed "Old Rough and Ready," a sobriquet gained from his exploits during the Mexican-American War, his White House had about it a quiet, demure air.[1] This was largely due to the ministrations of Taylor's wife, Margaret, who, having traveled from one military post to another during her husband's military years, and having watched him face certain death on numerous occasions, now preferred to avoid "all gaiety and excitement." Guests to the White House were given glasses of muddy water and "embalmed" beef to consume before being invited to sit on hard-backed chairs and offered socks to darn. Conversation was disapproved of, though guests were encouraged to raise their eyes to heaven and mutter dark words about the dire fate awaiting their loved ones, before crying themselves to sleep.[2]

In the White House garden a more pastoral scene was on view. The former general's favorite horse, Old Whitey, had been granted special dispensation to graze on the lawn, and it was with Old Whitey that Fillmore found his most receptive audience.[3] The two could often be seen wandering around the lush grounds, Fillmore speaking with one hand behind his back and the white stallion idly chewing the petunias.

1. President Taylor was also known as "Old String 'Em Up and Cut Their Ears Off" due to certain obscure events that took place at the Battle of Buena Vista in 1847.
2. While the White House under the stewardship of "Miserable" Margaret Taylor was a remarkably staid place, the title for running the most tedious White House in American history must go to President Rutherford Hayes (1877–1881). Hayes, along with his wife, known as "Lemonade Lucy," served only soft drinks and sang hymns constantly. Such was their hatred of "the foolish and wicked practice of profane cursing and swearing" that they refused to speak any four-letter words at all, including the words *four* and *word*.
3. "Whitey's Law," as it was commonly known, was a piece of hidden legislation snuck into the Hawaiian Islands treaty. The law allowed for all "ashen, herbivorous quadrupeds" owned by the head of state to graze on the White House lawn. Despite the seemingly unique nature of the dispensation, the law was revived fifty years later when Theodore Roosevelt's pet albino rhinoceros could be seen roaming the White House grounds. When a White House clerk was unfortunately gored to death, Roosevelt was forced to keep the animal in the Lincoln Bedroom.

"Miserable" Margaret Taylor: referred to laughter as "the devil's hiccups."

This quiet routine was to change with the arrival one morning of Dorothea Dix. Dix had come to the White House to plead for more funds to aid her in her reformation of insane asylums. From the age of seventeen she had worked in houses of correction, teaching Sunday-school lessons to the prisoners every day of the week. However, she had been appalled by the misery of the insane held there.[4] From that time on she had devoted her life to the building of new hospitals for their care. Now, at twenty-six years of age, Dix was a beautiful spinster. She had been refused entry to see the gruff president and, at a loss, had encountered Fillmore on the White House lawn in deep conversation with Old Whitey.

"We shook hands and he asked me what I was doing there," Dix wrote in a letter to her grandmother. "I replied that I had been refused entry to see the president, at which he let out a great sigh and sat down looking most despondent. He is a most pleasant man to look at," she continued, "of strong build, with the most dazzling blue eyes. I warrant I should be more nervous conversing with a man of such exalted position,

---

4. The most common treatment for the insane in the mid-1800s was "abandonment therapy," in which patients were left chained to the floor for days, without food or water, until they "came about of an improved outlook on their situation." See Nicholas Ratchett's *Mental Infirmity: Are Splints the Cure?* (1845).

and yet seeing him walking in the garden, talking to a horse, he does so remind me of my charges at the hospital."

Dorothea Dix: enamored of Fillmore's "special" qualities.

Although Fillmore does not mention the occasion of their first meeting in his journal, it seems that greetings were exchanged, for soon he was writing frequent letters to Dorothea. With Abigail returned to Buffalo—on the express orders of Thurlow Weed—Fillmore found himself alone once more, and hungry for companionship. In one letter to Dix he described a typical day as vice president: "Dear Miss Dix: I do thank you for your kind letter of the tenth of March. It is most refreshing to be asked the questions you pose. In truth, it is thrilling to be asked any questions at all. In the morning, shortly after my daily ablutions and breakfast, I arrive at the White House. The president and his cabinet are very busy men and so I repair to the garden and discuss the latest news with my colleague, Mr. Whitey. He is a Whig by happenstance rather than conviction, yet I do believe I can convince him to the cause. Yesterday, he stamped his foot in disgust as I explained to him the forthcoming ratification of the Clayton-Bulwer Treaty. And this very morning he let out what can only be termed a snort of approval when I told him of the publication of Miss Amelia Jenks' new temperance journal, *The Lily*. It is wise to stay close to one who has the ear of the most powerful man in the country."

The correspondence blossomed, and for Fillmore the days at the White House seemed to slip by all the quicker for his newfound friendship. Dix wrote to Fillmore often, telling him of her campaign to separate the criminal from the insane in jails, "so that the mad should not be made to share space with the merely bad."[5] On visits to the White House, Fillmore would take Dix for rides on Old Whitey, and on one occasion he even whittled Dix a small wooden plaque for her desk that read, "It is not required that one is mentally deranged to labor here, but being thus disposed surely ameliorates the situation."

While Fillmore's journals dutifully report his meetings with Dix in the fall of 1849, he is strangely reticent on the exact nature of their relationship. In fact, rather than revealing his state of mind, Fillmore's journal for this period concerns itself solely with a long, rambling story entitled "The Runaways of Fern Hollow; or, It's Never Too Late, Lucretia!"[6] Little could Fillmore have known it, but the tranquility that he now enjoyed was about to be shattered forever.

Accounts of President Zachary Taylor's demise differ, but what is known for certain is that Taylor had been attending a Fourth of July celebration at the base of the Washington Monument under a scorching noonday sun. The highlight of the festivity was the attendance of three individuals who had known George Washington: Dolley Madison, wife of James Madison; Elizabeth Hamilton, wife of Alexander Hamilton; and George Washington Parke Custis, adopted grandson of Washington, whom the public were encouraged to poke and prod.

5. Dix's later attempts to separate both the "mad" and the "bad" from the "dangerous to know" would be less successful.
6. *The Runaways of Fern Hollow* concerns two ponies, one of whom is the chief of all the ponies in the land, and the other a pony who looks after sick ponies. In the story, the two ponies leave their responsibilities behind them and run away to a distant land, where they spend much time chasing each other and lying down on bales of straw, gazing into each other's eyes.

After two hours of this veneration, not to mention what Taylor called the "execrable nonsense" of the Marine Band's performance of "Nelly Was a Lady," the president tired. But his return home was severely delayed when a wagon hauling a giant stone of Maryland marble broke through the bridge that crossed the city canal. By the time the bridge was mended, President Taylor was hot, thirsty, and hungry.

Returning to the White House, he found a table loaded with cherries and wild berries—an unusual feast, considering his wife's penchant for boiled boot leather and raw turnips. There were gallons of chilled milk instead of the usual tepid ditchwater, and the president quaffed and feasted eagerly until dinnertime, when he began to complain of cramps. Under the rolling eyes of his doom-fearing wife, Taylor heard the White House doctors dismiss his problem as "acute indigestion."

By the following Monday his condition had worsened, and his wife had begun to darn furiously. The White House doctors concurred—by a three-to-two majority—that Taylor's indigestion had developed into "bilious fever" (with Dr. Abraham Witherspoon writing a dissenting opinion diagnosing mumps). Upon hearing the news, Fillmore hurried to the White House, but he was refused entry by Taylor's strict instruction.

Fillmore had good reason to be alarmed. Was it just a coincidence that it had been stonemasons who had broken the canal bridge, thus forcing President Taylor to stay longer in the hot sun, and inspiring in him a longing for cool cherries and cold milk? Could it be that beneath the seemingly accidental poisoning of the president lay a plot of labyrinthine intrigue, created by the master builders of conspiracy, the Freemasons themselves?

On Tuesday the ninth of July, at half past ten in the evening, President Zachary Taylor died. The five doctors present respectively recorded the reason for his death as "cholera," "typhoid," "beriberi," "the uncommon cold," and "a fall from a great height." Fillmore's journal reports his own emotions on that sad day. "I tour the cabinet rooms without impediment," he wrote.

"The riding crop that once chided me hangs limp and lifeless on the wall. Old Whitey is inconsolable. Who shall be president now?"

Following a restless night, Fillmore was greeted at the door of his boardinghouse by an escort of congressmen and was walked briskly to the House chamber.[7] The *Congressional Globe* spoke of a "strange, disbelieving silence" in the Capitol. Yet despite the solemnity of the occasion, Fillmore remarked how cheering it was that his congressional friends should greet him. "There was Black Dan, staring at me as if he could not quite believe his eyes, and Mr. Clay, shaking his head, evidently still unable to believe that dear President Taylor was dead." In particular, Fillmore recalled Thurlow Weed "gripping my hand most powerfully. He was trembling, and his face was red with a seemingly volcanic sadness. He was so overcome with emotion he could not say a word." Surrounded by his peers, Fillmore took the presidential oath of office. The simple country boy whose lifelong dream had been to destroy tyranny and injustice and to defeat evil and oppression had just been given the perfect opportunity to do so.[8]

It was obvious to President Fillmore that his first action should be the formation of a new cabinet, the former cabinet having been buried alive with President Taylor in accordance with his last wishes. Fillmore suffered an initial setback when Old Whitey, Taylor's horse, refused the post of secretary of the Treasury. But the most vicious intelligences of Congress rallied round to offer support. The House Bully, Black Dan, was aging, but the crack of his whip could still drum up support for the most unpopular of bills put before the House, and he graciously accepted the post of secretary of state. "He now refers to me as 'President Bernard,'" recorded Fillmore, "which, I suppose, is an improvement."

Yet despite all the wise minds Fillmore could call upon, the issue of

---

7. The presidential phalanx, made up of Congress' heaviest-set members, had been implemented after John Tyler had attempted to flee his own swearing-in ceremony in 1841. It existed until the Secret Service presidential protection detail was created in 1902, since when no president has ever managed to escape his own inauguration.

8. Fillmore's journals tell of one other lifelong dream in which he is "playing pat-a-cake with a sea-lion."

slavery still seemed an intractable confusion. How could he reconcile the abolitionist North with the slaveholding South? The answer would come to Fillmore in a moment of inspiration as he moved into his new home, the White House.

Upon her husband's death, Margaret Taylor had immediately broken camp, scorching the carpets behind her and scuttling the presidential toy boat collection. She had also carefully booby-trapped the building, and a trip wire she had left caused Fillmore to stumble as he was carrying a large box of his possessions into his new office. With the contents spilled across the floor, Fillmore's eye was immediately caught by one of his old inventions. The rubber band had been created in an afternoon during his innovative "rubber days" of the late 1830s. Fillmore had intended it to be used "in the holding of like objects together," yet now as he sat on the floor of the presidential office, toying with his device, he had a breakthrough: "Just as my rubber band is pliant and stretches with ease to encompass anything," he told his journal, "so a political solution of equal malleability is needed to resolve the slavery farrago."

Fillmore immediately called for another aging congressional giant, Henry Clay, and implored him to put all his rhetorical and political skill toward the prospect of creating a piece of legislation that had the same qualities as his rubber band, "a Compromise, if you will, with all the give and take of my malleable loop." Grunting acknowledgment, Clay loped off to his offices to begin his work, swatting smaller congressmen out of his way like flies.

When not solving the nation's problems, Fillmore was busy settling into his new home. He had decided to install a bath—a radically new and untested contraption—in the White House, and his every spare moment was spent wrestling with the building's byzantine plumbing system. When Abigail returned to Washington as the new First Lady, she wrote a letter to her mother depicting her overawed reaction to their new situation: "Millard has somehow become president, although this does not seem to have prevented him from getting his arm stuck in a U-bend. God have mercy on us all."

Amidst the general upheaval in Fillmore's life, there was still time for entertainment. In the fall of 1850, Jenny Lind, the famed soprano known as the "Swedish Nightingale," arrived in the United States under the auspices of the promoter P. T. Barnum, and the country became gripped by "Lindomania." New dishes were concocted in her honor ("songbird meatballs" were the pièce de résistance at Delmonico's), new diseases were named after her (the "Lindy bug," a virulent form of streptococcus, became the contagion à la mode), and so besotted did the nation become that a motion to rename the country "the United States of Lind" was only narrowly defeated in Congress. Even the most cynical critics were limitless in their praise. The *New York Tribune*, which earlier in the year had lambasted Nathaniel Hawthorne's novel *The Scarlet Letter* as being "shallow and derivative," wrote of Lind, "Whoever knows her and has been able to experience her has experienced perfection itself."

By December her tour had made its way to the nation's capital, and Fillmore and Abigail were present at the first night's show. Fillmore was transfixed. The *Washington Report* noted how at one point "the president's admiration for her singing was so great that he stood up and sang along with her, despite displaying a profound unfamiliarity with both the words and tune of Meyerbeer's 'Ein Feldlager in Schleisen.' The president's wife could be seen pulling on his coattails; finding this ineffective, she walked from the auditorium, her fingers in her ears."

Fillmore's enthusiastic response to the concert led to an invitation being extended to him to meet the singer at her hotel later that evening: "I arrived slightly early, as was my wont, and as I approached her door thought I heard a female voice say, 'I will have him eating out of my hand.' I was mightily glad to hear this, as I was devilishly hungry. Imagine my surprise when the door should swing open and none other than Mr. Weed

Jenny Lind: Swedish Nightingale.

should appear in front of me! He explained that he been paying Miss Lind his respects and that she was expecting me.

"The charming Miss Lind was wearing a red silk dressing gown and gazing into a mirror. Such was her splendor that it took me a few moments to realize she was surrounded by a menagerie of bizarre creatures. A tiny man in military costume was sitting on her lap twirling an even tinier moustache. 'So good to see you, Mr. President,' she said without looking at me. She gestured to the little man on her lap. 'This is General Tom Thumb, Mr. President. Mr. Barnum has lent him to me for my security.' She clapped her hands absentmindedly and two pigtailed Chinamen, who appeared to be joined together at the waist, lurched forward from behind a drape and displayed the most remarkable dexterity in pouring me a cup of tea. 'Mr. Barnum is paying me one thousand dollars a night to sing for all you lovely American people. He lent me a few of his exhibits to amuse me. Do they amuse you, Mr. President?' I must admit to being quite transfixed with a creature named Jo-Jo the Dog-Faced Boy, who was completely covered in hair and was curled up in front of the fire snoring. I was patting his head and rubbing his belly when a grotesquely corpulent child waddled into the room and began banging a toy drum. 'Ah,' said Miss Lind, 'that would be Master Allie Turner, the mammoth fat infant. I do not know why Mr. Barnum lent *him* to me.'"

Fillmore's journal continues: "Miss Lind picked up a letter from her bureau and waved it in the air. 'Do you know who Hans Christian Andersen is, Mr. President? He says he is in love with me,' she stated tonelessly, looking at the letter with some contempt. I congratulated her on having an admirer of such fame, but she cut me off. 'Have you seen him, Mr. Fillmore? He is so ugly. And with Hans you are never sure if it is the boys or the girls. He is so confused.'

Hans Christian Andersen: Ugly Duckling.

"With that she threw the letter into the fire and turned her full attention to me, seemingly for the first time. I must admit I found her most compelling. 'Is it true,' she said as she walked over to me, 'what they say about you American presidents?' I told her that I was not sure what they had been saying, but that there was indeed a lot of responsibility attached to the post, not to mention the long, arduous hours. This, however, did not seem to satisfy her. 'Mr. Thomas Jefferson was well known throughout Europe for his excitability and amorous adventures,' she purred into my ear. 'Do you have amorous adventures?' I was so startled by the question that I took a step backward and stepped on the foot of the fat infant, who let out a scream so loud that the twins from Siam dropped their tea tray, startling the Dog-Faced Boy, who sprang up on all fours and began savaging General Tom Thumb, who desperately tried to protect himself with his tiny bugle. Miss Lind screamed for 'Constentenus' and from out of nowhere a muscular man covered in tattoos rushed into the room. But instead of helping part the combatants, he grasped Miss Lind, hoisted her over his shoulder, and carried her off into an adjacent chamber, despite her protestations that 'now isn't the right time for that.' Seeing the maelstrom before me, and not wanting to get bitten by the enraged Jo-Jo, I made my excuses to no one in particular, and left."

Lind was only one of many dignitaries whom the new president met during his first months in office. Well-wishers such as the ever-faithful Dorothea Dix mingled with politicians and emissaries from around the globe. On open day at the White House, when members of the public were allowed to meet the president, Fillmore was approached by a twelve-year-old boy who asked Fillmore for his autograph, as well as those of his cabinet members. Fillmore asked the boy's name and was told it was John Pierpont Morgan, although "his friends called him J.P." With the cabinet holding session in an adjacent room to the greeting parlor, Fillmore decided to fulfill the boy's wish immediately. "I had soon collected everyone's signature, including a bloody handprint from Black Dan," he recalled, "but was shocked upon returning to surprise the little robber in the act of stuffing his pockets with the White House cutlery!" In no short order Fillmore put him across his knee and spanked him thoroughly, and Morgan "ran from the White House in tears. I trust," wrote Fillmore, "that my actions have corrected his thieving ways."

*   *   *

Throughout the spring and summer of 1850, Fillmore's cabinet had been in perpetual session, as Henry Clay's compromise bill was taken through its final stages. Although Fillmore had not been involved in the niceties of its construction, he had provided his cabinet with inspirational leadership, constantly firing rubber bands across the room to remind them of the nature of their task. Finally, on September 9, 1850, the bill was ready. Surrounded by his advisors, Fillmore was slowly led through the epic piece of legislation, which he would have to sign if it was to pass into law. Concessions were made to both the North and the South, and it was clear that Henry Clay had displayed remarkable sensitivity for a man with such a prominent brow; no one could be offended by this bill. By September 18, Fillmore needed to put his name to only one more article of legislation, entitled the Fugitive Slave Act.

In his journal, Fillmore recalls asking for an explanation of what this act was to entail, "because I would hate to see the slaves treated in a worse manner than they are already." There was a pause as the members of his cabinet looked nervously at one another, but the silence was broken by the entry of none other than Thurlow Weed. "I was surprised to see Mr. Weed here, but as he is my old mentor, friend, and companion, I felt his advice could be of the greatest use to me now. I asked him his opinion of the Fugitive Slave Act, and he informed me, 'It is to help all those slaves that have become misplaced. We cannot very well have them running around like kittens lost in the wild without providing for them, now can we?' His words seemed to make sense, and the image of kittens lost in the wild touched my heart. Yet I still sensed a certain apprehension in the rest of my cabinet, and when I asked them if this was untrue, they each in turn looked at Mr. Weed, who returned their gaze with his powerful gray eyes, and then shook their heads in dumb silence. Mr. Weed looked back at me and implored me to 'think of the kittens, dear Fillmore,' and with the sound of contented purring in my ears I signed the paper, and suggested three cheers be given to Mr. Clay for his wonderful compromise, and Mr.

Weed and his kittens. There was a notable lack of enthusiasm amongst my fellows, which I put down to the many hours they had devoted to this great work. Only Mr. Weed congratulated me, shaking my hand with the utmost passion and laughing madly with joy."

Fillmore recalls there being a strange quiet about the White House that evening. Many of his staff had returned home claiming illness, and Old Whitey bit his hand as Fillmore attempted to feed him a sugar cube. "If this should be a time for celebration," wondered Fillmore, "why do I feel so glum?" He would find out the reason the very next day.

"I was taking morning tea in my office when my beloved Abigail burst through the doors, grasping a newspaper in her delicate hands. She asked me how I could have put my name to the Fugitive Slave Act. I relaxed a little and began to show her my rubber band, which I thought would help her simple female mind understand the complexities of the compromise. But as I was beginning my demonstration she looked at me with an uncomprehending stare. 'Millard,' she said, not without some firmness, 'do you know what a fugitive is?' I replied that I believed it to be a cleansing uncture or ointment designed for the evacuation of the bowels. Abigail stared at me for some time before saying, 'The Fugitive Slave Act requires federal agencies to assist in the capture of runaway slaves. It punishes any-one who collaborates in an escape, denies accused runaways the right to testify in their own defense, and thus makes it possible for free blacks to be kidnapped and enslaved. Have you not seen the newspapers? They are call-ing you a man who will compromise his most sacred morals. The south-erners are laughing, saying you are "their man." What have you to say for yourself?' Under this barrage of information my attention had drifted and the rubber band I held snapped back against my face. I tried to tell Abigail about Mr. Weed's comparison of the slaves with lost kittens, but she cut me short and replied that whatever kittens I was talking about had surely been tossed in a bag and drowned. She left my room, slamming the door behind her. What have I done?"

As federal marshals began to hunt down escaped slaves, often coercing local law enforcement officials into helping them, anti-slavery groups denounced Fillmore. He began to receive threatening mail, and it was generally acknowledged by both supporters and denigrators of the bill that Fillmore's name was now "shrouded in wickedness." His former political allies deserted him, and many of his so-called friends from Congress stopped visiting the White House. "I am sure that the advice Mr. Weed gave me was sound in theory," wrote Fillmore in his journal, "but it does not seem to work in practice."

Approximately three weeks after the signing of the Fugitive Slave Act there is a lacuna in Fillmore's diaries. The White House logbook seems to show that he was absent from the building for days at a time, although there is no mention of any official travels in the presidential record. Oddly enough, at the same time that the president was away from Washington, strange reports began to crop up in newspapers stretching along the eastern seaboard. The *New York Star* described how a "portly man" wrested the fugitive slave James Hamlet out of the clutches of a federal agent. In Baltimore, the escaped slave Rachel Parker was broken out of jail by a man described simply as "very polite." In Boston, two federal marshals who had captured the escaped slaves Shadrach Minkins and Thomas Sims were knocked unconscious by a man who "left a long and seemingly sincere note apologizing for his actions." A signature at the bottom of the note had been hastily crossed out.

If only Fillmore had been in his office and thus able to steamroll emergency legislation through Congress, it seems certain that these terrifying acts of vigilantism could have been halted. If that had been the case, then perhaps the Compromise of 1850 would have gained greater acceptance, Fillmore would have been reelected, an era of peace would have spread across the country, the Civil War would never have happened, and all men, regardless of their race, creed, or color, would now be living together in brotherly harmony. As it was, Fillmore was nowhere to be found, and when his journal begins again—four days after the Boston incident—it is baffling to find him just outside Buffalo.

Fillmore had been riding Old Whitey along a road by the light of the full moon when he saw ahead of him three figures, one lying prostrate on the road. "I called out to see if help was needed, but upon hearing my voice the two standing persons ran away. I rode to one side of the prone figure and saw that it was a young female Negro who had evidently fallen unconscious. I dismounted and helped her sit up, and as I did so her eyes opened. I smiled to show I meant her no harm, but in an instant she had grasped my crotch and hauled herself to her feet. I crumpled to the ground in pain, but my assailant had not gone ten paces from me when she too fell down, clutching her head. Doubled up as I was, I crawled toward her and asked her who she was and what ailed her.

"She told me her name was Harriet Tubman, an escaped slave, and that her 'damned dizziness' was due to having been struck on the head by her owner when she was young. She informed me, not without some pride, that she was the best conductor on the 'Underground Railroad' and had transported over one hundred slaves to freedom in Canada. I was amazed, and enquired with disbelief about this railroad that ran under the ground, for who would have thought that a race in servitude was capable of such technological wizardry! Miss Tubman shook her head as if she too could not believe it. At that moment the two figures who had run away earlier stepped out of the darkness toward us, and Miss Tubman scolded them most fiercely. 'We call her Moses,' one of the men told me, pointing at Miss Tubman. 'Because she is a man?' I asked hesitantly, for Miss Tubman looked every inch a woman. 'No,' he said, and then it dawned on me: 'because she is a Jew!' Although she did not bear the traditional Semitic complexion, nor the usurer's long crooked nose and sharp fingernails, I thought how right it was that the persecuted race of antiquity should now be helping the persecuted race of today. The male Negro tried to explain something to me, but I was so caught up at once with the spirit of the universal brotherhood of man that I embraced him in a tearful hug. I vowed that I would be their guide to Lake Erie, whence they were set to be transported by boat to Canada. Placing Miss Tubman on Old Whitey, I walked alongside her with her two colleagues.

"On that walk we talked of many things: the unjustness of slavery, man's yearning for freedom, and the best recipe for Irish stew. Miss Tubman announced her preference for adding turnips and barley to the mixture, and we both agreed on the need for additional stout. When I bid them a tearful adieu, Miss Tubman gave me a kiss on the cheek and said that if I was ever in Canada I should call on her. We left agreeing that there are three things all people have a right to: life, liberty, and hot pot pie."

10.

Fillmore Abroad

(1850–1853)

Defusing Tensions—A Great Voyage—Master of Disguise—The

Peculiar Commodore Perry—A Misunderstanding with the

Mikado—Battle Royale—Inconstant Time—Homeland

Insecurity—Standing Down—Tragedy

*F*illmore toiled hard to right the wrongs of the ill-starred Compromise of 1850, but the damage had been done. The president's annual message to Congress, delivered on the subject "What I Did During My Summer Holidays," was not well received, and already the fickle Whig Party was trying to find a successor, untarnished by the slavery debacle, in time for the elections of 1852. With unscheduled scuffles breaking out in both chambers of Congress, Fillmore realized that his divisive figure was best kept out of public view.

Shunned by his former political aides, alienated from his colleagues in Congress, and with talk of the House Subcommittee on Assassinations being resuscitated once more, Fillmore took the fateful decision to leave the inflamed passions of the country he presided over. But where could he go where he would not be recognized? What virgin land had not been penetrated by the illustrious name of Fillmore? After consulting with the Office of the Geographer, only one country seemed suitable for such a retreat—Japan.

In 1638, the Tokugawa shogunate had recognized the danger that foreign influence represented to its rule, and sealed Japan off from the outside world.[1] Foreigners were expressly forbidden from stepping upon the country's shores, and death sentences were routinely imposed on any Japanese citizen foolish enough to provide information about the island to

---

1. Tokugawa Ieyasu (1543–1616) was a great warrior, ruthless strategist, and obsessive decapitator. It is said that during his reign there were so many decapitations that the average height of the Japanese population shrank by a foot. The Tokugawa shogunate's decision to cut Japan off from the rest of the world was an attempt to extend this proclivity onto a geographical level.

outsiders.² Cut off from Western civilization, and with no need for an army or navy, Japan became the most urbanized, literate, and peaceful nation in the world. Such a barbaric backwater would prove the perfect place for Fillmore's escape.

With his plan hatched, Fillmore summoned Commodore Matthew Perry to the White House. A commanding presence, Perry's scowling mouth and luxuriant coiffure had seen action in both the War of 1812 and the Mexican-American War. He had commanded vessels in the Mediterranean and off the coast of Africa, and such was his fame that he had even been offered a commission in the Russian navy.³

Fillmore informed Perry that he was to deliver a letter he had written to the Mikado of Japan, in which he called for the opening up of trade routes between the two countries. Thus on November 13, 1852, Commodore Perry set sail at the head of a squadron of black-hulled steam frigates, Fillmore's letter locked in his cabin's safe. Yet Perry's boat carried a far more precious cargo aboard it: the president himself.

Not wishing to draw attention to himself, Fillmore had decided to travel completely incognito. He had obtained a midshipman's uniform and a fake naval commission from the secretary of the navy under the name Pilchard Dillmore. "In my coat of blue cloth and squeezed into my white breeches I am freed from the weight of office, and from the presidential chain mail," he wrote in his journal. "The open sea is a balm to my soul

---

2. There was one exception to this rule. A small Dutch trader's post was allowed to operate on a prison-like island in the middle of Nagasaki Bay. One foreign ship a year was allowed to visit this outpost, exporting Japanese silks and importing the one thing the Japanese could not create for themselves: little Dutch boys. Famed for their dyke-repairing ability, and chosen specifically for the length and breadth of their fingers, Dutch boys were a much sought-after commodity throughout East Asia. The pernicious trade continues to this day, and it is rumored that China's mammoth Three Gorges Dam has over three hundred illegally imported Dutch boys on call twenty-four hours a day, in case the dam walls should spring a leak.
3. Perry's reason for turning down this commission stemmed from a case of extreme degenerative solipsism. As a child he had been fascinated by the many different countries of the world, and the navy had proven a natural outlet for this enthusiasm. But the older he grew, the more his horizons diminished. By the age of twenty he was describing his childhood interests as "nonsense," by the age of thirty he had begun to mistrust the concept of Australia, and by forty he no longer believed in the existence of Asia and much of northern Europe. Thus when informed of the offer to join the Russian navy, he dismissed it as a puerile joke. As he grew elderly, Perry retreated into a completely solipsistic state, believing only in what he could see from his bedroom window in New York (although on clear days he was said to have mentioned the possibility of Canada).

Perry: New York, New York?

and my absence is, I hope, a salve to the country. Let wounds heal, not least the chafing given me by my abrasive unmentionables."[4]

The journey to Japan was to take five arduous months, with the squadron traveling eastward around the Cape of Good Hope.[5] Accidents and deaths were all too common on the high seas, and the president provides a unique perspective on the harsh life of a sailor in the United States Navy: "Woke up at ten in the morning. Pleasant dream involving talking beetles. Reported for duty. Excused from heavy labor, again. Lucky me! Took the sun, and ate mango until luncheon in lieutenant commander's rooms. Excused from scrubbing of floorboards. Sighted pod of dolphins and asked commodore if he would pursue. Commodore somewhat bad-tempered. Perhaps he is homesick? Invited to dine at commodore's table for forty-fifth day in a row. Enquired as to the playing of cribbage with officers; won again! Others appear seasick. Marine band still practicing 'Hail to the Chief.' If only they knew! Excused from night watch."

4. Metal undergarments had been worn by presidents ever since 1801, for the express purpose of protecting the presidential reproductive organs, and thus ensuring a son and heir to the presidency.

5. Since it was first sighted in 1488, the Cape of Good Hope had been known respectively as the Cape of Shipwrecked Souls, the Cape of Drowned Sailors, and the Cape of Splintery Death. A precipitous decline in trade with the Orient saw its name changed to the present appellation.

As the squadron approached Singapore it came across an American survey barque engaged in a scientific expedition in the Pacific Ocean. With the waters so unknown, Perry was keen to gain information from them, and Fillmore was equally excited to meet the naturalists on board. "We were receiving instructions from their navigator when I came upon the boat's captain and first mate leaning over the gunwales and enquired of them their thoughts on their naturalist trade. 'Oh, Mr. Dillmore,' the captain said dreamily, 'it is the finest occupation in the world. The dolphins leaping out of the water, the giant turtles swimming beside us, the funny little fishies with their bright colors and their mouths opening and closing. Always opening and closing!' I must admit I had to stifle a chuckle at the very thought of them. 'And can there be anything finer to mortal eye than the whale?' the captain continued. 'Their big flippers, all that cuddly blubber, and those blowholes. Poof! Poof! Always making such humorous noises! Surely they are the most peaceable beasts on God's earth.' The first mate was equally enthusiastic, and said that he had never seen a whale become angry, except, that is, when they were being hunted. This observation seemed to perturb the captain. 'Well, yes, Mr. Starbuck, that may be true,' he said, stroking the thin black beard on his chin, 'but I warrant, you or I might be a bit of a handful if we had nasty metal harpoons sticking out of us.' The first mate inclined his head in agreement, and the captain, continuing to lightly chide his companion, suggested that 'we would probably wiggle a bit, and kick up a bit of a fuss, if our blubber was being turned into oil for streetlamps.'[6] Both men went suddenly quiet and looked out to sea. There were tears in the captain's eyes. 'The inhumanity of man to God's greatest creatures never ceases to perplex me,' he whispered. Not wishing to see such sweet men so despondent, I suggested that perhaps the only other animal on God's earth of such interest to watch was the sheep, thoughts of which suddenly seemed to flood the

6. Whale oil was used for a vast array of purposes in the nineteenth century, including greasing, slicking, smearing, creaming, and all manner of embrocating. Such was the size of the trade in the 1850s that 1854 was declared Best Lubricated Year Ever.

captain's mind and calm him, and with which statement both he and the first mate happily concurred. Soon we were talking about how close to Eden this world would be if sheep were but a hundred feet long and could swim.

"The captain informed me that his boat was traveling to the east coast of Japan, where it had been rumored many different types of whales lived, 'of all different shapes and sizes.' The first mate said that he had even heard rumors of a large white whale that lived there, to which the young captain raised his eyebrows in wonder and proclaimed he would give his right leg to see such a marvel. At that precise moment a young pilot whale appeared miraculously between our two boats, rising high out of the water, and the captain leaned over the side and patted its forehead. And with that our two boats separated, and I waved goodbye to the good ship *Pequod* and its gentle, whale-loving crew."

On May 26, 1853, the American squadron entered Japanese coastal waters and dropped anchor in Naha harbor. It was raining heavily, but from the mainland a small boat was paddled out to Fillmore's flagship. Perry was in the middle of explaining to his crew that they were about to encounter "a singular people" and for this reason everyone was to behave with the greatest "prudence, forbearance, and discretion," when two Japanese officials climbed aboard. Perry took one look at them and was so horrified that he "screamed out loud" and ran to his cabin, bolting the door behind him. The Japanese were somewhat baffled by this greeting, and once again Fillmore's diplomatic skills were desperately needed.

"Whilst I had taken this journey in order to remain inconspicuous," reads his journal, "Commodore Perry's hitherto unsuspected fear of the Japanese endangered our mission and I realized that I would have to reveal my true identity. Thus ripping off my top and pantaloons, I declared myself not Midshipman Dillmore but President Fillmore! The American sailors did not bat an eye—confused beyond belief as they probably were—while the Japanese merely looked even more puzzled. After being handed a towel I demanded that I be introduced to the Mikado."

Unfortunately for Fillmore, the faltering English of the Japanese envoys meant they were somewhat puzzled by the definition of a "president," and although he did his best to explain to them the concept of a federal republic, his definition of Section I of Article II of the United States Constitution seems only to have made matters worse. After nearly three hours of explanation, during which time he had declared himself the "king of Washington," "lord of the West," and "number one politician," Fillmore's explanation of himself as "America's champion" finally seemed to impress the Japanese. "The emissaries began to circle me, prodding my belly gently with their sticks, and speaking to each other in what seemed to be approving tones, before scurrying off the boat." A diplomatic incident had been narrowly averted.

Later that afternoon an arrow was fired onto the deck of Fillmore's ship announcing that the Mikado would meet "America's champion" the following day. The meeting was at such short notice that Fillmore desperately sought a suitable gift to present to the Mikado. Catching sight of the ensign hanging from the stern of the ship, "I determined there could not be a better way to extend a hand of international brotherhood to this remote land than by the gifting of Old Glory."

The following morning a Japanese delegation was sent to escort Fillmore and his honor guard to the mainland. Overnight, a large pyramid-shaped building, bedecked with colorful flags and banners, had been built on the seashore. Surrounding it now were hundreds of Japanese with bows, muskets, and spears. Inside the building, Fillmore was surprised to see that a large platform of earth had been erected, overlooking which sat the Mikado, "resplendent in a maroon silk robe and little cloud-blue socks." Fillmore was ushered forward, and he offered up the ensign he had taken from his ship. Unwrapping it, the Mikado seemed to laugh. "I was asked whether I would 'ozumo,' and the Mikado repeatedly pointed at my belly. Identifying this as an invitation to dine, I strongly nodded my assent, for I had not eaten any breakfast. The Mikado pointed to the earthen stage, where I presumed we would be dining, and then clapped his hands, at which I was half led, half dragged to an antechamber by three Japanese women.

"Before I knew it, all my clothes had been removed and the ensign I had gifted to the Mikado had been wrapped around my waist. I wondered what savage rite this was where one was made to dress in the flag of one's country while one dined, but then I remembered that similar events were almost obligatory at the House of Representatives Christmas party, and I felt a little more at ease.

"A large drum was now being beaten, and I was led out onto the mound, despite there being still no sign of tables or plates. I had heard rumors that the Japanese would gorge themselves on a type of flying lice, displaying their remarkable dexterity by grabbing the parasites out of the air with chopped sticks. I very much hoped I would be given a knife and fork, or better yet, a large butterfly net, for I was terribly hungry. The drumming stopped, and into the building walked a Japanese considerably different from any other I had yet seen. Each of his footsteps seemed to shake the room, and his vast girth—compared to that of the slim little Japanese that we had met previously—immediately identified him as the chef."

Japanese court records made available to this author suggest that Fillmore was somewhat mistaken in his deduction. The man now approaching him was none other than Hidenoyama Raigoro, the greatest sumo wrestler of the age. Hidenoyama had been retired for three years after crushing all competition in the sport. He had since taken to wrestling inanimate objects, and his spectacular defeats of "Elm Tree" and "Large Boulder" were legendary.[7]

Fillmore wrote how the giant wrestler "took a handful of salt from a large bowl by the side of the earthen platform, which I hoped was the prelude to our feast. But instead of waiting to garnish his dishes with it, he began to throw it all over the ground. I, on the other hand, kept the salt in

7. In 1864, Hidenoyama Raigoro's emaciated body was found at the base of Mount Fuji in the full costume of the sumo. To this day, Japanese geographers claim he had wrestled the sacred mountain three and a half feet to the east.

my hand and was looking around for the pepper bowl when a gong sounded. Startled, I spun around and saw the chef crouch down, touch his fist to the ground, and charge at me! He grasped me by the throat and began to lift me into the air, to enthusiastic applause from the Mikado. Had I taken too long in ordering my food? But where was the menu, and what was the *plat du jour*? I tried to signify my ignorance by throwing my hands up at the behemoth but accidentally threw a handful of salt straight into the chef's face, causing no small aggravation to his eyes. He released his grip, and after regaining my breath, I went to offer the poor fellow the corner of my ensign with which to wipe his face clear. As I did so, however, the flag came undone at my waist, and stepping upon it, I tripped forward with some force into the back of the disoriented cook.

Katsushika Hokusai's The Heimlich Maneuver.

"With the long journey to Japan having prevented me from partaking in my usual morning constitutionals, I had flirted with corpulence on the high seas. As such, my body was of no small consequence, and the blinded chef was thrust out of the ring by the intimation of my weight upon him. He crashed into the Mikado's throne. There was the sound of splintering wood and a shrill, high-pitched yelp, but all that could be seen of the

Mikado from beneath the chef's considerable bulk were his two little blue socks. A strange quiet fell on the room; sensing that protocol had been breached in some way, I thought it best to take luncheon aboard my ship. Being handed a hat by one of my naval officers with which to cover my modesty, we shuffled out of the building, waving at the awestruck Japanese, and promising we would return 'in a bit.'"

Fillmore spent the next few days aboard his frigate in deep thought. He began to doubt whether Japan was a suitable place for his concealment after all: "The essential differences between our two cultures require more exploration than I can give them time," he wrote in his journal. "It seems that while I say *potato*, they say ポテ. I say *tomato*, they say トマト. It is better we call the whole thing off." So Fillmore gave the order to return home, much to the relief of the still-trembling Commodore Perry.

Returning home via the Pacific, Fillmore wondered ceaselessly about what events had taken place at home during his many months abroad. Had his absence helped heal the wounds within the Whig Party? Had his mistaken signing of the Fugitive Slave Act been forgiven? Had Dorothea Dix knitted him the hat she had promised? One can only imagine Fillmore's disappointment, after so long abroad, to arrive in Washington in December 1852 and discover that little had changed.[8]

Fillmore's credibility had not improved a jot. Indeed, while Fillmore was delighted to read in the newspapers that "a band of abolitionists and

8. This was not entirely surprising. A temporal anomaly plagued all voyages to the Far East during this period, due to Japan's refusal to replace its traditional lunisolar calendar with the Gregorian calendar until 1873. Those traveling to Japan before this year were thus forced to endure a small time inconsistency. This inconsistency was further aggravated by crossing the International Date Line, which had yet to be permanently anchored off Kiribati, and thus floated uncontrolled across the Pacific, sometimes looping as far west as Japan and, on one occasion (1772 or "the Lost Year"), being found terribly knotted on a beach in Chile. The free-roaming date line was often sought by sea captains, who were notorious for weaving back and forth across it during Pacific journeys in an attempt to grow younger. Being fifty-eight years old and suffering from acute rheumatism at the time of the trip to Japan, Perry appears to have been no different. (It should be noted that Commander John Aulick had been the first choice to command Fillmore's expedition, but his last foray into the Pacific had left him and his entire crew aged between four and sixteen years old. They had refused to return home, and had since become pirates.) Thus while Fillmore would leave for Japan on November 13, 1852, on a round trip that would take the better part of fifteen months, he would actually return only one month after he had initially left. Such temporal distortions were not fully untangled until the International Meridian Conference of 1884 (1882).

southern slave owners" had recently met together "under President Fill-more's name," he was less happy that the meeting had been held purely to announce the groups' joint condemnation of him as "a traitor to freedom, principle, and party." With his tenure as president coming to an end, he found himself vilified by both his party and the voting public.

It was to be a grim autumn. In the presidential elections of 1852, Fillmore was not even considered as a candidate for president, despite his creation of a new dance step for the party called the Whiggle.[9] Devoid of his experience and wisdom, the Whigs were soundly beaten by the Demo-crat contender, Franklin Pierce, whose decision to run on a ticket of unre-pentant alcoholism and internecine racial violence proved particularly popular with an increasingly polarized electorate.

It was not only the Whigs' political ambitions that were expiring. While Fillmore had been away, many of his party's greatest heroes had died. Senator Henry Clay, who had worked so hard on the Compromise of 1850, and who had been voted Congressman Most Likely to Succeed every year from 1834 through 1850, had been mauled to death by a giant black dog in front of the Capitol steps. Soon after, Black Dan Webster, secretary of state for two presidents and undefeated House Bully of the last two decades, was thrown from his horse at his home in Massachusetts and died soon after strangling the recalcitrant beast to death.[10] Meanwhile,

---

9. Fillmore described the dance as "one step forward, two steps back."

10. Twelve years after Daniel Webster's death, the House Sub-Sub-Committee for Séances and Hoodoo received a com-munication from a place they described as "Hell" informing them that Daniel Webster was now one of the most signifi-cant reformers in the lower regions of the Inferno. Using his strong-arm tactics and great rhetorical skill, he had apparently pushed through swingeing reforms to Hell's constitution. In *The Devil v. Daniel Webster (II)*, he successfully con-vinced a jury of imps that all souls should suffer "finite damnation" not to exceed 3,000,000,000,000 years. Other great legal battles fought in the underworld included *Beelzebub, Lord of the Flies v. Webster*, in which he argued that the depths of Hell's piles of excrement be made fathomable, and *Moloch, Prince of Child Sacrifice v. Webster*, on the age of consent. Meanwhile, Webster and his old political rival John Calhoun (who had died in 1850) had locked the Demonic Parliament in a series of heated debates over Hell's temperature. Webster contended that "all hellish environs, not excluding the obstreperous eighth circle faction, should have their temperatures lowered to a clement 76 degrees Fahrenheit" (Celsius being used only in Heaven). John Calhoun, who had previously suggested "it will be a cold day in Hell before it is a mild day in Hell," argued loquaciously, in the midst of being torn apart by wild horses, that Hell's temperature should be maintained at the current 831.2 degrees, declaring a toast with his one attached arm to "the burning heat; next to our perpetual torture most dear."

Thurlow Weed, his Whig Party crumbling around him, had left on an extended trip to Europe for reasons unknown. Standing on the porch of the White House, Fillmore came to the grim conclusion that he might well be the last in the long illustrious line of Whig presidents.

In the remaining weeks before he left office, Fillmore prepared himself for his role as a private citizen. Ever conscientious, he replaced all the items he had taken from the White House stationery cupboard, deconstructed the fortress he had built out of cushions and blankets in the living room, and vainly tried to collect the hundreds of rubber bands that were scattered across the Oval Office.[11] In the White House garden, he bade a sad farewell to Old Whitey, his faithful advisor and confidant, untethered the noble horse from his gilt post, and watched him gallop down the Mall to pastures new, scattering schoolchildren in his path.

Pierce, in a favorite pose, reaches for his gin flask.

On the morning of Franklin Pierce's inauguration, the president and the president-elect were to ride in the same carriage toward the Capitol.

---

11. Fillmore was particularly proud of the fortress he had constructed, and would often hold Cabinet meetings within it. This upset some of his Cabinet, especially Charles Conrad, his secretary of war, who was always made to stand lookout, in case "Abigail, Dorothea, and the girls" should launch a surprise attack.

Fillmore was his usual avuncular self—even seated next to his successor—and noted in his journal that Pierce was also affecting a cordial tone, carefully vomiting out of the carriage's windows rather than on Fillmore's shoes, as had happened at the pre-inauguration dinner party the night before.[12]

Upon arriving at the Capitol, Pierce scrambled up the steps toward the chief justice. Slurring his words, he began his inaugural address, which was delivered as a string of ribald limericks, in which the citizens of Nantucket were accorded particular attention. As he spoke, dark clouds blackened the sky and a biting wind swept across the Mall and the city. Fillmore recalls feeling Abigail's hand clutching his sleeve. He looked down and saw that his usually ebullient wife was pale and shivering. "Abigail told me that someone had snatched her coat from her as she left her carriage. She had bravely tried to withstand the elements, but with snow now falling heavily, I could see her shivering. Who would do such a thing on a day as cold as this? I wondered if we should break with protocol to get her inside. But at that moment President Pierce gestured in my general direction, and as I attempted to edge off the platform with Abigail, he approached us both and threw his arm around us, declaring me his 'bestest friend' and Abigail the most beautiful woman he had ever seen." By the time Pierce's oration had concluded, Abigail was cold as ice.

Fillmore rushed his wife to their hotel, but she had caught a severe cold and suffered a high fever. Over the next few days, Fillmore talked to her a great deal, in the hope of inspiring in her the fiery disdain she had so often felt for him in the past. But when, while reading to her from the Bible, he asked "who the Christians were, and were they the heroes?" he was shocked to see his wife respond with only a weak smile and a gentle

12. Pierce's future life was to be a tragic one. After losing the Democratic nomination in 1856, Pierce reportedly quipped, "There's nothing left to do but get drunk." Unlike his pre-election promises, this was one he intended to keep. He would be drunk for the next thirteen years, his fortune slowly dissipating, and when he mistakenly declared his support for Canada during the Civil War, he alienated his few remaining supporters. With his political credibility destroyed, he was bought by P. T. Barnum in 1868 and exhibited in a cage as "The Great American President." He died in 1869.

pat of his leg. Physicians were called, but her cold had rapidly become pneumonia. On March 29 she worsened; the next day, at nine in the morning, Abigail Fillmore died. "For twenty-seven years, my entire married life, I was always greeted with a shake of her head, a rolling of her eyes, or a low-muttered comment I could not quite hear," Fillmore wrote in his tearstained journal. "Alas, no more." A tearful Dorothea Dix visited him and offered her condolences, but deep in his grief, Fillmore seemed terribly changed to her. "Poor, sad, beloved Mr. F. does not respond to my friendly caresses," she wrote. "Gone is the glint in his eye at the mention of small befurred creatures. He looks into the distance and says nothing." Even Thurlow Weed, who had returned to Washington for the inauguration, came to pay his respects to his former protégé. "He had found my dear departed Abigail's coat," Fillmore noted. "How thoughtful of him to return it."

Despite his friends rallying around him, the death of Abigail devastated Fillmore. "I feel I have no strength—no resolution—no energy—the prospect is gloomy," he wrote. On April 12, 1853, he appears to have wandered out of his Washington hotel with only the clothes on his back; on foot he left behind him the city of his presidency.

11.

Fillmore Agonistes

(1853–1859)

*T*he ethnological notes of Captain John G. Bourke, of the U.S. Army's Third Cavalry, assert that on the evening of November 17, 1853, during his stay amongst the Zuni Indians of New Mexico, "the *Nehue-Cue*, one of the secret orders of the Zunis, sent word that they would do us the unusual honor of coming to our house to give us one of their characteristic dances." Soon twelve dancers had arrived. "The center men were naked, the hair was worn with a bunch of wild turkey feathers tied in front, and white bands were painted across the face at eyes and mouth."

Bourke's attention was particularly caught by "an older man, lighter of skin and more strangely attired than the rest, who wore a pair of goggles, painted white, over his eyes." The Zuni began to dance to the traditional accompaniment of drums, rattles, and hysterical screaming, yet to Bourke's mind the older man seemed somewhat out of place "in manner and action; his pontificating strides forward and gesticulations of the arm brought to mind not so much a dance as the worst grotesqueries of the demagogue." After some time, in which the dance reached a fevered pitch, it was announced that a feast had been prepared and, recalled Bourke, "a squaw entered, carrying a large tin pail of what appeared to be urine. The older man who wore the white goggles stepped forward and, grasping the pail firmly, as if in a trance, began drinking from it. I could scarcely believe the evidence of my senses! The other Zuni looked on in awe and a chant began to rise in their throats: 'Fill! More! Fill! More!' and continued even after the pail had been replenished. Despite the depravity of the scene, the older Indian struck a chord of familiarity within me, and I determined to speak to him. But, fully sated by now, he began to pour the remnants of the urine over his head to even greater cheers from the Zuni. So foul and filthy did the room become that I felt compelled to run into the refreshing night air. By the time I had returned, the Zuni and the mysterious man had departed."

Two months later, Lieutenant John Page, of Fort Laramie in Wyoming, filed a report of his investigation into the tipping of Mormon cows by members of the Brule Sioux. Upon visiting the Sioux village, Page's attention was distracted from the task at hand by one of the tribe's traditional rituals. "It was approaching the summer solstice and the Sioux were indulging in the barbaric practice of the Sun Dance, in which the young men of the tribe present themselves to a medicine man, who then takes between his thumb and forefinger a fold of loose skin from their breast, and runs a very narrow-bladed but sharp knife through it. A stronger skewer of bone, about the size of a carpenter's pencil, is then inserted, and tied to a long, thin rope fastened, at its other extremity, to the top of the 'sun pole.' The whole object of the devotee is to break loose from these fetters by tearing the skewers through his skin, a horrible task that even with the most resolute may require many hours of torture." As Page attempted to communicate with the Sioux chief, he noticed that one of the men involved in the ritual "was not young, but old." Despite his advanced age, writes Page, "he wheeled with great vigor as the drumming and singing continued, and the Sioux medicine man paid close attention to his steps, tracing them out in the dirt before him. Struck by this curious irregularity in such a revered ritual, I attempted to get closer to him, for I was certain I had seen his likeness somewhere before. As I reached the front of the watching crowd he passed quite close to me, his body streaked with blood, his eyes rolled back in his head so that all one could see were the whites, and I could swear that I heard him reciting snatches of the Constitution, in particular the Eighth Amendment. Suddenly, his dancing stopped, and with one swift motion he tore himself free from his bind- ings, spattering the crowd with his blood. He teetered on his slim white legs but was immediately caught by the Sioux, who treated him with great respect and laid him down upon a bed of sage, on which he began slowly to chew."

Shortly after this, on the Great Plains, the famed hunter William "Buffalo Bill" Brooks recalled in a letter to his brother seeing "a herd of about forty head, bulls, cows and calves, running in madcap panic toward us.[1] As the stampeding herd drew closer, what should I see atop the leading bull but a man, his thick, white hair flowing behind him, and his body adorned with the painted stripe of the Sioux. He was clinging to the beast's huge frontlet of shaggy hair, and I ventured to gallop next to him to grasp him to safety. He was quite insensate to my cries of alarm and inter-mittently sang out a song of which I only heard the lines 'give me a home' and 'antelope play' above the roar of pounding hooves. He was obviously a madman, and yet I could not help but think that there was something dig-nified in his aspect. He rejected all help, and we could do nothing to pre-vent the herd from charging headlong over a precipice, the crazed man clinging on to the very end. When we had worked our way down the chasm to acquire the animals' pelts, we could find no trace of his body."

Could Fillmore have been the old and portly gentleman who drank urine with the Zuni, danced with the Sioux, and rode a buffalo over a cliff? Almost categorically perhaps. While we do know that grief from the death of Abigail seems to have thrown him into a state of semi-seclusion, no journals survive for the year 1853 to shed light on his possible movements. What is known for certain is that Fillmore's journals begin again on July 4, 1854, when he writes of coming in a distant second in the city of Buffalo's "Look Ye Like a President" competition.

While Fillmore had been recovering from his grief, a new and unseemly breed of enmity had begun to spread its way across the country. Prompted

---

1. "Buffalo Bill" Brooks was the first of an eventual thirty-three Buffalo Bills to wander the Great Plains in the nine-teenth century. William Cody, the most famous bearer of that moniker, was the sixteenth to bear it, having been known throughout his early years as "Bovine Bill," "Bison Bill," and, for a brief experimental period during his teens, "Jemima Puddle-Duck."

by the desolation of the Great Potato Famine, thousands of new Irish immigrants had been flooding to America's eastern seaboard in search of new beginnings and fresh russet potatoes. Yet the Irish willingness to work for low wages, combined with their incomprehensible brogue and facility at dancing without moving their arms, angered many Americans, especially frontiersmen, who had previously held a monopoly on extreme poverty, impenetrable drawls, and ludicrous barnyard dancing.[2] When Catholic schools and churches began to be constructed to cater to these new arrivals, it became immediately evident that every new immigrant arriving on America's shores was an agent of the Pope, sent to subvert America into becoming a vassal state under the silken hoof of the Holy Pontiff.

Such was the uproar that a new political party was formed to counter the Irish threat. Named the American Party, although its detractors termed it the "Know-Nothing Party" because of its extreme secretiveness, it made rapid political gains thanks to its supporters' penchant for violently racist hijinks. Catholic churches were vandalized, priests were attacked, and pitched battles were fought within the new immigrant communities, most notably at the Battle of Our Lady of the Bleeding Face in 1855.

Hearing of these latest troubles to beset his beloved nation, and with news of the Supreme Court's ruling on the Dred Scott case pushing the slavery debate to ever greater heights, Fillmore grew increasingly impatient in Buffalo.[3] Whilst his travels seem to have calmed his sorrow at Abigail's death, they had not dampened his need for excitement. Despite himself, Fillmore was pining for the presidency once more: "You will call me foolish, but I miss the Oval Office," he wrote to Dorothea Dix. "In particular, I miss the little diagonally cut sandwiches that were served before state dinners." The mild-mannered Dix invited Fillmore to visit her in Virginia,

2.   While the wave of Irish immigration infuriated many Native Americans, Native Americans maintained the unswerving political position on paleface immigration they had held for the last three hundred years, which consisted of shaking their heads ruefully and repeating the old Indian incantation "Are you fucking kidding me?"

3.   In *Dred Scott v. Sanford*, the Supreme Court ruled that the slave, Scott, be returned to his owner, Sanford, since Sanford was still in possession of a receipt and the original chain packaging in which Scott had come to him.

where she was working on a string of new asylums. "Here you could delight in my affection for you," she wrote, "as I have always hoped you would." But an offer from a very different lady was about to rid Fillmore of all thoughts of repose.

Anna Ella Carroll was the eldest daughter of the governor of Maryland and had been trained from birth in the pugnacious and contrary attitudes needed to succeed in politics. At the age of sixteen, while the nation celebrated the Fourth of July holiday, she had organized a group of women suffragists to bind themselves in tiers up the entire length of the Washington Monument, forcing its customary floral decoration to be abandoned. The following year, she led a march of twenty thousand protestors *against* women's rights, and ended her demonstration by demanding a police officer imprison her for marching without a license. Fair, petite, and curvaceous, she had spent her adult life flattering to deceive, disparaging to enlighten, enlightening to flatter, and deceiving to mislead. Under the auspices of Thurlow Weed, she had become a vital cog in the Whig Party apparatus and had been responsible for organizing the public humiliation and eventual suicide of presidential hopeful Emmanuel Roth at the national Whig convention of 1844.[4] Now, at the age of thirty-eight, she was the consummate political animal.

Following the implosion of the Whigs, Carroll had become heavily involved with the Know-Nothing movement, and with the election of 1856 fast approaching she was now seeking a figure of national stature for her new party to rally behind. With that in mind she paid a visit to Fillmore in Buffalo, suggesting he return to the political fray. She could not have found a more receptive audience: "Miss Carroll believes I am destined to run for president once more," wrote Fillmore. "Goody!"

Fillmore's journals paint a vivid impression of Carroll's intelligence

---

4. She had also been responsible for the convention's spectacular bunting.

Anna Ella Carroll: Men not wrapped around her finger were secured under her thumb.

and acumen: "I tried to concentrate on what she was saying, but her lips were so red and moist and parted that I was filled with strange and distracting thoughts," he wrote. "She told me once again that I should love her like a daughter, and clasped my head to her bosom so tightly that I could feel her heart beating, very slowly." Amidst her "sighs and tender protestations" he was eventually persuaded to the cause.

Fillmore seems to have taken a somewhat eccentric position on his new political party, possibly due to some subtle plan that went unrecorded in his journals. Writing to Dorothea Dix after Carroll's visit, he apologized for not being able to visit her, but happily explained his new predicament: "The party is called the 'Know-Nothings,' and so I take it to mean, and you will be glad to hear, that its main objective is to help addle-heads and ignoramuses of all kinds. Miss Carroll spoke to me of a particularly virulent type of lunacy in which the afflicted believe that normal bread and wine is actually the body and blood of some strange edible god! If we do not nip this in the bud soon, people may start believing in all manner of ridiculousness—talking bushes, virgin births, the living dead—which cannot be of advantage to anyone's healthful mental state."

If Dix wrote a reply, it did not arrive in time; Carroll, noticing Fillmore's enthusiasm about taking a hands-on approach in his new party,[5] suggested that he travel to Europe while she arranged the details of his nomination. On May 17, 1855, Fillmore, with a small entourage, once again took to the ocean waves.

As a former president, Fillmore was accorded all the respect due to a visiting head of state. In England, he was excused the traditional pickpocketing by a street urchin, and was accorded an audience with the young Queen Victoria, whom he described as "short and round, like a lacy cannonball."[6] Fillmore relates how the two spent hours amusing themselves in the gardens of Buckingham Palace.

Queen Victoria: big, but fun.

"Her Majesty is a great enthusiast of our dime novels and insisted that we act out her favorite story of Malaeska, the Indian wife of the white

5. From a letter to Carroll: "I have devised a straitjacket bedecked in the Stars and Stripes with which to show my solidarity with the retarded electorate."
6. Queen Victoria was granted a number of affectionate nicknames during her reign, such as the "plum dumpling," the "frosted orb," and the "ruling dollop."

hunter. One of her servants tied her to a tree, from which I was then to rescue her. The servant, stiffly taking on the role of an Indian chieftain,
insisted that I hit him on the chin. As the queen cried out, 'Show no mercy,
Mr. Fillmore!' I hesitated, but the servant was most insistent, whispering
into my ear, 'She'll never let up until you do, sir.' Her Majesty was most
game, and as I untied her and declared her free, she fell into my arms,
declaring, 'Oh! But don't ravish me! You can't! I won't allow it! Not here in
front of everyone!' I attempted to say something, but she cut me off: 'I
know, I know, I know I cannot stop your livid American passion. All right,
then. Take me! Take me now!' Our scene was abruptly curtailed when
Albert, the prince consort, stormed out of the palace and confronted us,
demanding in a high-pitched German voice, 'Viccy, vy do you tease me so?'
Her Majesty could not contain her giggles."

Fillmore's arrival in France went less smoothly. The French affected
never to have heard of the United States, and when Fillmore finally
pointed it out on a map, he became engaged in a "somewhat heated debate
about whose revolution had been better." In Paris, his journal alludes simply to the "wonderful views," although his activities gain a fuller telling in
the writings of the famed French diarists Edmond and Jules de Goncourt:
"At the American ambassador's party we had been discussing art. Jules had
suggested that any picture that produces a moral impression is a bad picture, when a fat American man, whom we were told had held some political position in his homeland, tripped on the carpet—a priceless
Savonnerie—and knocked that tedious arriviste Count Montgolfier into
the punch bowl. Montgolfier, as was typical, insisted that a duel be fought
in hot-air balloons high above the city, and we all appeared the next morning in the Jardin de Luxembourg to watch the combatants ascend. The
American seemed to believe he was on a sightseeing trip and continually
waved off the pistol handed to him. Before long the two balloons drifted
high into the air and out of sight. Having declared that a poet is a man
who puts up a ladder to a star and climbs it while playing a violin, Jules

became bored, so we went to eat breakfast. Upon our return we were told that Montgolfier's balloon had been punctured, and he and his second had plunged half a mile to their deaths. It seems that the count, seeing that his opponent was much more interested in waving at people below him than in dueling, had fired his pistol above his head. How we laughed! We left to drink absinthe, whereupon Jules suggested that all debauchery is an act of despair in the face of the infinite."

In Rome, Fillmore was granted an audience with Pope Pius IX to discuss the matter of his Know-Nothing nomination.[7] Upon meeting, the Pope and the president were amazed to find they looked almost identical. "There was much laughing and prodding," wrote Fillmore, "and turning around quickly trying to catch the other one out." Yet Fillmore, with his usual perceptiveness, noticed that something seemed to be troubling his holy doppelgänger. "Although His Holiness is fortunate enough to share the Fillmore features, he seemed strangely unhappy. When I asked him why this was, he said that he yearned to wander freely amongst his flock, and to smell air free from the stench of frankincense. He explained morosely that the only fun he enjoyed these days was making his cardinals bend over so that their hats fell off."

Upset to see the Holy Father so distraught, Fillmore was struck by what—considering his situation—can only have been divine inspiration. "So similar were we in features that I suggested we swap clothes for a day. He could thus be a touring ex-president, able to move around the city at his leisure, and I would be Pope. Once His Holiness had ushered his attendants away, we exchanged clothes, he wearing my suit and I his papal tiara. Then, with nothing more than a wink, he left the room and I remained— Millard Fillmore, Supreme Pontiff of the Universal Church!"

Fillmore's journal for the day continues: "I soon came to see why

7. Pope Pius IX was the ninth Pope to follow the Papal Nomenclature Bull of 1724. This had been implemented following a succession of unorthodox papal titles such as Pope Superb, Pope Above Suspicion, Pope Tyrannosaurus Rex, Pope Your Name Here, and Pope Poppet.

Fillmore (right) *and Pius* (left): *even Mary, Mother of God, couldn't tell them apart.*

Pius had been so miserable. After I had been taken for a few laps around the Vatican City seated on my portable throne, I too grew restless. When night fell and there was still no sign of His Holiness, I began to wonder what might happen if he did not return. Would my nomination for the Know-Nothing Party be affected? If not, how would I fit my title of Bishop of Rome, Vicar of Jesus Christ, Successor of the Prince of the Apostles, Primate of Italy, Archbishop and Metropolitan of the Roman Province, Sovereign of the State of the Vatican City, and Servant of the Servants of God onto the ballot slip? What's more, I began to realize that my dining habits would have to improve if I was to wear white vestments for the rest of my days. The future looks bleak," concluded Fillmore, "although I am looking forward to feeding the papal bulls and bathing in the Holy Sea."

A relieved Fillmore wrote the following day, "As it turned out, His Holiness was as good as his word. He staggered back into the papal apartment at six o'clock in the morning. By then I had accidentally excommunicated Emperor Franz Josef of Austria and condemned as heresy the idea that baked potatoes are not delicious. His Holiness seemed to have had a wonderful time. He had rouge on his collar, and said in slightly slurred tones that he had crammed enough fun into one day to last for all of heavenly eternity. He did not elaborate on his pursuits, but after we exchanged clothes and I took my leave of him, my traveling companions gave me strange looks for the rest of my trip, and Jonathan, my private secretary, burst into tears whenever he spoke to me."

Fillmore's trip to Europe was called to an end when Anna Ella Carroll sent him a telegram announcing he had been accepted as the Know-Nothing presidential nominee. Fillmore was delighted, and Carroll informed him that his chances of becoming president a second time had improved considerably following the vicious beating on the Senate floor of Massachusetts senator Charles Sumner by Preston Brooks, a Democratic senator from South Carolina. As Carroll and the Know-Nothings had foreseen, random acts of violence were set to be *the* hot campaign topic of 1856.

Upon his return to the United States in June of that year, Fillmore was greeted by over three thousand people at the New York docks. "As I got off the boat, fireworks were lit and my hand was shaken by numerous persons unknown to me. Such support for the mad cheered me tremendously. Miss Carroll suddenly appeared next to me and, winking at me in her deeply confusing manner, led me through the fray, despite her petite size and the tightness of her figure-revealing corset."

Yet Carroll was not the only one of Fillmore's female admirers to have appeared at the dock. "As Miss Carroll dragged me through the crowd, I also saw a tearful Miss Dix standing to one side. I stopped and enquired of her the reason for her distress, to which she replied that in order to gain the presidency I had made a deal with the devil. I attempted to tell her that, following my Roman escapades with the Holy Father, quite the opposite was the case, but she ran from me crying hysterically. I did not know quite what to make of it, but Miss Carroll soon diverted my attention by tugging me toward a podium."

The city's newspapers reported on the subsequent events: "Quieting the crowd with her hands," wrote the *New York Advocate*, "Miss Carroll spoke in a low-pitched husky voice, but with a vehemence that was astonishing, of the work now being performed by the Know-Nothings in search of the great moral reform against the purveyors of popery. With indisputable logic Miss Carroll declared that each papist killed was one less servant of Satan, and with fire in her delectable chestnut eyes and perspiration on her perfectly smooth forehead, she told a heartbreaking story concerning a former nun who was forced to breed babies for ritual murder by Catholic priests."

Fillmore's journal relates how he was surprised at the hostile reaction to "potpourri" in New York, and felt somewhat confused as to what "dried fragrant plant petals had to do with aiding the mentally deficient." Fillmore realized, though, that having being traveling for some time, he had probably lost touch with his fellow citizens' concerns. As he stood on the podium, gazing at the thousands of people who had come to listen to him speak, Fillmore recalled hearing a large sheet being unfurled behind him, "and turning around saw a vast banner emblazoned with a picture of a shamrock with a red line passing through it. This seemed to reinforce the anti-potpourri message and, heartened by this, I thus began to extemporize a speech as best I could."

The next day's issue of the *New York Advocate* recalls that Fillmore's speech was "peculiar." The *New York Sun* was no kinder: "While Miss Carroll displayed a fine turn of phrase, and ankle, in her sensual preamble, Mr. Fillmore showed himself quite aloof from the issues that concern today's East Coast papist-haters." Only the *Brooklyn Daily Eagle* gave it a positive review—its botanical expert, Walt Whitman, whose recent book on lawn foliage had gained him some infamy in horticultural circles, termed it "electric!"

Fillmore recalls that when he stepped off the stage he was met by Anna Ella Carroll, who, he wrote, "seemed flushed with excitement, but before she could congratulate me who should rush up to me but a still tearful Miss Dix. Now she was laughing aloud, saying she had mistaken my intentions completely. Such are her terrible mood swings I worry she has caught a bout of hysteria from one of her patients."

Dix was to join Fillmore as a traveling companion for the rest of his presidential campaign, during which his unaffected speeches in the run-up to the election were described by more than one observer as "political suicide." With Dix's help, Fillmore propounded a message of fresh flowers and mental hygiene, equating potpourri increasingly with "mental mustiness." In Baltimore, his speech was entirely about the beneficial psychological effects of flower arranging; in Pittsburgh, he talked passionately about poseys, nosegays, and tussie-mussies; in Philadelphia, when asked—to his surprise—a question about the Pope, he declared that "some of my best friends are Catholic." As such, the Know-Nothings, their message of racial hatred brilliantly undercut by Fillmore, failed to carry the electoral votes of any state in the 1856 election.[8] Fillmore would not be president again. Nevertheless, traveling the country with Dorothea Dix, he seemed truly happy for the first time since Abigail's death.

On January 2, 1857, Fillmore bade farewell to an emotional Dix and traveled to Saratoga Springs to recuperate from his fierce election campaigning and to address a meeting of the Florists of America, who had been one of two national organizations to have endorsed his presidential run.[9] Saratoga Springs was the gaudiest of America's nineteenth-century resorts, with casinos, saloons, music halls, and brothels lining its streets. But it was the mineral baths that gave the town its fame, and which Fillmore now sought for physical and mental restitution. The latest scientific studies had conclusively proven that water, far from being bad for the health, could, in the

8. Except those of Maryland, Anna Ella Carroll's home state, in which it was said she had batted her eyelids at over two-thirds of those eligible to vote.
9. The other being the politically promiscuous National Council for Endorsements.

service of hygiene, be good for it. And it was while taking one of the town's hot mineral baths that Fillmore was to have an encounter that would shape the rest of his life.

"I had asked for a curative to a sore throat, as I had been campaigning for months nonstop," he wrote in his journal. "Thus when a man approached me from behind, and with one tremendously strong hand began to massage my neck, I took this to be the treatment I had asked for. Yet as the massage grew more robust, I began to feel increasingly uncomfortable. Perhaps it was the crushing of my windpipe that caused such unpleasant sensations, or possibly the fact that my masseur was dunking my head repeatedly under the water—no doubt as part of the curative effect—that produced such a feeling of discomfort in me. I attempted to communicate as much, but realized I could not make a sound other than some unintelligible spluttering noises, so intently were my vocal cords being kneaded into a healthful pulp. It was at this point that I began to lose consciousness, and thought it best, at the risk of insulting my well-intentioned therapist, if I freed myself from his grip. Fortunately, before entering the bath I had been advised to lather myself in a strange fatty substance called 'soap,' which afforded my skin a certain silkiness, and allowed me to slip out of the iron grasp. I wish I had chosen another way of expressing my displeasure, for upon turning around I found that my masseuse, a bearded gentleman who wore a full military uniform while performing his therapeutic marvels, was seething with anger! Perhaps it was the fact that he had only one arm that had upset him so, as I imagine it was a hard life being a one-armed masseuse. But before I could compliment him on his skills, he had leapt through a closed window to the street below without even asking for a gratuity."

For the next week, Fillmore's journal is filled with narrow escapes and close shaves. A runaway carriage almost ran him down while he listened to a piano recital in the Saratoga theater. On being shown around the Saratoga casino, a roulette wheel spun off its spindle and almost decapitated him. On his last day in town he discovered three small holes, "like those caused by bullets," in his hat. "Moths?" he wrote questioningly.

Even as imperturbable a man as Fillmore began to suspect that some-one wished him ill, and his suspicions would be confirmed upon visiting New York City a month later. "I was taking a happy repast, having just delivered a rousing lecture on dandelions, and was finishing off my glass of elderflower water when the room began to sway about me. I began to see two of everything—two bartenders, two tables, two mugs in front of me. I was feeling quite light-headed, and was just beginning to enjoy the symmetry of it all, when I looked up at my two waiters and realized that, between the two of them, they only had two arms. I remember something of a struggle and stumbling into the street, but the rest is lost to me."

It is truly unfortunate that Fillmore should have been battling for his life at this moment, for he was thus denied witnessing one of the most dramatic events ever to occur in New York's history. At approximately the same moment that Fillmore was grappling with his single-appendaged opponent, a near-riot was sweeping the rarified environs of nearby Wall Street. The famed banker Mordechai Johnson recalled what happened in his best-selling memoir, *So Very Rich*.[10] "The securities were being called out in the afternoon session when a great disturbance erupted and an old man, stout and with a thick head of gray hair, rushed into the exchange and began shouting in frantic terms, 'The Mexicans have invaded! All is lost! Sell! Sell! Sell!' before running out again. There was a pause of a few seconds, at which point a one-armed man carrying a sword-stick burst into the room in a fury. No sooner had he done so than a blizzard of paper flew into the air, a vortex of humanity swamped the floor, making it quite impassable, and the market descended into chaos."

This bizarre intrusion into the stock exchange triggered the devastating

10. Although *So Very Rich* does contain small passages of remembrances, the bulk of the book consists of an inventory of everything Johnson owned at the time of the book's publication in 1888. Two more books would follow: the vellum-bound *Even Richer* in 1891, and the slim pamphlet *Poor*, published subsequent to the financial panic of 1893.

Panic of 1857, the third major financial crisis the United States had suffered, prompting over five thousand businesses to fail within a year, unemployment to rocket, and the decade of prosperity that had begun with the
California gold rush to come juddering to a halt. One can only wonder
whether a man of Fillmore's authority and standing in the community
could have prevented the markets from panicking.

Instead, Fillmore's journal next recalls him "waking in a strange bed,
in an unfamiliar house, with a lady to whom I had not been introduced
staring down at me with a rather severe look on her face." The lady was
Caroline McIntosh, the forty-four-year-old widow of a railroad magnate,
whose recent death, society magazines sniffed, had left her "with a surplus
of riches and a shortfall of grief." She explained to Fillmore that her servants had found him curled up on the doorstep of her town house, and
enquired "whether I was the same Millard Fillmore that had once been
president, or if I was one of the Philadelphia Philmores whose gala dinners were so scrutinized by the fashionable dailies. I replied that I was the
former, and she seemed somewhat disappointed."

Fillmore spent several days convalescing after his struggles. He was
fifty-seven years old, and although still strong, he lacked the recuperative
powers of his youth. During that time McIntosh quizzed him endlessly on
the attendees of his state dinners.

"She asked whether the Remsons were really worth one million dollars, as they claimed, but all I could recall was that Mr. Remson ate with
his fingers for fear of sharp-edged cutlery. When she enquired as to
whether the Schnecks had really bought a third estate in Philadelphia, all I
could remember was that due to some Old World superstition, they only
passed the salt to their right, and never spoke during dessert. As for the
Schermerhorns, I knew nothing of their West Indian assets, nor the scandal involving Mr. Schermerhorn and the bootblack, but I had noticed that
when Mrs. Schermerhorn was served lobster she would not eat it, but
instead whispered into its ear throughout the meal."

By the time McIntosh had exhausted Fillmore's knowledge he was fit once more and ready to leave. "I gave Mrs. McIntosh my word that I would do whatever I could to repay her for her kindness and discretion. I was somewhat unprepared for her immediate response that she had always wanted a president of her own but—with the exception of a summer timeshare she had recently taken out with the Vanderbilts on President Pierce—she had never had the chance of having one all to herself. She asked, therefore, if I would marry her.

"I must admit to feeling rather awkward at this proposition. Mrs. McIntosh reassured me that I should see it merely as a marriage of convenience, a little something to tell her friends about, as well as a way of showing up Lena Van Rensselaer, who had married King Zog of Albania two years ago and had been dining off it ever since. This appeased my soul somewhat, for my heart still belonged to dear, departed Abigail. Not wanting to go back on my word, I reluctantly agreed. Mrs. McIntosh later brought me something called a 'prenuptial contract,' which I am to sign. It is written in a legal language my provincial law career has not prepared me for, although it seems that I am not permitted to reveal where Mrs. McIntosh buys her drapes, nor the present disposition of her cook."

There is little further mention of the passionate affair Fillmore began with McIntosh. Suffice it to say that the happy couple would be married on February 10, 1858, in a private ceremony for 1,500 of their closest foreign royalty.

The honeymoon was to be taken at Niagara Falls, then the most fashionable honeymooning spot in North America, but before the blissful couple left, Fillmore was paid a visit by Dorothea Dix. Under McIntosh's strict instructions, neither Dix nor any of Fillmore's other friends had been invited to the wedding. "Dorothea greeted me civilly," recalled Fillmore, "but she was clearly unhappy. I ushered her into my study in the basement, where we sat alone together for some time, no words passing between us. Eventually she began to talk of 'a tempest of feeling' in her

Caroline McIntosh: keeping up with the Joneses, Asquiths, Cabots, Delanos, Lowells, Winthrops, Baldwins, Evarts, Hoars, Tafts, Lippitts, and Chafees.

breast and, tears welling up in her large, soft eyes, spoke of 'an opportunity missed' and 'what might have been.' It was all I could do to hug her and tell her that she was still young, and no matter what had prompted her despair, she still had plenty of time to devote to her work for the insane. She eventually managed to compose herself, and told me she hoped that I would be happy in my new life. I promised her I would write, and she nodded and smiled."

Whatever misgivings Fillmore may have had about his sudden marriage, they were soon forgotten amidst the thundering magnificence of Niagara Falls. Couples strode the promenade, gazing up at the massive waterfalls, marveling at their power. Yet the rumbling grandeur of the falls had not scared off a host of daredevils looking to make a name for themselves. Going over the edge were tightrope walkers, men in barrels, small children caught in the current, professional divers, and amateur suicides. At the time of Fillmore's honeymoon, all talk was of Arthur "the Salmon" Lemont's recent ill-fated attempt to swim *up* the falls.

Fillmore had been in Niagara for three days when he caught sight of an old friend on the promenade—Anna Ella Carroll. She was "greeting a man who seemed shockingly familiar to me. Whether it was the beard, the hair, the suit, or the lack of an arm that first caught my eye, I do not know, but I could swear that this was the same man who had attacked me in Saratoga and New York! Alarmed for Miss Carroll's safety, I immediately excused myself from the new Mrs. Fillmore—who was in any case deeply engrossed in a copy of *Debrett's Peerage & Baronetage*—and hurried to Miss Carroll's aid. The one-armed man saw me coming and ran, confirming my suspicions, taking with him a roll of Miss Carroll's money in his hand. Miss Carroll spun around, saw me, and then raised her arm to her forehead and fainted dead away."

Fillmore saw that the one-armed man had boarded the *Maid of the Mist* tour boat and was heading to the Canadian side of the falls. "I realized I must follow," wrote Fillmore, "but how?" Luckily, Fillmore's honeymoon coincided with the arrival of the French acrobat Charles Blondin, who was amazing audiences by walking along a steel cable stretched across the falls. Fillmore, whose sense of balance and proportion had always been exemplary, realized that this was the only way to pursue his mysterious assailant. Snapping a branch off a nearby tree to use as a balancing pole, he edged his way onto the cable. "The mist soaked my clothes within seconds, and made walking extremely difficult," he recalled, "but with fear and terror driving me onward I was soon halfway across." At that point Fillmore felt a sharp blow knock the branch out of his hands. Looking down at the tour boat, he saw the one-armed man was on deck and shooting at him with a pistol. "My fingers were still numb from the blast when I heard another bullet hurry past my ear. A third shot sounded and, unable to maintain my balance a moment longer, I plunged from the wire, one hundred feet down into the whirlpools of the falls."

Fillmore recalls, "I remember sinking down, being pushed deeper and deeper by the incessant pounding of the water. It got darker and darker until my head seemed to touch the riverbed. I floundered, trying to make out which way was up and which was down, when I felt cold fingers grab hold of my arm. I opened my eyes, and amidst the bubbles and tumult of the water I saw a skeleton reaching toward me. Around its neck was hung a millstone. Despite my lungs being fit to burst, I peered closer and saw the stone held an inscription. I just managed to make out 'William Morgan—TRAITOR' before I was swept away by a powerful current. My lungs burned with exhaustion, but a thousand questions flooded my mind. If a fish could talk, what would it say? Would I prefer to have fins or tentacles? Was this the same William Morgan whose disappearance at the hands of the Freemasons over twenty years ago had set me on my quest to fight injustice and tyranny? If so, had the one-armed man been sent by the Freemasons to kill me? All was growing hazy when suddenly I felt a strong arm pluck me out of the water by my collar and a French voice mutter what sounded like '*les amateurs*' before everything went black."

Fillmore awoke surrounded by doctors and a large Frenchman wearing a leotard. He was relieved to hear that Anna Ella Carroll had staged a remarkable recovery shortly after fainting and had promptly disappeared. Similarly, his new wife, Caroline, had insisted on returning to New York in order to attend a ball, leaving a note for him in which she hoped "nothing was broken or chipped." But Fillmore was more concerned with the questions that continued to spin through his mind. Only one thing was for certain: the one-armed man held answers to them all.[11]

---

11. Except to the question of whether Fillmore would prefer fins or tentacles, which Fillmore would later decide was fins.

12.

Fillmore Errant

(1859–1866)

Private Eyes, Missing Arms—The Paternalistic John Brown—

A Pyrotechnic Display—Debunking Myths—The Civil War

(Abridged)—Lincoln, Imitator—Accidental Assassinations—

A Lesson in Authenticity

*I*t is a truth universally acknowledged that a man in search of a one-armed assassin must be in want of a good detective, and Fillmore was no different in this respect. Fortunately, as a former president, he was provided with the services of the most famous detective agency of the era.[1]

The Pinkerton Detective Agency was the creation of Allan Pinkerton, a bearded, stocky Scotsman who had left his homeland in the late 1840s to set up business as an optician in Chicago. However, the shock of moving to a city that was colder, grayer, and more miserable than even his hometown of Glasgow caused him to become afflicted with intransigent insomnia. Although he sought to keep his optician's shop open twenty-four hours a day, adding to his sign the phrase "We never sleep," his nighttime hours were generally lonely, desolate times that stretched before him like the bleak Highland landscape for which he still pined.

In an attempt to amuse himself during his sleepless hours, Pinkerton had begun spying on his neighbors' nighttime activities. Within three months he had exposed a counterfeiting operation, broken up a white slavery ring, observed twenty-five improper acts involving farmyard animals, and forced the youthful evil mastermind Adjunct Professor Moriarty to flee to England. Word soon got out that Pinkerton "had an eye on everyone." Famed for his discretion, Pinkerton became known as "the private eye doctor," later being shortened to just "the private eye," and it was only a matter of time before Pinkerton's Opticians was quite overshadowed by Pinkerton's Detective Agency.

---

1. This presidential privilege was often abused, most notably by Franklin Pierce, who was constantly calling on his detectives to help him find his keys.

Pinkerton: ironically, never discovered the whereabouts of his own moustache.

By 1859, Pinkerton had a vast network of detectives spread across the country, and Fillmore now asked him to inform him of any armless men his agents might come across. Within days, he received a telegram from him stating that a man without an arm had been sighted on the banks of the Potomac in Maryland. Fillmore hurried to the destination, arriving late on the night of October 16, 1859. There was no moon, and after a brief scare in which he was unable to make out his own hand in front of his face ("and wondered, for an awful moment, whether I was the pursuer or the pursued") he regained his senses and saw the lights of a farmhouse beckoning to him.

Throwing himself upon the mercy of the farmhouse's owner, Fillmore saw the door opened by "one of the most singular men I have ever had the chance to meet, of about my age, and looking somewhat like an eagle, with a long bushy beard that makes me sorry that I resolved to go clean-shaven through my years. He asked me straightaway in a very harsh tone of voice whether I thought slavery was the most despicable practice ever to be perpetuated on this earth, or whether I was one of the damned and should be put to death. After some deliberation I chose the former answer, and my inquisitor seemed to soften. I introduced myself and found that the man went by the name of John Brown.

"He led me into the house, where I was amazed to find the main room filled with boys and young men. 'These are my sons, Mr. Fillmore,' said Mr. Brown, and then proceeded to introduce me to them all. 'Here is John junior,' I remember him saying with pride, 'and here are Jon, Johnny, Johnnie, Jonnie, Jonathan, Jonathon, Johnathan, Johnathon, Jonson, Johnson, Johnsen, Johnston, Jonas, Jonah, Jonald, Jonnifer, Jondeleeza, Littlejohn, and Salmon.' He said I was more than welcome to rest here but that he and his sons were rather busy, as they were planning an excursion to the town of Harpers Ferry across the river. I told him not to mind me, and he began to hush the children and bade them sit down in rows in front of him.[2]

"It so transpired that Mr. Brown likes to plan his family outings with almost military precision," wrote Fillmore, "although I imagine with a family that size such foresight is necessary. It seems it was to be an educational trip, beginning with the entire family visiting the armory in Harpers Ferry before embarking on a circular journey, or 'revolution' as Mr. Brown put it, through the southern states. I was busily engaged in removing a pebble from my shoe, and so missed many of the details of the trip. Surprisingly, his sons did not seem terribly excited by the prospect, but Brown did not seem to notice. His speech ended with the exhortation 'Now go out there and make your pappy proud.'

"It was then that the boy called Jonah, who was only thirteen or fourteen years old, put up his hand. 'Do we *really* have to liberate the Negroes, Father?' he said. 'I want to go fishing.' 'By God, boy,' roared Mr. Brown, 'you'll liberate the Negro and you'll like it! I didn't spend years bringing you up in the abolitionist cause so you'd waste your days in idle pursuits of

---

2. It is said that Brown had longed to father a full company of children but had had to settle for a mere platoon upon the expiration of his wife from exhaustion.

John Brown: Abolitionist Beard of the Month,
January 1858.

the flesh! I'm giving you a chance for heavenly immortality!' 'But I don't want heavenly immortality,' responded Jonah, 'I want to go and play with my friends.' At this Mr. Brown walked over to him, grabbed him by the ear, and dragged him to a table. Despite Jonah's protestations, Mr. Brown insisted that the boy arm-wrestle him, and when the boy reluctantly assented, Mr. Brown slammed his son's hand into the table with such force that the young fellow fell off his stool. Mr. Brown then stood up and placed a foot on Jonah's back: 'Now, boys, when one of you can whip me, you don't have to do a damn thing, but until that time you'll do what I say!' A groan slunk through the whole group, except for John junior, a young man in his middle twenties, who beamed with pride at his father. 'I won't fight you, Father, ever!' he said. 'Good boy,' replied Mr. Brown before turning to the rest and adding, 'Why can't you all be like John junior here? He's been fighting the abolitionist struggle since he could walk, and he isn't finished yet, are you, son?' 'No, Father,' said John junior happily, 'not until I am baptized again in a tide of blood.' Mr. Brown nodded in approval.

"The other boys were reluctantly beginning to pull weapons out of a large crate when I heard a whisper from behind me. Turning around, I saw it was Jonald, who was aged about sixteen years. 'It's horrible, Mr. Fillmore, sir,' he said under his breath. 'He wanted us to invade Atlanta last week, and it took all of our pleading to get him to try something a little smaller. I tell you, if we're not burning some slave owner's house to the ground, then we're being forced to intimidate members of the Missouri legislature. Sometimes, Mr. Fillmore, just sometimes I wish my father's body lay a-moldering in the grave.'

"'I heard that, Jonald,' said Mr. Brown from the center of the room, causing me to jump and Jonald to turn white as a sheet. 'If you think you can do better without me, then why don't you begin tonight's attack without me? In fact, why don't you begin tonight's attack without any of us, eh, Jonald?' Jonald attempted to protest, but his father fixed him with the most piercing stare I had ever seen, and pointed to the door. His head hung low, Jonald walked slowly out, a few of the other boys wishing him luck. 'And as for the rest of you'—Mr. Brown turned and faced his other children—'you'd best not think of showing your faces around here until a free state for the poor enslaved blacks has been established in the southern Appalachians. Now git!'

"'Right away, Father, sir,' said John junior. 'Come now, brothers—follow me.' The last boy to leave the room was seven-year-old Salmon, the youngest of the group, whose red hair Mr. Brown mussed as he passed, saying as he did so, 'Show no mercy, young Salmon, and if you should die in battle, or are captured and hanged by the neck, just think that your pappy is pleased with you.' Salmon looked up at his father with big tear-filled eyes and stretched out his arms to embrace him, but Mr. Brown pushed him away. 'You're weak, boy! Just like your dead mother. Go now and fight—your hour has come! Farewell!' The small boy ran sobbing out of the door, leaving Mr. Brown shaking his head. 'You've got to be tough with them,' he said to me confidingly. 'They'll thank me for this one day.'

"Mr. Brown began strapping his own body with knives and bullets, and as he did so I thought it time to ask if he had seen any one-armed men in the vicinity. He said he had not, but I noticed that he walked almost everywhere with one hand in his pocket, which might well have given that illusion to Pinkerton's agent. Mr. Brown eventually left, and I spent the night in the empty farmhouse somewhat depressed, although later on that night I heard all sorts of fireworks and loud bangs, which cheered me some, as Mr. Brown's hardworking boys certainly deserved a treat."

A few weeks after his meeting with John Brown, Pinkerton sent Fillmore another telegram that a one-armed man had recently been sighted in Charleston, South Carolina, and Fillmore hurried there at great speed. Along the way he noted how the entire countryside was buzzing with political rumor. "All the talk is of 'Sir Session,' a powerful member of the British aristocracy, I presume, whom the South Carolinians have great hopes for. It is remarkable how easily we forgive and forget the horrors of the War of Independence."

Fillmore arrived at the city's harbor at half past four in the early hours of April 12, 1860. "There was plenty of commotion down along the waterfront, with men manning cannons and soldiers running to and fro," recalled Fillmore. "Announcing myself to a passing sergeant, I was taken to see one General Beauregard, whom I questioned as to the uproar. 'He's hiding in there, sir,' said the general, pointing to Fort Sumter, which lay in the middle of the harbor. 'We've been calling on him to surrender for weeks, but he ain't budging none.' I was amazed—the good citizens of Charleston had obviously heard of my search for the one-armed man and had trapped him. I felt I had to make certain they had the correct villain. 'Is he armless?' I asked. 'Why, yes, sir, we believe he has very few arms since the blockade, sir,' replied General Beauregard. 'Couldn't hurt a fly if he wanted to, sir.' I was so grateful at the way the good southerners had rallied behind my search that I became quite flushed with enthusiasm. 'Why don't you attack?' I asked, for it seemed strange to me that one man could hold off an army. 'Well, sir,' said the general, 'we don't feel we can make a move without the authority from someone higher up, sir. After all, sir, the future of our nation hangs in the balance.' Overcome by his eloquent concern for my well-being, I cried out, 'And what of the authority of a former president?' Grasping a torch, I rushed to one of the cannons and lit it. A cannonball roared out of the gun straight at Fort Sumter. That would show my mysterious assailant what happens when a democratically elected government official is attacked! General Beauregard came racing after me, a wide grin on his face. 'Well, sir, I guess that settles it. We'll have at them now!' he cried. 'You mean *him*,' I corrected. 'We'll have at *him* now.' 'Why, no, sir,' he replied, slightly surprised. 'I mean *them*, the Yankees, sir, and especially that damned Unionist Major Anderson and his troop over there in the fort, sir. He's been refusing to come out of it for weeks.' I was flabbergasted by what he was saying. 'Can I just say, sir,' he now said, removing his hat from his head, 'that we always knew you'd side with the South in the end, Mr. Fillmore, sir. Why, ever since that wondrous compromise of yours, we knew you was a good 'un.' At that the general rallied his men around him and called for 'three cheers for Mr. Fillmore, boys.' As more explosions sounded around the harbor and Fort Sumter began to fire its own cannons in return, I thought it best to leave Charleston, and hoped that come the morning, everyone would have forgotten all about this little incident."

These would prove to be only two of numerous mistaken sightings that would follow. Pinkerton, a stickler for detail, had insisted that his agents report not just on missing arms but on missing legs as well, "in case, to avoid suspicion, the malefactor be walking on his hands." At a time when the national limb count was barely three times that of the population, Fillmore's search rapidly spread across his entire homeland. His now white hair streaming behind him, Fillmore bestrode the land, peering into the nation's hearts, minds, and sleeves in search of the man who he believed was the key to the most damaging conspiracy his beloved country had ever been forced to bear. For the next six years his journals bulge with the trials and tribulations, the detours and diversions, and the breakfasts, lunches, and dinners he faced along the way.

Under an unceasing stream of telegrams from the Pinkerton agency, Fillmore traveled to the West once more. There he prowled the unruly cow towns of the frontier for any sign of the one-armed man, meeting a whole host of frontier luminaries along the way. He played cards with "Wild Bill" Hickok ("who, with his deep interest in the fine arts, is more 'mild' than 'wild'") and mud-wrestled with Calamity Jane ("who, I observed as she snagged her pistol on her skirt and shot herself in the foot, is not so much calamitous as unfortunate"). In Mississippi, he met the sharp-shooting Reverend Cleophas Dowd, who would administer the last rites to people he had shot, then call on himself to repent before begrudgingly hearing his own confession. And confronting the famed outlaw Billy the Kid, he was shocked to discover that Billy was in fact a dwarf and almost forty years old. "Mr. Kid was thoroughly upset by his nickname," wrote Fillmore, "and stated that he wouldn't be such a 'red-eyed son of a she-cat if people weren't so darned insensitive.'"

His remarkable presence of mind was on display when he solved the riddle of the Spinks—a quarrelsome Tennessee family famed for killing anyone who failed to answer their conundrum (the answer, Fillmore records, was "sesquipedalian"). And his remarkable presence of body saw him bridge a gap in the transcontinental railroad in Iowa, saving a trainload of nuns and orphans from certain delay. In a saloon in Kentucky, he was asked to referee a bizarre boxing match between the Sultan of Muscat and the Rajah of Lombok, after the two sovereigns—who had each been attempting to balloon around the world—crashed into each other above Louisville. And while taking a steamship along the East Coast he helped extricate the newly laid transatlantic cable from "the grip of an aroused kraken" by his gentle tickling of the monster's belly.[3]

And what of the Civil War? you may ask. How did this most tragic and bitter sectional conflict affect Millard Fillmore? Curiously, not very much at all. In fact, from 1861 to 1865, Fillmore seems to have been strangely oblivious to the violence that erupted around him. Although his diary refers to sightings of many troops, "some wearing gray and others wearing blue," he seemed confused that "rarely do you see the gray troops and the blue troops together." On the rare occasions that he did stumble upon the aftermath of combat, he would presume it was caused by "one of the infamous feuds you hear happen so much in the hot-blooded South." He would often aid the wounded he came across as best he could, stanching wounds and singing calming cowboy songs to the mortally wounded while preaching the gospel of "forbearance and brotherly love to these quarrelsome young men."

By 1865, with the war winding down, Fillmore had investigated more than 760 sightings across the country, and felt he was beginning to know all the habits, haunts, and hobbies of one-armed men.[4] His clothes had grown ragged, his gait was not quite so jaunty, but his spirit was undiminished. It might seem reasonable to ask whether this single-mindedness was in some way a sign of mental instability. The change in his appearance led some contemporary commentators to believe that the death of Abigail had irretrievably unbalanced him. Others suggested a physical rather than mental affliction, pointing to the large candle he had been forced to consume in Congress under the orders of Black Dan Webster back in 1836. Yet

---

3. Fillmore's travels in these years—spread over almost forty-five journals—are far too many to include within this present volume. For a full and unexpurgated look at the never-before-published details of Millard Fillmore's later life, please see the forthcoming *The Complete Unpublished Remarkable Millard Fillmore: Author's Edit*, which is typeset in a new font (Millardia) and includes deleted typographical errors as well as annotated marginalia by Millard Fillmore's great-great-great-grandniece, Mildred Fillmore. One thousand limited editions will contain a lock of genuine hair, and a 3D hologram of the four Whig presidents.

4. "Archery," wrote Fillmore, "is not a common pursuit."

Fillmore's journals never complain about physical or mental distress. Even when one of Pinkerton's agents sent him on a fruitless journey to Nebraska—a state that Congress had recently tried to force to secede—he seemed overwhelmingly optimistic. "I feel I am getting very close," he wrote.

While Fillmore had been traversing the country, Abraham Lincoln had been elected president. For all his alleged ethics and morals, Lincoln was not an original thinker. From birth, he had modeled his own life on that of Fillmore, nine years his senior. He had made sure he was born in a log cabin, and insisted that he grow up in poverty-ridden circumstances similar to Fillmore's. Following Fillmore's lead, he had become a lawyer and joined the Whig Party. He was not even averse to pilfering Fillmore's rhetoric; in 1862, Fillmore's journal recalls an off-the-cuff speech he gave to a gaggle of street urchins in Washington, D.C., on "the delights of dessert." The "Pudding Address," as he termed it, began, "Fourscore and six years ago our fathers brought forth on this continent a new confection. . . ." [5] The rest is history.

Whether it was an attempt to exorcise his own guilt over this gratuitous pilfering of Fillmore's character or his genuine wish to praise Fillmore's exploits as an angel of mercy on the Civil War's battlefields, President Lincoln would extend a fateful dinner invitation to his inspirational predecessor on April 14, 1865.

It felt peculiar for Fillmore to return to his former residence, largely because when he arrived, Mary Lincoln had locked her husband out of the building and "was throwing pots and pans at him as he desperately tried to regain admittance." The Lincolns' marriage had been fraught with difficulty from the start. While Lincoln was tall and thin, Mary was short and round, and their clashing physiognomies brought out the worst in each other. Mary took to wearing rounder and rounder clothes to accentuate Lincoln's thinness, while Lincoln took to wearing a stovepipe hat to accen-

5. It seems Fillmore was referring to the invention of flan.

Abraham Lincoln: not so much honest as opportunistic.

tuate his wife's rotundity. "Standing together," wrote the congressional wit Glenn Beaux, "they are dead ringers for the letter *d.*"

When Lincoln noticed Fillmore he drew him to one side. "He said that he was awfully sorry but Mary was upset at his recent purchase of a pair of stack-heeled boots, and would I mind proceeding to the after-dinner entertainment he had planned. As Mrs. Lincoln had come upon the steak knives, I thought his suggestion most amenable."

Lincoln was an avid theatergoer and could regularly be found in his box at Ford's Theatre when he sought to escape the pressures of the war, or his wife. He was in the custom of asking friends to accompany him on the condition that they wear a bonnet, so that theatergoers might think all was well in the president's marriage. Fillmore assented to this stipulation happily, writing, "It quite reminded me of old times with Mr. Crockett."

Ford's Theatre had recently staged a groundbreaking version of William Shakespeare's *Hamlet*, the text of which had been significantly modified for the rough and rowdy American audiences of the time. Renamed *That Crazy Prince*, Elsinore Castle was transformed into Eleanor's Saloon, Ophelia performed a risqué dance to the tune of "Yankee Doodle Dandy," Laertes shot Fortinbras after drinking Polonius to death, and

Hamlet's famed "To be or not to be" soliloquy was replaced by the lines "Prithee, sirrah, inquire of thyself a question: / Dost thou feel fortunate? Well, dost thou, my taffeta punk?"

The play being performed the night Fillmore and Lincoln attended the theater was not, alas, this groundbreaking tragedy, but rather a farce entitled *Our American Cousin.* Its depiction of Americans as being brash, vulgar, and greedy had made it a huge hit, and it was now into the seventh year of its run. Lincoln had seen it thirteen times and could be heard shouting, along with the main actor, the play's most famous line: "Don't know the manners of good society, eh? Well, I guess I know enough to turn you inside out, old gal—you sockdologizing old man-trap."

Fillmore's journal recalls, in detail, the events of the evening: "The first act of the play was a masterpiece, producing a uniquely soporific effect upon me. I soon found myself wafted into a deep sleep in which I was granted a strange vision. I was traveling in a black steel wagon at great speed, yet I could see no horses pulling me. Sitting to my right was a handsome man wearing strange clothes, who seemed to be of some importance, and who was waving to the crowds that thronged the streets. I began to wave as well, and giggle in a high-pitched breathy voice, when suddenly a gunshot rang out and the head of the man next to me was thrown backward. Everything seemed to slow down as if in a dumb-show, and I saw blood was covering the pink skirt suit and hat I was wearing. I looked to my left and saw a shadowy figure with a rifle aiming at me from a small grassy hillock, and at the same moment I felt a hand grip my thigh. I turned around and was startled to see the man who had been shot smiling at me as blood streamed from the huge wound in his head. 'Pucker up, Jackie,' he said, and I awoke with a start.

"Mr. Lincoln had gripped my thigh in anticipation of his favorite speech, but such was the shock imparted to my half-dazed self that I tumbled backward in my chair and crashed to the ground. Luckily, my fall was softened somewhat by a young moustached man I had previously not been aware of in the box. I swiftly readjusted my bonnet, curtseyed, and extended my hand to the young gentleman. But he was frantically scouring the floor as if he had lost something. I endeavored to help him, and when I saw a small pistol lying underneath Mr. Lincoln's chair I reached under and retrieved it, without disturbing the president. Tapping the young man on the shoulder, I proffered the gun to him, and he grasped it eagerly. Unfortunately, at that very moment, Mr. Lincoln began to chant out his favorite lines from the play, and as the line reached the crescendo of "sockdologizing old man-trap" the young man must have been so shocked at the coarse language that he accidentally discharged the gun into the back of poor Mr. Lincoln's noble head. There was a pause, and a scream, and the young man, distraught with horror, leapt from our box onto the stage, shouting, 'Sic semper tyrannis,' which I sincerely hoped meant 'Send for a doctor' in Latin."[6]

As the theater emptied on that grim April night and Lincoln's body was taken to a nearby house, a despondent, still-bonneted Fillmore was left alone in the theater box. His journal relates how he suddenly felt much older, as if his sixty-five years had sprung upon him all at once. "Poor Mr. Lincoln's death seems to have taken the wind from me," he wrote in his journal. "I feel more tired than I have ever felt before."

The next morning, as word of Lincoln's death spread across a horrified country, Fillmore's own state of mind had not recovered. The Civil War had created thousands of new amputees across the country, and looking at the vast pile of telegrams sent to him from the unceasing Pinkerton, Fillmore's optimism faltered. "I have decided to halt my pursuit of the one-armed man and return to Buffalo," he wrote, "where I think I will spend my last years in quiet contemplation."

6. John Wilkes Booth—the "moustached man" in Fillmore's retelling of the event—was an up-and-coming young actor whose status as a theatrical heartthrob had seen doctors prescribe his performances to those suffering from poor circulation. His signature role as Merkin Dasher, in *Puny Feelin'*, only increased his fame and recuperative powers, and he was besieged in public by doe-eyed admirers and wall-eyed invalids. Booth was not content. At the age of twenty-two he personally bankrolled a production of *King Lear* in which he was to play the title role. Critics described it as a "placebo performance," and he was rejected by audiences and physicians alike, fatally unhinging him.

It was to be a slow journey. Fillmore wrote that he "could not stomach the hectic pace of the train or stagecoach," and so instead hired a small cart, drawn by a mule, to take him home. Up until this point Fillmore's journals reverberate with curiosity and inquiry, yet in these pages they are bled of all enthusiasm, stating simply the hour of his waking, the towns he rode through, and the time of his going to bed. Nothing, it seemed, could stir him from his torpor. There is a fleeting reference to his traveling through the town of Pieville, the center of New York State's pastry industry, yet he writes of "not feeling terribly hungry." On one other occasion he recounts seeing "an elephant, most probably escaped from a traveling circus and in need of help," but Fillmore's journal continues, "I thought it best to leave its safe return to others, and continued on my way." What are we to make of such uncharacteristic disinterest? It was as if the lifeblood had been sucked from the most dynamic figure of the nineteenth century, leaving the hollow shell of a man behind.

In the depths of this depression, Fillmore was forced to ford the great Ohio River, when he caught sight "of a strange old man, older even than I, standing on a keelboat, cursing, spitting, and shouting at his equally old dog. The old man was trying to place a cup of whiskey on the dog's head, and when he was successful he would hobble back to the other end of the boat, pick up an old musket, and aim it at the cup. But every time he lifted his musket, the dog—who obviously had some intelligence—would drop its head, spill the whiskey, and proceed to lap up the liquid. I saw this happen two or three times, with the old man getting angrier and angrier and the dog getting drunker and drunker, and I was about to continue on my way when the old man saw me and beckoned me over. He asked me, in a scratchy rasping voice, if I would be kind enough to balance a cup of whiskey on my head, just for a moment. I tried to protest, but with a burst of surprising speed the old man hurried up to me, placed the cup on my head, and scurried back to his musket. I wanted to say no, but my voice was lost. Perhaps, I thought, this was the way I was meant to die. Then, rid-ding myself of this silly notion, I shouted at the old man to stop. But as the words left my lips there was a loud bang and a puff of smoke; the old man was thrown backward into the bottom of the keelboat, and I was knocked flat by a tremendous jolt to my chest. 'Did I hit ya?' the old man squealed. 'Oh, Lord, did I hit ya?' I was spread-eagled on the ground, whiskey covering my face. The breath had been quite knocked out of me, but somehow I was alive. The old man hurried over to my side, and his dog began licking my cheeks. 'Well, I never,' said the old man, and he lifted from my chest the amulet Poe had bequeathed me so many years ago. It had been squashed flat by the large round musket ball lodged into its side! 'Wowee!' cried the old man, helping me up. 'I never seen anything like that before!' I thanked him for his help but said I must be on my way. He looked at me strangely. 'Don't you know who I am?' he asked. Getting slowly to my feet, I replied I was sorry but I had no idea, and as I steadied myself on my cart he shook his head and, drawing himself up as straight as his old bones would allow, announced, 'Mike Fink, king of the keelboaters, at your service!' His name seemed to spark a vague memory in my mind. Had Mr. Crockett mentioned him all those years ago? I introduced myself, but before I could say another word he had launched into a long speech interrupted only by huge gobs of spit and the occasional belch.

"'Pah, war! Ain't good for nothing but to make people forget stuff, not least who they are and who they want to be. Once everybody wanted a piece of me, but then the war came and . . . well, who remembers Mike Fink now? They all got scared, Millard, too scared to think. Too scared to remember. I used to make 'em laugh like crazy. Then they started saying I was oh-fence-iv, that I wasn't good for the children, that I wasn't 'onorable. Can you believe that? But I say honor's for the birds, Millard. Honor's what gets a man killed for doing something he doesn't understand. Honor's what we say we have when we got nothing else to back us up. Honor, Millard, is the most scoundrelous thing I ever heard. And they called me oh-fence-iv, hell . . . Sure, I told some tall tales in my day, but I'll vouch there's more truth in one sentence of them than in all your so-called noose-papers of nowadays. Heck, Millard, it's getting to the point where people just don't know how to *believe* anymore. I always thought that a straight-up lie is a darn sight better than something pretending to be a truth. But hell, since the war all people want is what they call awe-then-tissity. I hear you can pipe it and pump it into your rooms, or maybe I'm getting confused. But I tell you, there ain't ever been anything truer than lying, gambling, bragging, cowardly Mike Fink!' "

Fillmore recalled being transfixed by the speech as the river rolled quietly by and the old dog lay by his side, occasionally licking his outstretched hand.

"'Why,' Fink continued, 'they're all so busy chasing real life that they forget they can still enjoys the phony stuff. Heck, Millard, they've forgotten how to forget themselves. When Mike Fink was wrestling an alligator you never thought of no one but Mike Fink. Now it's all "me" and "you" and la-di-da. Why, they might even forget you one of these days. They'll probably think you're some good-for-nothing polly-tishun 'coz their minds are so full of fear, fear put there by good-for-nothing polly-tishuns! A fella once told me that there was only one cure for fear and that was rattlesnake blood. Hell, I must have drunk gallons of the stuff and scared every rattler halfway to Canada before I realized what he meant. Fear's what we make it, Millard. Mark my words. You and me'll have something to say about fear yet. Yes, by God we will. There's always time for one more adventure, Millard, no matter how old we are. Always time for one more adventure.' And with those words he cast off his keelboat and sailed down the river, his old dog barking and snapping at his heels.

"I looked down at the crushed amulet, and as I did so it flicked open to reveal the picture of the Great Seal of the United States that Poe had bequeathed me all those years ago. There was the great pyramid, with the strange floating eye atop it. Perhaps Mr. Fink was right," wrote Fillmore, "perhaps there was time for one more adventure."

13.

Fillmore Unbound

(1866–1874)

*F*illmore's next journal entry places him at sea, on an ocean voyage to the East. Gazing at the amulet Poe had given him had triggered a moment of revelation: the answer to the Freemason riddle lay in Egypt. But how was Fillmore to visit the country without alerting the secretive and suspicious fraternity to his presence? Through Pinkerton he had heard that a number of former Confederate and Union troops had been traveling to Egypt at the request of the country's all-powerful leader, the Khedive. Thus, disguising himself as a captain in the Union Continentals, Fillmore made full speed for the port of Alexandria.

Fillmore: an officer, a gentleman, a little teapot.

In its three thousand years of existence, the Great Pyramid of Giza had been witness to human ambition in all its tawdry variety. But perhaps even it had never beheld anything as grand as the works being carried out under the rule of Ismail Pasha, the Khedive of Egypt. Known as "Ismail the Magnificent," the Khedive had worked relentlessly to deserve this honorary title.[1] Declaring that "my country is no longer in Africa; we are now part of Europe," Ismail was intent on transforming his country into one awash with European culture and technology. In particular, the Khedive was obsessed with European railways, and soon hundreds of miles of train tracks sprang up across the desert country. Perhaps the greatest example of the Khedive's commitment to Europeanization could be found on Egypt's north coast, where his engineers had begun laying huge railway tracks running from the port of Alexandria to Syracuse in southern Italy, in the hopes of transporting his entire nation to Europe. And even in the royal palace, a miniature railway snaked through the ornate rooms and sculpted gardens, the Khedive driving it himself, his legs up about his ears, the tassel from his fez streaming behind him.

Such was the Khedive's commitment to cultural improvements that he had hired Giuseppe Verdi, the greatest composer of the age, to write an opera for the grand opening of the Khedivial Opera House. The Khedive was disappointed when Verdi rejected his suggestion that the opera be about "a kindly steam train who assists other engines, and a portly sultan who acts as their firm but fair leader," and at the premiere of the resulting opus—*Aïda*—the Khedive showed his still-lingering resentment by blowing on a whistle and making loud "choo-choo" noises throughout the entire performance.

Nevertheless, the Khedive's Europeanizing instinct only went so far. Pinkerton's information had been correct: the Khedive *had* paid for fifty Civil War soldiers, drawn from both sides of the conflict, to travel to Egypt. But his reasons for doing so were much darker than the detective could possibly have imagined. The terrific ferocity with which the Civil

---

1. Beginning as "Ismail the Insignificant," he had rapidly become "Ismail the Noticeable," then "Ismail the Conspicuous," before emerging as "Ismail the Magnificent" in 1863. In later years, as his influence declined, he would be known as "Ismail the Erstwhile."

Ismail the Magnificent searching for belly button fluff on one
of his less magnificent days.

War had been fought was well known, and the Khedive, a fanatic of blood sports, now planned to pit northerner against southerner in gladiatorial combat in his newly built Italianate coliseum.[2]

The first combat was scheduled to pit Beverly Kennon, a Confederate lieutenant, against Thaddeus Mott, a Union colonel. Unleashed into the arena to a roar from the massed crowd, Kennon and Mott approached each other, grasped each other by the hand, exchanged cordial salutations, and began to walk around the arena seemingly engrossed in remembrances of the Battle of Mobile Bay. It was immediately clear that the Khedive had sorely underestimated the gentlemanly etiquette of American officers. A shiver of excitement ran through the impatient spectators when Mott finally withdrew his sword from its scabbard. But it seemed he only wished to point out the delicate engraving on its pommel, much to Kennon's delight. The entertainments did not improve when the much-touted "rank match" between Private Dennison of the Union and Brigadier General

---

2. The Khedive was renowned for the ingeniousness of his bloodthirsty temperament. Other gladiatorial bouts he had planned included women versus men, children versus adults, thin people versus fat people, short people versus tall people, people with no arms versus people with no legs, and, in possibly his finest moment, a short, fat, male child with no legs versus a tall, skinny adult woman with no arms.

Colston of the Confederacy ended with the two men sitting cross-legged on the coliseum floor playing gin rummy, and an infuriated Khedive was forced to cancel the rest of the season.

But what was Ismail to do with all these soldiers now that he had transported them to his country? Realizing that if Egypt was to become a modern European nation it would need an army competent in performing untold acts of savagery, he ordered the American soldiers to help train his troops in the latest killing techniques being utilized by more advanced countries. The Khedive's request seemed, on the face of it, a simple undertaking, but all did not go smoothly. The American soldiers did not fully understand the religious culture of the land they were in. "The soldiers pray constantly!" wrote an outraged Wilburn Hall, a former Union lieutenant, in his much-admired memoir of the time, *Filthy Savages.* "What kind of insecure deity needs devotion paid to him five times a day?" James Basel, a former captain for the South, agreed: "They got right huffy when I used their 'Holy Book' for target practice." Major Vanderbilt Allen was equally shocked, and in a letter to his wife he wrote, "We are accused of religious intolerance, which could hardly be further from the case, for it is *they* who are intolerant for not believing in the one true God, the Lord Jesus Christ, and it is *they* who will join their savagerous prophet in hell for their bigotry."

Amidst this ideological friction, a disguised Fillmore arrived in Cairo. He was having his own difficulties, not least in the matter of his diet: "I had read of the fabled Sahara Dessert, which was described as one of the greatest confections in the world. Yet when I asked my guide where I could find an establishment to consume it, he ignored me." Forgoing this delicacy, Fillmore threw himself into his investigations of Freemasonry, spending days wandering the bazaars enquiring after the devilish organization. He soon realized that such a search was hopeless: his hotel room was rapidly filling with carpets he had been cajoled into buying, and to make matters worse he had become accidentally hypnotized while watching a snake charmer and had developed a worrying tendency to hiss. Relinquishing his disguise, he went to ask the Khedive for help in person.

The Khedive was overjoyed to have a former president of the United States visiting him.[3] He listened intently as Fillmore described his life's battle against the Freemasons, from William Morgan's disappearance, through the rise and fall of the Anti-Mason Party, to his suspicions about the death of Zachary Taylor, his travels across the country in search of the one-armed assassin, and finally the amulet Poe had given him linking the Masons to the pyramids. After he had told his life story—repeating, at the Khedive's request, the part about the transcontinental railroad—the Khedive looked Fillmore up and down and said that he would certainly help him uncover "this ghastliness," if only to "free the pyramids from the taint of such decidedly un-European mumbo-jumbo." At that moment, one of the Khedive's American soldiers stormed into the room. "Ah, Mr. Chaillé-Long," said the Khedive, "how go the preparations?" Fillmore recalled that the American was beet red with rage and did not even register his former president sitting in the room, instead bursting into a furious harangue about the queen mother's chief eunuch, who, Chaillé-Long said, had been "giggling" at him again. The Khedive desperately tried to interrupt, but to no avail, and Chaillé-Long declared he was returning to his home in San Francisco, "where men acted like men." Turning on his heel, he stormed out, leaving the Khedive looking "quite dejected." Fillmore asked the Khedive what was the matter, and was informed that Chaillé-Long had been due to head an expedition to discover the source of the Nile. "When he said this my heart skipped a beat," wrote Fillmore. "Ever since I was a child I have been in awe of the majestic Nile. From what mysterious valley or mountain did it stem? And to what strange and unknown sea did it extend? Seeing as how the Khedive had been so agreeable in

---

3. Court records show that the Khedive's joy might have been partially due to the upcoming series of gladiatorial combats he had planned that winter, entitled "Supreme Monarchs versus Elected Heads of Government." He had already gained tentative acceptances from King Carol I of Romania and William Gladstone, the British prime minister.

offering his help to me, I immediately told him that I would take over the leadership of the expedition!"

The Khedive was exultant at Fillmore's generosity, promising that he would work ceaselessly to capture the Freemasons while Fillmore was away, and taking the time to show the American the picturesque location of his tomb in the Cairo graveyard should he never return. The ex-president soon found himself in the midst of preparations for his voyage, although it seems that Fillmore was somewhat nonchalant in his planning. "It seems a simple enough task of following the river's path for two or three weeks," he wrote in his journal. "After all, how long can a river be?" Little could Fillmore have known as he departed ceremoniously from Cairo on the back of a camel and at the head of a small force of Egyptian soldiers that he would not return for three long years.

The journey would be arduous, stretching over two thousand miles through both baking desert and inhospitable rainforest. He traveled south through Egypt and downward through the Sudan before bottoming out in the land of the Unyoro and Yunbarri in what we today call Uganda. There were blood-sucking insects to contend with, and man-eating snakes, not to mention the dangerous natives and the ever-present threat of a topical disease.[4] All of these would certainly have destroyed the body and soul of a weaker man, but Fillmore seemed to be cocooned against danger. It was as if the spirit of his youth, the same spirit that had watched over him in his parents' log cabin as he clung to every word of James Bruce's *Travels in Abyssinia*, was once again protecting him. As his companions succumbed to fever or exhaustion, Fillmore continued blissfully unruffled. At Foweira, Egypt's southernmost point, he describes smearing himself in cow dung to ward off the mosquitoes, happily noting, "It is much more pleasant a chore when Black Dan is not standing over your shoulder obliging you to do it." In El Obeid, in the Sudan, he writes of being tricked into eating his

4. Leprosy—very topical. Dengue fever—not so much.

camel, "for when I awoke the next morning and asked where Humpty might be, the soldiers pointed to my belly and laughed." Outside of Gondokoro, a thousand miles south of Khartoum, he saw his first hippopotamus, and was so delighted that he had to be restrained from leaping into the river, "for I did so want to splash about with it." Meanwhile, his noble appearance saw him christened M'Bugaru, "the white prince," by the tribes he met along the way.[5]

Another month's journey south and he was in the kingdom of the Grand Kahotah, M'Tesa, where Fillmore dazzled the tribesmen with his remarkable rubber band tricks. Visiting the province of Makraka, he angered the terrifyingly overcourteous Niam-Niam, refusing a third helping of their famed eyeball stew, and causing them to attack. Fillmore was hit by "at least six poisoned arrows," but rather than killing him, the poison only seemed to make him "ecstatically happy," and he recalls chasing the attackers off in a frenzied attempt to "hug every last one of them."

As the Nile shrank in size, Fillmore recalls the ground becoming steeper and the vegetation thicker. Leaving the remnants of his party on the jungle floor, Fillmore followed the river up into the mountains, carefully watching as it became narrower and shallower, until finally, on July 3, 1872, in the heart of the Nyungwe Forest, Fillmore saw it turn from a river into a stream, and from a stream into little more than a rivulet, which seemed to dry up in a small clearing directly in front of the door of a small mud hut.

Fillmore relates how he was most puzzled at this sight and called out, but there was no reply. Peering through the hut's door, he saw the glowing embers of a fire, some animal bones and skins, and three large wooden buckets. He was about to look further when he heard the sound of someone approaching and darted into the surrounding undergrowth. "Imagine my surprise when I saw a white man, very thin, although with a thick

---

5. Depending on the word's inflection, *m'bugaru* can also mean "he who eats camels."

moustache, walking up to the hut. He wore little more than a loincloth and carried in his hands a bucket filled with water. When he reached the rivulet he carefully poured the contents of the bucket onto the ground. 'There you go, my pretty,' he said, 'hurry along now.' I felt compelled to introduce myself and, stepping out of the bushes, called out to the man. He seemed quite startled, but then gave me a kind smile, and in a booming English voice exclaimed, 'Oh, well done! I thought I had you quite beaten.' I was perplexed by this strange greeting, but before I could say a word the man announced cheerfully, 'Your turn,' turned his back on me, put his hands over his eyes, and began to count out aloud. When the man had reached 115 and still showed no sign of stopping I tapped him lightly on the shoulder. He lifted up one of his hands and looked at me quizzically. 'Well, aren't you going to hide, then?' I asked him why I should do such a thing. 'You are Mr. Stanley, I presume?' he said, turning to face me completely now, although I noticed he was still counting on his fingers. I replied that I was not. 'Oh, my dear fellow, I'm terribly sorry,' he exclaimed, reaching out his hand. 'My name's Livingstone. One of your countrymen and I have a little wager. I said he couldn't find me before the end of the century, and he said he jolly well could. I haven't heard dickens from him for six years, and since I've got five pounds staked on the outcome, I very much hope it stays that way.' He began stroking his chin thoughtfully. 'He probably followed those footsteps I left for him in the snow back in Turkistan. The funny thing was, I was actually walking backward.'[6] He chuckled to himself, and I felt I had to ask how he had come by his most peculiar situation. He picked up his bucket and motioned me to walk with him.

"'When I first happened upon this bolt-hole there was a little native fellow here, old as the hills,' he explained. 'Upon seeing me, he gurgled something about being "freed from a curse" and "the spell being lifted," or

---

6. Hide-and-seek, known as "The Great Game" throughout the Victorian era, was so popular it was played on both individual and national levels—most notably when the hiding city of Tashkent was found by Russian seekers in 1865 and quickly annexed.

some other Johnny Foreigner nonsense. Anyway, before I knew it, he was dead as a doornail. Well, I couldn't just leave the bally river to dry up, and having nothing better to do with my time, I thought I'd keep up the custom. When in Rome, and all that . . .' We had by now arrived at the shore of a great lake, and Mr. Livingstone filled his bucket with water and turned back toward the hut. 'Admittedly, the work is rather grueling, and the hours are quite long,' he said, carefully pouring the water out and watching it run down the hill, 'but the job satisfaction is tremendous.'

"I spent a most entertaining day walking back and forth between the lake and the hut. Informing me that he was a doctor, Mr. Livingstone kindly took a look at the leech that had become my ever-faithful traveling companion over the last year. I told him all that had occurred in the world since he had begun hiding in 1865, although I was not able to name the winners at Royal Ascot, nor tell him who had won the University Boat Race. As the sun sank beneath the hills I said I had to rejoin my expedition, and we parted cheerily, I swearing that if I ever saw Mr. Stanley I would mention I had seen the good doctor on a freighter bound for Australia."

Delighted at having succeeded in his task, Fillmore turned north and

Dr. Livingstone: the source of the Nile, I presume?

returned home. The journey seems to have passed in an instant. The only significant mention in his journals is of his stay in Monbutto, where he met the fabled Aka pygmies. No taller than children of six or seven, but blessed with great endurance, the Aka patiently suffered Fillmore's barely suppressed giggles at their size. The Aka attempted to trade one of their own, a pygmy woman, "as broad as she was tall," for all of Fillmore's journals, with which they were enthralled.[7] Fillmore was reluctant, but when he awoke one morning to find himself tied to the ground, the pygmy chief straddling his chest, poking him in the throat with a spear, he graciously acquiesced. Traveling downriver with the pygmy woman, whom he christened Tiki-Tiki, Fillmore soon returned to Cairo.

"When I arrived back at the royal palace," wrote Fillmore in a new journal, "the Khedive was exultant. In particular, he gained great pleasure from Tiki-Tiki, exclaiming, 'Look how she dances, look how she dances!' while clapping his hands together. I tried to tell him about my remarkable meeting with Dr. Livingstone and my discovery of the source of the Nile, but he no longer seemed interested in it, preferring to ogle the shaking of the little pygmy woman. When he had signaled that Tiki-Tiki should be placed in his harem, he turned to me, wiping tears from his eyes. 'Oh, Mr. Fillmore, you have made me very happy. Now I will show you that I have kept my end of the agreement.'

"The Khedive led me down a set of stone steps that took us deep beneath the palace and eventually stopped in a corridor, lit only by torches, along which were many large metal doors. From the moans and groans I could hear from within I presumed it must be the Khedive's infirmary, where the benevolent sultan treated his sickly subjects. The hunchbacked doctor who accompanied us thrust one of his many keys into a lock and swung the door open. There, huddled in the corner, was none other than

---

7.   In the Aka pygmies' primitive religion, cloth binding is a manifestation of the jungle god Binda.

the one-armed man I had long been searching for! I immediately protested to the Khedive that this man needed no medical attention, for his arm had been like that for years. 'He has been in Egypt for some time,' explained the Khedive. 'His name is Major General William Loring. He arrived to help train my armies, but my spies informed me that he was involved in other, more scurrilous activities.'[8]

William W. Loring: the one-armed assassin, armed.

"Before I could say a word, the one-armed man looked up at me, and I regretted having accused him of malingering, for indeed he did look unwell, his face having broken out in a rash of cuts and bruises. 'You have made powerful friends, Mr. Fillmore,' he said, gesturing at the Khedive, 'but you cannot stop our leader.' I wanted to know more. Had the Freemasons killed President Zachary Taylor and Edgar Allan Poe and John Quincy Adams because they had gotten too close to the truth? But Major General Loring folded his arm and would not say another word. 'He has

---

8. The Khedive was bending the truth somewhat, for Loring had originally been scheduled to fight in the Khedive's "righties versus lefties" gladiatorial series.

not told us their designs,' said the Khedive, 'but we will know soon enough.'
He looked toward the doctor, who smiled happily.

"When I returned to my rooms, stunned by this revelation, and keen
to wash myself clean of the dung that still covered me from the expedition,
I found a card left on my pillow. It was an etching of the Great Pyramid
with an arrow pointing to its summit, next to which was written the word
'midnight.' Whom could it have come from? There was only one way to
find out, but the hotel clerk had seen no one enter my room, and the servant boy kept holding his nose and laughing at me. Could light be shed on
the matter by climbing the pyramid itself, perhaps at the suggested hour?"

It was dark when Fillmore began the long ascent up the side of the Great
Pyramid. Each stone was over five feet tall, but fortunately Fillmore still
had the strength of youth in his arms and legs. The 450-foot climb took
him almost an hour, and he cursed himself many times for "not bringing a
light refreshment." When he eventually hauled himself onto the small platform at the pyramid's summit he was "somewhat surprised to see another
figure standing there with his back to me, and wearing a long hooded robe.
I asked who he was, but garnered no reply. I asked the same question again,
thinking the cowl he wore about his head might have blocked out my voice,
but still no answer. Walking up to him, I tapped the strange man on the
shoulder. Then his hands went to his head, and pulling down the hood, he
turned around. Imagine my surprise when my gaze was met by a pair of
gray eyes. It was none other than my old mentor, Mr. Thurlow Weed! I was
so startled I could hardly speak, but Mr. Weed smiled and put me at my
ease. 'So, Fillmore,' he told me, 'we are finally alone.' Upon regaining my
voice, I told Mr. Weed that it was a remarkable coincidence that he should
be here on the Great Pyramid at this very moment, because I felt certain I
was about to uncover a conspiracy that dated all the way back to our time
together in the Anti-Masons. He shook his head as if he could not believe
it either. 'Fillmore, Fillmore, Fillmore,' he said, 'I don't think you under-

stand. I formed the Anti-Mason Party to steer and control the investigation away from the concern to which I have always been utterly devoted.' 'You mean the Whigs?' I asked, slightly confused, but Mr. Weed did not answer my question. 'You cannot deny your country's history,' he said to me, and his eyes glazed over as he began telling me an odd story in which George Washington, James Monroe, and Benjamin Franklin were all Freemasons. It was diverting, in a fantastical sort of way, and offered me a chance to collect my breath after the long climb.

"When Mr. Weed finally looked at me again, his gaze had changed. It had become steely and hard, as when I had spilt hot wax on his head at one of our earliest meetings. 'Fillmore,' he now said, 'you have been a thorn in our side from the very beginning. We did not expect you to be so voracious in your quest for us, but you were, despite all the chances we gave you to stop.' I replied that I was beholden to Mr. Weed for his help and thus was only doing my duty, and that I had conclusive evidence that the Freemasons were responsible for the assassination of Zachary Taylor. I began to list the proofs, but Mr. Weed grew ever angrier. 'Be quiet!' he yelled. 'We didn't kill Zachary Taylor, you buffoon,' he said, seeming to have misheard me. 'Why, Fillmore, would I kill Taylor if it would make you president? We wanted you as far from power as possible!' My head began to spin under this onslaught of facts. 'Well, if the Freemasons didn't kill Taylor, then who did?' I enquired. I heard the rustling of a crinoline petticoat at my back, and a woman's voice spoke up softly: 'It was I.' When I spun around, who should be standing behind me but dear demure Miss Dorothea Dix, looking quite delectable in the midnight air! 'I did it because I loved you so much, Millard, so very much. I only wanted to make you happy, to make you president. I hope I have not made you sad. Have I?' Her countenance was so fair, her confession so heartfelt, that I could hardly bring myself to condemn her. 'Miss Dix,' I spluttered, 'I never knew you held such affection for me.'

"'Oh, Fillmore, you fool,' said yet another woman's voice, this one coming from behind Miss Dix. I strained to see who it was, but the lady revealed herself soon enough as Miss Anna Ella Carroll! She was holding a pretty little pistol that accentuated the fineness of her hands, the pearl handle beautifully complementing the delicate silver filigree on her bodice. 'I gave you the presidency on a plate!' she cried. 'We could have ruled the country together, arm in arm. But you thwarted my plans. No man has done that to me before.' I didn't know quite where to look or what to say. 'I found an ally in my hatred for you in the ever-generous Mr. Weed,' she continued. The two of them exchanged knowing glances, and I must admit to being quite dizzy with revelation.

"Mr. Weed now gestured for me to look down at the ground far below us. This suggestion did not help my dizziness; in fact, it made it considerably worse. But as I teetered on the brink, I could just make out that the base of the pyramid was flecked with hundreds of figures carrying flaming torches. Was it a trick of the light, or did I perceive the glint of razor-sharp trowels in their hands? A sound seemed to come to my ears, a low chant that sounded awfully like 'Kill more! Kill more!' What could this mean? I was about to give up and ask the pale Miss Dix if she could explain everything to me at a slightly slower pace when Mr. Weed, who had been talking all the while about the need for a 'blood sacrifice' to usher in this 'new age of humanity,' pulled from his cowl a large blade and leapt to attack me!

"Perhaps it was the altitude or the effects of the previous day's sun, but Mr. Weed seemed convinced that I was not his old friend Millard Fillmore but instead some 'enemy of the brotherhood.' We rolled about on the top of the pyramid as if engaged in a melodramatic fight to the death, as I desperately tried to persuade him of his error. I saw out of the corner of my eye that Miss Dix was also wrestling with Miss Carroll, and the two were pulling each other's hair and screaming in a most unladylike fashion. All the while the chanting from below was getting louder and louder, and Mr. Weed seemed to grow in strength with each moment. In one swift movement, which quite belied his advanced age, he pinned me to the ground and, placing the knife to my neck, began saying something about getting me 'out of the way' and 'killing the new president' and 'reinitiating slavery,' and perhaps even something to do with 'persecuting the Jews.' In fact, I wish I had had a chance to write it all down, but I must admit that my attention had wandered during Mr. Weed's lecture and had become quite transfixed by a small circle of lights that had appeared high in the sky above him. As Mr. Weed continued to tell me of the 'destruction of democracy' and the rise of a 'new world order,' I noticed another circle appear. Then there were three, then five, then seven, then eleven. In an instant, they had filled the sky above us. The chanting had stopped, and Mr. Weed suddenly realized that something was amiss. Looking up, he staggered to his feet, his mouth agape, and began to threaten the circles of light with his knife, screaming out that he 'was so close' and 'it wasn't fair.' And so it was that, staggering backward on the pyramid's peak, poor Mr. Weed lost his footing and disappeared over the edge, his hideous screams growing fainter, and then louder, and then fainter, and then louder, and then fainter again, as he tumbled down the pyramid's side to his certain doom. Exhausted, I crawled to the edge and saw that the torch-carrying men were running off in all directions, scattering white aprons behind them. Miss Carroll had disappeared too, leaving just myself and a similarly fatigued Miss Dix lying atop the pyramid.

"Turning onto my back, I looked at the circles of light above me and wondered what they were and why they looked so familiar. The lights seemed to grow brighter and brighter, and I began to lose consciousness, my body feeling as if it were floating through the air quite weightlessly. Was it a dream, or did I see figures inside those circles of light—figures, it seemed to me, wearing feather headdresses and clutching tomahawks? Could that have been the fair Matoaka, blushing at me from behind a collection of curiously colored flashing lamps? Was that good Chief Osceola, laughing at me with his arms crossed? And in amongst them did I really perceive the figure of mad old Mr. Emerson, smiling broadly and waving to me? I was just wondering what these creatures were, where I might be taken, and whether there was a buffet car onboard, when blackness enveloped me."

Fillmore awoke in a Cairo hospital, "although quite different from the one I had seen in the Khedive's palace, being both clean and devoid of manacles." He felt exceedingly well, he wrote, and the "bruises and nicks I had suffered at the hands of the sadly deranged Mr. Weed had quite disappeared." The Khedive came to visit Fillmore, hand in hand with Tiki-Tiki, whom he said he was taking as his wife. He explained that Miss Carroll had been captured after attempting to flee the country disguised in the long, all-enveloping robe Egyptian women wear. The shapeliness of her ankles had, however, caught the attention of the Khedive's guards, and she had been arrested. The Khedive went on to explain that Fillmore had single-handedly prevented the overthrow of his government. His spies had reported that the Freemasons had been scattered to the four winds. "If only Mr. Weed could have lived to see this day," wrote Fillmore sadly. The Khedive then handed Fillmore a letter; it was from Dorothea Dix. Although the original is lost, Fillmore's journal quotes a small section of it. "'Although I know you can never forgive me for what I have done, and although I know we can never be together, I will be with you always,'" which, wrote Fillmore, "confused me greatly, for how could we never be together and yet she be with me at all times?"

His mission accomplished, Fillmore left Egypt in August 1873, bound for New York City and his beloved homeland. Greeted by a delegation at the city's docks, Fillmore was asked whether he would do the city the great honor of ringing the opening bell at the New York Stock Exchange. Fillmore was excited—he had never been to the exchange before—and was thrilled to hear the stirring tales of profit and loss that had occurred in the country since his departure. In particular, he was fascinated by tales of

Black Friday in 1869, when the big-game speculators James Fisk and Jay Gould had attempted to corner the Gold Market.[9] He was also hopeful of petting "the bulls and bears that I am told live there."

Fillmore's visit was recalled by Marcus Goldman, a broker of IOUs, in his best-selling tell-all, *IOU Nothing:* "The securities were being called out in the afternoon session when a great disturbance erupted and former President Fillmore, elderly but still graceful, was ushered into the exchange after some time abroad. There were cries of 'Speech! Speech!' from the brokers, and quiet fell on the floor. At this point the former president seemed to drift into a reverie, and as every man waited with expectation to hear his words, he announced in a booming voice, 'The South is invading! All is lost! Sell! Sell! Sell!' There was a pause of a few seconds, at which point the president turned on his heel and teetered out of the room. No sooner had he gone than an eruption of paper flew into the air, a flood of humanity swamped the floor, making it quite impassable, and the market descended into chaos."

Fillmore's extraordinary words at the stock exchange triggered the terrible Panic of 1873, the fourth major financial crisis the United States had suffered, prompting a nationwide financial depression and mass bankruptcies across the country. Although seemingly irresponsible, Fillmore's warning seems to have prevented any chance of a second Civil War taking place. With the South's economy ruined, any type of attack that might have been in the planning was forsaken. With heroic understatement, Fillmore wrote of his outburst: "It seemed like the right thing to do at the time."

Returning to Buffalo, Fillmore was surprised to discover that his wife, Caroline, was there to welcome him. It transpired that she had been

---

9. Despite their best efforts, the elusive metallic beast had escaped, ripping a hole in the wall of the New York Mercantile Exchange and bounding free into the countryside, causing massive financial uncertainty. It was not until the construction of the United States Bullion Depository and Petting Zoo at Fort Knox in 1923 that Gold was finally captured and price fluctuations were eased.

banished from New York society after using the wrong fork at a charity luncheon, and had compounded the error by suggesting that one could eat caviar off silver. Chastened by the fickle nature of her peers, she had thrown off her pretensions and returned to a simple country life, baking bread, hand-washing her own clothes, growing vegetables in her garden, and holding gala balls only twice a season. Thus it was that Fillmore, surrounded by friends and loved ones, settled into a life contentedly devoid of adventure, satisfied that he had "finally managed to express my hatred of injustice and tyranny."

On the morning of February 13, 1874, while trying to shave a bearded pig he had been sent by the Rajah of Lombok, the seventy-four-year-old Fillmore felt a sudden sharp pain in his neck, and found his left arm had gone numb. A doctor was called for, but upon being given medicine Fillmore was forced to take to his bed. Despite the remedies being pressed upon him, the paralysis soon spread to the rest of Fillmore's body. "I cannot fathom what the trouble is," wrote Fillmore in one of his last journal entries, "for I have been in perfect health for almost my entire life." By February 27, Fillmore's journal entries consist solely of the word *gooseberry* spelled over and over again. By March 8 he could no longer write, and was having great difficulty doing his favorite animal impersonations, being forced to confine himself to cows and sheep. The doctor in attendance brought him a bowl of soup to eat, and this seemed to briefly revive him, for Fillmore managed to whisper enigmatically, "The nourishment is palatable." These would prove to be the last words he ever spoke. At ten minutes past eleven, as death comes to all men, so it came to the remarkable Millard Fillmore.

Postscript

As tears poured down the faces of the friends and family who had gathered around her husband's deathbed, a brokenhearted Caroline Fillmore thanked the doctor for his aid and walked him to the door. "He had been with us almost every day since the illness had struck, and was so polite and kind," wrote Caroline to her sister. "Indeed, poor Millard's death seems to have affected in the most powerful of ways even those who barely knew him. Some time after I had shown the doctor to the door I looked out and saw that he was still standing in front of the house, his gaze transfixed on the bedroom window as if he half expected to see Millard standing there waving to him. I watched the doctor for some time, and eventually, having satisfied himself that dear Millard would not be arising, he turned and walked away. Even so, all the way up the street, he continued to look over his shoulder in a most tentative and uncertain manner, his gray eyes flickering with doubt."

Notes

"Is it real or is it humbug?" asked one visitor of P. T. Barnum upon viewing the signs for his *American Museum* of human oddities, to which Barnum replied with a smile, "That's just the question: persons who pay their money at the door have the right to form their own opinions after they have got upstairs."

Seeing as readers have paid their money (or at least made the trip to the library), it is thought that perhaps they could do with a little help in coming to their own opinion. For while the author's conclusions are, at times, eccentric, they are by no means the "stuff of dreams," "grand delusions," and "execrable tittle-tattle" that his peers have accused him of writing.

Unfortunately, since the return of the entire Fillmore archive to the surprisingly litigious Aka pygmies, we are unable to offer facsimiles of the Fillmore journals as direct evidence. Nevertheless, while the arc of Fillmore's life portrayed in *The Remarkable Millard Fillmore*—his upbringing, his legal and political careers, his roles as vice president and president, his leadership of the Know-Nothings, his death, and so forth—can be well attested to in any standard historical reference book (in particular Robert Rayback's *Millard Fillmore: Biography of a President* and Robert J. Scarry's *Millard Fillmore*), it is hoped that by pointing out how some of the less famous circumstances mentioned in *The Remarkable Millard Fillmore* also adhere to known historical fact—despite their seemingly bizarre nature—that the reader might be persuaded to adjudge the rest of the book's account not humbug, but undoubtedly real.

Author's Note

•   The epigraphs to this book are all taken verbatim from their quoted sources. That the White House itself should be so faint in its praise merely goes to show that one should not look for solidarity amongst presidents. (Harry S. Truman would write of Fillmore, "At a time when we needed a strong man, what we got was a man that swayed with the slightest breeze.")

•   *Woodworth's Youth's Cabinet* was a dour children's periodical, focusing on the wholesomeness of a Christian life. It was one of the few places to offer Fillmore any praise whatsoever, not only for the upstanding message his vertiginous climb from apprentice to president gave American youth ("You look astonished, and wonder how it was possible for him to work his way up to the Presidential chair; but he did it, nevertheless. Would you like to know how? I can tell you, and I will tell you, if you will promise to remember it. He did it by making the most of his time") but also for his own abstemious character ("The new President, besides being a good statesman, is a man of excellent moral principles, and, if I am correctly informed, is a signer of a certain declaration of independence, known as the pledge of entire abstinence from all that intoxicates").

•   The Aka pygmies are a wandering African people, although more often found in the Western Congo Basin than in northern Uganda. Their worship of cloth binding has heretofore been kept secret.

•   Lincoln's patent no. 6469, for a device to lift boats over shoals, did exist. It was the result of the future president having his boat become stranded on a sandbar on a voyage home to Illinois. Until the discovery of Fillmore's journals, he had been the only U.S. president to hold a patent.

Chapter 1: I, Fillmore

•   As far as the author's description of Millard Fillmore's family tree goes, it is entirely accurate. Millard Fillmore's great-grandfather was captured by the pirate Captain John Phillips (a former carpenter) and press-ganged into joining his crew. Before long he led a mutiny against the merciless pirate and sliced Phillips' head open with an axe. That head would stand trial next to the surviving pirates in a Boston court. Similarly, Millard Fillmore's grandfather Nathaniel was left for dead in the woods of New York State while fighting in the French and Indian War and was forced to eat his own shoes and blanket to survive.

•   Harry S. Truman did not have a middle name, but only a middle initial. Although Truman claimed that taking an initial was a common practice in southern states, the exact provenance of his *S* has never been ascertained.

•   Fillmore was brought up, as stated, in a log cabin in the Finger Lakes area of upstate New York. He was a great devotee of adventure novels, and recalled reading *The Voyages and*

Adventures of Captain Robert Boyle (1776), a best-seller of the age, which crudely mixed historical fact with outrageous fiction. Conversely, James Bruce, the remarkable Scottish explorer of the eighteenth century, actually did search for the source of the Nile. But upon publishing accounts of his journey in *Travels to Discover the Source of the Nile, in the Years 1768–73*, he was accused of inventing the whole expedition and dismissed as a fraud.

• While the feud between the American explorers Lewis and Clark is not recorded in traditional histories, Meriwether Lewis was shot in the leg after being mistaken for an elk during their famed expedition. Certainly it seems as if somebody had it in for Lewis. Three years after the expedition he really was found dead on the Natchez Trace with his wrists cut and bullet holes through his head and chest.

• At five feet four inches, James Madison remains the smallest man ever to become president. He weighed just one hundred pounds.

• During the War of 1812, General William Hull did launch an abortive assault on Canada before surrendering his much larger army—as well as the city of Detroit—to the British without firing a shot. Convicted of cowardice and neglect of duty, he was sentenced to be executed. But the elderly general was reprieved at the last moment by President Madison and allowed to retire.

• Fillmore was unhappily apprenticed to a cloth-dresser, and it is true that Britain had placed restrictions on the emigration of skilled mechanics (and machinery designs), to prevent the loss of their trade secrets. Fillmore did win a turkey raffle at an apprentices' New Year's Day party, after which he peculiarly decided never to gamble again. As remarked upon by the author, Fillmore was so unhappy at his place of work that he threatened his employer with an axe. Both his pronouncement that he would "split down" his employer and his decree that "I have an inborn hatred of injustice and tyranny which I cannot express" are word for word accurate, and can be found in the autobiographical work *The Early Life of Millard Fillmore.*

Chapter 2: Fillmore, Man of Law

• Abigail Powers, Fillmore's first wife, was actually his first schoolteacher.

• Judge Walter Wood did introduce Fillmore to the law, the judge's generosity making Fillmore burst into tears as stated. Fillmore did help Wood in evicting tenants, although whether Wood persuaded Fillmore to fight in bare-knuckle boxing matches in New York is unverifiable except through the missing Fillmore journals. Fillmore would eventually leave the judge's service and move to East Aurora because he suspected Wood "was more anxious to keep me in a state of dependence, and use me as a drudge," a common complaint amongst boxers to this day.

• Fillmore's fearsome opponent in the boxing ring appears to have been Tom Molineux, a freed slave who bestrode the boxing rings of New York and London like a colossus in the early nineteenth century.

• The Panic of 1819 was the first major financial crisis the United States ever faced. Some suggest it was the result of the massive governmental borrowing that occurred during the War of 1812, although due to a general uncertainty on the exact causes of the panic, the intoxicated ravings of a youthful Fillmore should not be entirely discounted.

• The Battle of New Orleans really did take place two weeks after a peace treaty had been signed at Ghent. The city of Ghent is allegedly located in Belgium.

• Andrew Jackson was a serial duelist, fighting 103 duels throughout the course of his life. These were mainly held in the defense of his wife's good name, who was, as stated, accused of being a bigamist for not having divorced her previous husband before she married Jackson. Jackson was wounded so frequently that it was said he "rattled like a bag of marbles" from all the bullets lodged in his body. He regularly coughed up blood and suffered chronic pain from his wounds throughout his life.

Chapter 3: Fillmore the Explorer

• John Adams and Thomas Jefferson were fierce rivals in life and did both die on July 4, 1826, with Jefferson joining the choir invisible a few hours before Adams. This meant Adams' actual last words—"Thomas Jefferson survives"—were slightly wide of the mark.

• The kidnapping of William Morgan for writing an exposé of the Freemasons is as accurate as historians can know. It was rumored that he was drowned in the Niagara River, although some have suggested that he actually fled the country incognito. A number of Masons were convicted of kidnapping Morgan, but their remarkably lenient sentences resulted in a hue and cry over Masonic infiltration of the justice system. Morgan's body was never found.

• Fillmore's love of the city of Buffalo is entirely accurate and led him to declare: "Buffalo in the progress of history is destined by its position to be what Alexandria and Venice were."

• Thurlow Weed was Fillmore's mentor and sponsor to the Anti-Masons, a very real political party. While no evidence can be found in the traditional historical record of Thurlow Weed's broadsides against tight lacing, his thoughts on restrictive clothing were very much of his time. In fact, they are curiously similar to the writings of the enormously popular lecturer and phrenologist Orson Squire Fowler, whose seminal pamphlet *Intemperance and Tight Lacing* states: "The amount of air supposed to be breathed at each ordinary, natural inspiration, is found to average about six pints; while the amount usually inspired by a tight-laced lady, is only about three pints, or a diminution of about one half! Of course, tight-lacers have only half their natural powers of life, and are therefore only about half-alive, the other half being dead—dead while they live, besides the shortening of their lives by hastening death."

• On the night of New Year's Eve, 1826, Fillmore really could be found stalking the corridors of New York's capitol, although according to Robert Raybach's *Millard Fillmore*

(1992) he was not seeking Masons but planning for the coming session of the state legislature.

• The temperance proscription against "opium, tea, coffee, tobacco, snuff, condiments, mustards, spices, flesh, and everything heating and stimulating" is once again echoed in the stipulations of the indefatigable Mr. Orson Fowler.

• Alexis de Tocqueville and his friend Gustave de Beaumont originally traveled to the United States under the auspices of the French government to write a treatise on the state of American prisons. This was eventually published in 1832 as *Du système pénitentiaire aux États-Unis et de son application en France.* That the two men should—according to the Fillmore journals—have ended up in a prison would certainly explain the pair's deep understanding of the American penal system.

• The French Revolution ushered in many quantitative changes with it, most notably the adoption of the metric system in 1791, making France the first country to go metric. Possibly this had been caused by past discrepancies between the French inch and the English inch, the French inch actually measuring 1.0638 standard inches.

• The pig barbecue that Nat Turner and his fellow slaves held the night before their bloody slave rebellion did take place, although Fillmore's description of slavery as "perhaps the most beautiful example of domestic happiness and contentment that this fallen world has known" appears to have been taken from a pro-slavery tract written by none other than his future colleague Samuel Morse, who was famed for his anti-abolitionist stance. Nat Turner was deeply religious and became known as "the Prophet" by his fellow slaves. He frequently had visions that he presumed were messages from God. Curiously enough, these visions and messages largely suggested to Turner that he "kill all whites," the order he gave to his group of rebels before the rebellion began.

Chapter 4: Fillmore's Progress

• John Calhoun, the fire-breathing southern politician, was famed for the pro-slavery speech he delivered on the Senate floor entitled, "Slavery a Positive Good."

• The description of Daniel Webster—known derisively as "Black Dan" because of his dark skin and hair—is very close to the mark. A brilliant orator and fearsome pro-Unionist, he was with John Calhoun and Henry Clay part of the "Great Triumvirate" who ruled the Senate during its supposed golden age. For all his accomplishments as a lawyer, senator, and secretary of state, Webster is largely remembered today as the title character in the fantastical short story "The Devil and Daniel Webster" (1938) by Stephen Vincent Benét.

• As described, Congress was a rough-and-tumble place. When, in Fillmore's first year in Washington, D.C., Congressman Dawson of Louisiana was called to order by Congressman Arnold of Tennessee, the Congressional Record shows Dawson retorting, "If you presume to call me to order, sir, I'll cut your damnation throat from ear to ear," sparking a near-riot on the floor of the House.

• Davy Crockett, the "King of the Wild Frontier," was actually a member of the House of Representatives from 1826 to 1830 and from 1832 to 1835. An advocate of small government and a big critic of governmental spending, he supported the rights of squatters and opposed President Jackson's Indian Removal Act. A tireless self-promoter of his frontier image, on being defeated for reelection in 1835 he announced to his constituents, "You may all go to hell, and I will go to Texas." He did exactly that, joining the Texas Revolution and dying at the Battle of the Alamo, alongside Jim Bowie.

• Andrew Jackson really did suffer the first assassination attempt on a president. The assassin was a deranged housepainter by the name of Richard Lawrence. Both of Lawrence's pistols misfired, after which Jackson furiously attacked him with his cane. For some reason, most historical records fail to mention Fillmore's crucial intercession.

• At the Battle of the Alamo, Lieutenant Colonel William Travis is supposed to have drawn a line in the sand with his sword, and invited those who were willing to stay and fight the Mexican army to cross it. Hence his somewhat understandable anger at Fillmore's decision to leap back and forth across it.

• The siege of the Alamo occurred very much as described. About two dozen slaves, women, and children were set free at the battle's end. Curiously enough, a woman giving her name as Susannah Dickinson was amongst them.

Chapter 5: Fillmore Amongst the Natives

• The Great Patent Office Fire of 1836 saw the destruction of over seven thousand models and nine thousand drawings of pending and patented inventions. Also destroyed were thousands of file histories of inventions, leading to many patented inventions being copied illegally, among them, presumably, those created by Fillmore.

• The friendship between Samuel Morse and Fillmore can be attested to in the public record. In 1842, Samuel Morse called on Fillmore in New York City and showed him the operation of his telegraph, which Fillmore felt was "a national blessing." That Morse communicated only through knocks and taps has hitherto not been remarked upon by his own biographers.

• There has been much debate over the origins of *OK*, with the suggestion that it is a variation on the Choctaw word *okeh* being an oft-remarked-upon possibility. Indeed, Martin Van Buren is often mistaken as the originator of *OK* because of his home in Kinderhook. However, it has been more persuasively suggested that the word stemmed from an abbreviation for any of several different intentional misspellings of "all correct," including "oll korrect," "orl korrect," and "ole kurreck." Those still not satisfied should see the six articles published by the etymologist Allen Walker Read in the journal *American Speech* between 1963 and 1964.

• Martin Van Buren really did own two pet tigers, which he kept at his country home in upstate New York. He was also afraid of trains. The letter he wrote to Andrew Jackson, quoted in the footnote, is taken verbatim.

• In 1832, when Chief Osceola of the Seminole Indians was asked to sign a treaty ceding his tribe's Florida lands to the United States, he reportedly stabbed the treaty with a dagger, saying, "This is the only treaty I will make with the white man!" He was right to be skeptical. He really was taken captive under a flag of truce by the dastardly General Thomas Jesup at Fort Marion. The foul deed caused many protests amongst Americans, and Jesup was roundly condemned for his unsporting behavior. This did not prevent Osceola from dying of malaria, still a prisoner, in 1838.

• The Native American war pipe may not be as well known as the more famous peace pipe, but it did exist. In order that the reader should not make a mistake similar to Fillmore's, the peace pipe usually has a round stem, while the war pipe's stem is often flattened.

• The Second Great Awakening was the second great religious revival in United States history, the First Great Awakening having rather petered out in the late 1740s.

• The writer Ralph Waldo Emerson was a tireless champion of the dispossessed Native American tribes throughout his life. He seems to have been working on his famed essay "Nature" when Fillmore met him with the Cherokee, for it is in this work that the line "I am become a transparent eyeball" appears. In fact, all the phrases spoken by Ralph Waldo Emerson are verbatim.

Chapter 6: Fillmore the Kingmaker

• The Sultan of Java really did make a gift of a leopard to Congress.

• Despite flying in the face of the First Amendment of the Constitution, the gag rule, which prevented anti-slavery petitions from being submitted to Congress, actually was in place from 1831 to 1844.

• Fillmore was the head of the House Committee on Ways and Means.

• While Representative Cilley's practical joking cannot be verified, the consequences of his actions appear to be very real. There is a law in Ohio that prohibits attempting to get a fish drunk. What's more, under Alabama law, anyone who wears a false moustache in church and causes "unseemly laughter" is also subject to arrest. See www.dumblaws.com.

• It appears that log cabins had a similar pull on the nineteenth-century electorate as a war record has on today's voters, for President Harrison really was portrayed as having been born in a log cabin, despite his wealthy Virginian upbringing.

• Many histories of the Utopian movement in America point to the destruction of the Phalanstery at Brook Farm as the event that triggered the demise of George Ripley's Transcendentalist community.

• The Virginia Minstrels, the most famous minstrel troupe of the day, did indeed play in Boston on the night that Fillmore relates, and the newspaper reviews of the performance are verbatim. Emerson would deliver many of his famous transcendentalist lectures at the same venue during the 1840s. Curiously, if Fillmore had paid closer attention to his surroundings he might not have been so surprised by the devilish goings-on, for he would have seen that the concert was taking place at Boston's own Masonic Temple.

• Minstrel songs of the period were typically outrageous to today's modern sensibilities, including such titles as "Who's Dat Nigga Dar a-Peepin," "The Band of Niggers! From Ole Virginny State," and "De Coon Dat Had De Razor."

Chapter 7: Fillmore Goes West

• President Tyler really was thrown out of the Whig Party for relentlessly vetoing legislation. A cannon really did explode on the USS *Princeton*, killing the secretary of the navy and the secretary of state, while the president was down below. Tyler would marry Julia Gardiner, daughter of a senator also killed in the explosion.

• James Polk was the first presidential candidate to be labeled a "dark horse."

• The stagecoach driver Henry Wells actually did start a school for speech disorders in his twenties due to his own speaking problems. He would go on to found the American Express company and the Wells Fargo company, which held a monopoly on banking and express coach services to the West.

• From 1740 to 1790, Spain controlled half of South America, more than a third of North America—including the Louisiana Territory—and Mexico, of which California was a part. By the time of Fillmore's visit to California, the Spanish empire, under such terrible rulers as Ferdinand VII, had almost entirely been lost. Indeed, following the Mexican War of Independence (1810–1821) California became a Mexican province.

• Popular history states that the discovery of gold at Sutter's Mill in California sparked off the gold rush.

Chapter 8: Fillmore Restored

• Critics of the present administration should realize that fabricating a reason for invading a country is nothing new. Ulysses S. Grant, who fought under Zachary Taylor in the Mexican-American War, agreed that his force had been sent south "to provoke a fight." Similarly, critics of the present Congress should realize that not standing up to the president's demands for war has long been a tradition amongst elected officials. Even though James Polk had publicly coveted Mexico's land before he had been elected president, no one in Congress dared stand up to his fabricated reasons for invasion. Well, almost no one. A Whig congressman did dare challenge the president, in order that a war not be rushed into too suddenly or without just cause. He was roundly ignored. Who was this unpatriotic peacenik? Abraham Lincoln.

• John Quincy Adams did visit Fillmore in Buffalo, and it is possible the two men discussed the threat of Freemasonry, for Adams had described the organization as being a power-hungry "boa constrictor."

• President Zachary Taylor did refuse to tow the Whig party line on slavery, being much more sympathetic to the abolitionist cause than he originally professed. This led some to suspect he was murdered (some even suggested that Fillmore might have been responsible).

• John Quincy Adams' death on the floor of the House occurred as described, although whether it was caused by poison dart or his advanced years cannot be verified for certain.

• Shortly before his death, Edgar Allan Poe was found in Baltimore, in a state of great distress, wearing clothes that were not his own. The coroner declared the cause of his eventual death as "congestion of the brain." To this day nobody is certain how he came to be found in such a state, although foul play has never been entirely ruled out.

• The quotations remarking on the worthlessness of the vice presidency are, of course, all verbatim.

• Fillmore did indeed have a bad relationship with Zachary Taylor and was regularly locked out of cabinet meetings.

Chapter 9: Fillmore for President!

• President Rutherford Hayes' wife was known as "Lemonade Lucy," as she kept a "dry" White House, although the "foolish and wicked practice of profane cursing and swearing" was condemned by George Washington.

• Old Whitey, Taylor's horse, was indeed allowed to graze on the White House lawn.

• Dorothea Dix was a crusader for the creation of asylums for the insane. Even traditional histories have hinted that Fillmore might have conducted an affair with her.

• The circumstances leading up to Zachary Taylor's death are all true, including the July 4 celebrations and his consumption of cherries and milk. Shortly after his demise, Fillmore recalls receiving an anonymous letter saying Taylor had been poisoned. In 1991, Taylor's body was exhumed, and although traces of arsenic were found within it, the quantity was declared insufficient to be fatal.

• "Lindomania" was a very real phenomenon throughout the United States upon the arrival of the Swedish singer Jenny Lind. Hans Christian Andersen was completely obsessed with her. She did meet President Fillmore while visiting Washington, D.C., although what they talked of together is not recorded.

• A young J. P. Morgan did write to Fillmore, asking for the autographs of both the president and the members of his cabinet.

• Most history books state that the Compromise of 1850 was the defining act of Fillmore's presidency, and also the deed that forever damned him. On October 23, 1850, Fillmore attempted to justify his signing of it in a letter to Daniel Webster: "God knows that

I detest slavery, but it is an existing evil, for which we are not responsible, and we must endure it and give it such protection as is guaranteed by the Constitution, till we can get rid of it without destroying the last hope of free government in the world."

Chapter 10: Fillmore Abroad

• There has actually been a Select Committee on Assassinations within the House of Representatives—although, rather than calling for assassinations, it was set up merely to investigate the John F. Kennedy and Martin Luther King Jr. assassinations.

• Japan really was sealed off from the outside world for two hundred years as described, with the exception being the Dutch trader's post in Nagasaki Bay.

• Fillmore did send a letter to the Mikado of Japan, care of Commodore Perry. And the ensuing opening up of trade to Japan is perhaps Fillmore's greatest achievement, according to conventional textbooks of the period. Upon arriving in Japan, Perry actually did hide in his cabin, although he gave differing reasons than the author of this book does, stating, "I determined to practice upon them [the Japanese] a little of their own diplomacy." He would "confer personally with no one but a functionary of the highest rank of the empire. . . . I was well aware that the more exclusive I should make myself and the more exacting I might be, the more respect these people of forms and ceremonies might be disposed to award me."

• Hidenoyama Raigoro was indeed the greatest sumo wrestler, or *yokozuna*, of his generation.

• Henry Clay was savaged by a dog on the steps of Congress shortly before he died.

• The temperature of Hell that the author quotes—831°F—is, in fact, accurate. This calculation stems from Revelation 21:8, which speaks of how "the fearful and unbelieving . . . shall have their part in the lake which burneth with fire and brimstone." A lake of molten brimstone—that is, melted sulfur—means that the temperature of Hell must be maintained below the boiling point of sulfur, which is 832°F. Since Hell, being a notoriously uncomfortable place, would no doubt have the hottest temperature possible, it seems likely that 831°F would be the correct number, as above that point, the fearful and unbelieving would be tortured in something resembling a sauna of brimstone, not a lake.

• The tragic death of Franklin Pierce's children, combined with the fanatical religiosity of his wife, drove the fourteenth president to drink. His words upon losing the Democratic nomination in 1856—"There's nothing left to do but get drunk"—are precisely what he said, and did.

• Abigail Fillmore did die after picking up a chill at Pierce's presidential inauguration.

Chapter 11: Fillmore Agonistes

• Following Abigail's death, it is known that Fillmore embarked upon a southern tour, the known details of which do not necessarily exclude the possibilities laid out by this author.

• The grotesque urine-drinking ritual that Fillmore seems to have taken part in can be verified in *The Urine Dance of the Zuni Indians of New Mexico* (1885) by Captain John G. Bourke. The Zunis held these dances from time to time so as to inure their stomachs to any kind of food, no matter how revolting, in order to prepare themselves for famines. Similarly, the description of the Sun Dance is historically accurate.

• William Brooks was called "Buffalo Bill" long before William Cody famously made the name his own (having won it from Buffalo Bill Comstock in a buffalo-killing competition in 1868).

• The Know-Nothing Party was very real, and rabidly anti-Catholic. Fillmore became involved with them through the auspices of the spy and political Machiavellian Anna Ella Carroll. It was nicknamed the Know-Nothing Party (its official title was the American Party) because when members were asked about its activities they always replied, "I know nothing." The fact that Fillmore actually visited the Pope in Rome while running as presidential candidate for an anti-Catholic party ("and enjoyed it very much") is true.

• Queen Victoria is reputed to have called Millard Fillmore "the most handsome man" she had ever seen.

• *Malaeska, the Indian Wife of the White Hunter* (1860) is generally acknowledged as the first dime novel to be published.

• Although without Fillmore's journals we cannot tell if Fillmore actually did fight in a hot-air balloon duel, such events did take place in Paris. In 1808, M. de Grandpré and M. Le Pique fought such a duel over a young lady. Grandpré punctured Le Pique's balloon with a blunderbuss, and Le Pique and his second plunged half a mile to their deaths.

• Fillmore himself remarked upon the facial similarities between him and the Pope.

• The brutal attack by Senator Preston Brooks (D.-South Carolina) on Senator Charles Sumner (R.-Massachusetts) on the floor of the Senate in 1856 famously occurred. Sumner had described one of Brooks' fellow South Carolinian senators as a "noise-some, squat, and nameless animal," and another as taking "a mistress . . . who, though ugly to others, is always lovely to him; though polluted in the sight of the world, is chaste in his sight—I mean, the harlot, Slavery." An enraged Brooks, feeling bound to defend the honor of his kinsmen, hit Sumner repeatedly over the head with his metal-topped cane until the cane broke. To show their support for him, South Carolinians sent Brooks dozens of brand-new canes to replace it. It took Sumner three years to recover. Meanwhile, the *Richmond Enquirer* commented: "We consider the act good in conception, better in execution, and best of all in consequences. These vulgar abolitionists in the Senate must be lashed into submission."

• Fillmore was greeted by three thousand people at New York on his return from Europe. New York City was a hotbed of anti-Catholicism, and Fillmore did indeed give a speech to them. Walt Whitman did write about Fillmore in 1856, although he was less than complimentary. Casting his eye over the presidencies of Fillmore and Pierce, he declared: "History is to record these two Presidencies as so far our topmost warning and shame.

Never were publicly displayed more deformed, mediocre, sniveling, unreliable, false-hearted men! Never were these States so insulted, and attempted to be betrayed!"
•   Fillmore did sign a prenuptial agreement before marrying the wealthy widow Caroline McIntosh. He is the only president ever to do so.
•   In 1859, Jean Blondin crossed Niagara Falls on a steel cable 1,300 feet long. Enormous crowds watched. By the time of his death in 1897, at the age of seventy-three, he had walked approximately ten thousand miles on the high wire.

Chapter 12: Fillmore Errant

•   The Pinkerton Detective Agency had as its motto "We never sleep." Whether this was inspired by the founder's insomnia is not recorded in traditional histories of the organization.
•   John Brown did father twenty children, many of whom joined him on his abolitionist crusade. One of them was indeed named Salmon.
•   The Battle of Fort Sumter, in which Fillmore is shown playing a significant role, is generally acknowledged as the beginning of the Civil War.
•   Lincoln's favorite speech in the play *Our American Cousin* is taken verbatim, and was known to bring the house down. It seems that Wilkes had planned to shoot Lincoln just after this line had been spoken in the hopes that the uproarious laughter would drown out his gunshot.
•   Mike Fink was both a real person and a folk legend, a hard-drinking brawler and braggart who was renowned for his practical jokes and tall tales. He exemplified the rough-and-ready frontiersman of the early nineteenth century and was often portrayed as the foil to Davy Crockett, as he lacked that hero's admirable traits. In the immediate aftermath of the Civil War his popularity declined, as boastful, cowardly folk heroes fell from favor with the public, to be replaced by stories of pluck and heroism.

Chapter 13: Fillmore Unbound

•   The Khedive of Egypt was obsessed with Europe and with trains. Under his reign, Egypt went from having virtually no railroads to having more railways per habitable square kilometer than any country in the world.
•   The Khedive's cultural reforms included paying Verdi to write an opera for him. Verdi was initially hesitant, but upon hearing that his great rival Richard Wagner would be approached if he turned it down, he accepted the commission. *Aida* was the result.
•   The United States' first incursion into the Middle East can be traced back to the Khedive's hiring of Civil War soldiers to train his troops. It seemed to be the perfect arrangement: the Khedive wished to free Egypt from the rule of the Turks, and the Americans were eager for martial glory. In the early 1870s, more than fifty American soldiers could be

found modernizing the army, exploring new lands, and fortifying the delta of the Nile. However, the soldiers did bring with them the prejudices of being Christian and, for the most part, bachelors. Wrote one American soldier in a letter back home, "All the efforts His Highness can make to civilize his people will be useless until he abolishes all the Harems and EUNUCHS FROM THE LAND!"

• Fillmore's adventures in search of the source of the Nile closely mirror those of Lieutenant Colonel Charles Chaillé-Long, formerly a Union soldier from Maryland who, while being employed by the Khedive, would become one of the great unsung explorers of equatorial Africa.

• Dr. David Livingstone was a Scottish medical missionary and explorer. Taken sick near Lake Tanganyika, he lost touch with the outside world from 1865 to 1871. Henry Stanley, an American journalist, was sent to find him in 1869 as a publicity stunt for the *New York Herald* newspaper.

• William W. Loring did exist, although most history books fail to mention his career as an assassin for the Freemasons. Known as Old Blizzards, Loring had lost his left arm while fighting for the U.S. Army in the Mexican-American War. He had gone on to fight for the Confederacy during the Civil War, before ending his soldiering career as a general in the Egyptian army.

• Without the Fillmore journals it is impossible to say whether the famed New York political boss Thurlow Weed was indeed the leader of the Freemason organization engaged in a mission to take over the world. What is known is that George Washington, Benjamin Franklin, James Monroe, Andrew Jackson, and James K. Polk were all Freemasons. Curiously, Weed did have one important link to Egypt, though: he was born in Cairo—Cairo, New York.

• Fillmore's last words have not been improved upon.

Acknowledgments

Thanks to:

The Startling Robert Bush

The Incomparable Hugh Dancy

The Incredible Bo Ketner

The Unparalleled David Lamond

The Spectacular Annie Morris

The Indispensable Dr. Pepe Rockefeller

The Magnificent Matthew Semler

The Extraordinary Guy Walters

Special thanks to:

The Amazing Andrea Schulz

The Tremendous Lindsey Moore

The Astounding Kirsten Wolf

The Astonishing Jill Grinberg

The Outstanding Luke Dempsey

Picture credits:

Library of Congress; New York Public Library; Art Resource, NY; Picture History; Buffalo and Erie County Historical Society; Harry Ransom Humanities Research Center; Fillmore House Museum; Kevin Petersen.

Index

Printed in the United States
by Baker & Taylor Publisher Services